SOCIAL WORK
A Critical Turn

Steven Hick
School of Social Work, Carleton University

Jan Fook
*Centre for Professional Development,
La Trobe University*

Richard Pozzuto
School of Social Work, East Carolina University

Thompson Educational Publishing, Inc.
Toronto

Information on how to obtain copies of this book is available at:

Website:	www.thompsonbooks.com
E-mail:	publisher@thompsonbooks.com
Telephone:	(416) 766-2763
Fax:	(416) 766-0398

Library and Archives Canada Cataloguing in Publication

Social work : a critical turn / [edited by] Steven Hick, Jan Fook, Richard Pozzuto.

Includes bibliographical references.
ISBN 1-55077-147-7
1. Social service--Textbooks. I. Hick, Steven F. II. Fook, Jan
III. Pozzuto, Richard

HV40.S648 2004   361.3   C2004-905792-8

Copy Editing: Elizabeth Phinney
Cover Design: Elan Designs

Every reasonable effort has been made to acquire permission for copyrighted materials used in this book and to acknowledge such permissions accurately. Any errors or omissions called to the publisher's attention will be corrected in future printings.

We acknowledge the support of the Government of Canada through the Book Publishing Industry Development Program for our publishing activities. We also acknowledge the support of the Government of Ontario through the Ontario Media Development Corporation Book Initiative.

Printed in Canada.
1 2 3 4 5   08 07 06 05 04

Table of Contents

PART 4. The Future of Critical Social Work

Editors and Contributors

G. Brent Angell. Associate Professor and Director of the School of Social Work, University of Windsor, Windsor, Ontario, Canada.

Ben Carniol. Professor Emeritus at Ryerson University, Toronto, Canada.

Gerald de Montigny. Associate Professor in the School of Social Work at Carleton University, Ottawa, Ontario, Canada.

Paul K. Dezendorf. Associate Professor in the Department of Social Work, Winthrop University, Rock Hill, South Carolina, United States.

Brid Featherstone. NSPCC Reader, Applied Childhood Studies, University of Huddersfield, Great Britain.

Jan Fook. Professor and Director of the Centre for Professional Development at La Trobe University, Melbourne, Australia.

Karen Healy. Associate Professor in the School of Social Work and Policy Studies, University of Queensland, Queensland, Australia.

Steven Hick. Associate Professor in the School of Social Work at Carleton University, Ottawa, Ontario, Canada.

Jim Ife. Haruhisa Handa Professor and Head of the Centre for Human Rights Education at Curtin University of Technology, Perth, Western Australia.

Graham McBeath. Senior Lecturer, University College, Northampton, Great Britain.

Christine Morley. Lecturer at the School of Health and Social Development, Deakin University, Melbourne, Australia.

Richard C. Pozzuto. Associate Professor in the School of Social Work, East Carolina University, Greenville, North Carolina, United States.

Amy Rossiter. Associate Professor in the School of Social Work, Atkinson College, York University, Toronto, Ontario, Canada.

Brenda Solomon. Assistant Professor in the Department of Social Work, The University of Vermont, Burlington, Vermont, United States.

Trevor Spratt. Senior Lecturer, School of Social Work, The Queen's University, Belfast, Northern Ireland.

Sarah Todd. Assistant Professor in the School of Social Work at Carleton University, Ottawa, Ontario, Canada.

June Ying Yee. Associate Professor in the School of Social Work at Ryerson University, Toronto, Ontario, Canada

Stephen Webb. Senior Lecturer in Social Work and Social Policy, Brighton, University of Sussex, Great Britain.

INTRODUCTION

Towards "Becoming" a Critical Social Worker

Steven Hick and Richard Pozzuto

There is no single conception of critical social work — we are in fact looking at a number of critical perspectives, many of which do not use the term "critical" at all. They refer to themselves as structural, radical, progressive, anti-oppressive and so forth. So what do these different perspectives have in common? Perhaps only two things: that a better social world is possible and that the achievement of a better social world requires a qualitative change in current social relations. The focus and approach to change varies among the perspectives. Is it useful to try to piece these perspectives together and seek common themes or principles? The answer may depend upon the particular perspective of critical social work used in formulating the answer. Some of the contributors believe the task is possible and others do not. The editors believe that a dialogue among the perspectives, be it within these pages or within the actions of the readers, will enrich the perspectives and our capability for establishing a better social world. We hope this collection advances the dialogue.

A range of theoretical perspectives have informed, and continue to inform, critical social work. Among these are structural theories, feminist theories, phenomenology, social constructivism, postmodernism, post-structuralism and post-colonialism. These theories are not necessarily of the same level or emphasis. Each of these perspectives, though, contributes to a fuller understanding of critical social work and our current social circumstances. These theoretical perspectives focus on different aspects of life, at differing levels of abstraction, and from a different point of origin. A structural perspective, while concerned with the daily lives of individuals, emphasizes the institutional relations within a society. Feminist theories originate their analysis from the insights gained from a feminist perspective. A phenomenological perspective emphasizes direct lived experience.

These perspectives are not necessarily mutually exclusive and can be complimentary. They can also be in conflict, and when they are, the conflict can and often does advance each of them. The theoretical perspectives also provide diverse options for creating desired changes. All of these theories have challenged the exclusive focus of social work practice on helping people in their day-to-day lives. Practice, as conceived by critical social work, must contribute to a transformation of everyday lives; towards changes in economic, social and political structures, relations or organizations. The contributions in this volume make clear that critical social work at its base is about addressing and changing the factors underlying the lived experience of clients. Some call this social change. Others refer to it as promoting social justice, and still others refer to it as "linking the personal and political." In the end, all of the perspectives share the view that larger societal-level structures and relations should be addressed in some way.

Critical social work does not lend itself to a single understanding, and hence the perspective offered is one of multiple understandings. This is not to say that there are not common threads that run through the understandings. Critical social work does offer an analysis of the social context that includes an identification of oppressive elements and potential paths for their elimination. At times, parts of this analysis are implicit but the element of improving social conditions and the lives of individuals is constant. The method or focus of the analysis may vary as well as its scope, giving rise to various understandings.

Historically, the elements of critical social work are found in the origin of the profession, though they were not referred to as critical social work. Jane Addams's work at Hull House illustrates the analysis and practice with the intent of changing social conditions.

Earlier terms were "progressive" and "radical." For the U.S., Reisch and Andrew (Reisch, 2001) illustrate this history quite admirably. According to Fook (1993) this tradition of radical social work tends to share the following themes:

- a structural analysis of personal problems;
- an analysis of the social control functions of social work and welfare;
- an ongoing social critique, particularly regarding oppressive functions; and
- goals of personal liberation and social change.

For English-speaking audiences, the theoretical foundation for radical critiques began to change in the 1960s and early 1970s with the formation of the New Left. Marcuse's *One Dimensional Man* (1964) was a significant contributing influence. This work provided a broad audience with an introduction to critical theory, which was a product of the Frankfurt Institute. The early members included Max Horkheimer (philosopher, sociologist and social psychologist), Theodore Adorno (philosopher, sociologist and musicologist), Friedrich Pollock (economist), and Leo Lowenthal (cultural studies).

In 1937, Horkheimer published a seminal essay contrasting traditional and critical theory (Horkheimer, 1937). He criticized traditional theory as being formulated of general, internally consistent principles and with a primary objective of describing the world? (Jay, 1973, p.80).

Critical theory did not assume an exulted position for formal statements removed from social action. On principle, critical theory was suspicious of actions that assumed a naturalness of the social world. Horkheimer's position was one of being "wholly distrustful of the rules of conduct with which society as presently constructed provides each member" (Horkheimer, 1972, p.207). He derives this distrust from an understanding of the connectedness of systems of ideas and material conditions of life. Critical theory is no more divorced from the material conditions of life than any other set of ideas. It does not escape the relationship. It does, however, have the potential to be self-reflective and examine its connection to other factors. Among other things, this perspective anticipates change as the work itself changes. The idea of a single, constant perspective is inconsistent with the approach.

More so than many earlier radical perspectives, critical theory placed more emphasis upon examining and critiquing the ideology of a particular period.

The term "critical," borrowed from critical theory, became popular in intellectual circles and was attached to disciplines and professions to indicate an approach that adhered to a critical theory perspective. The formulators of critical theory never considered it a narrowly defined or closed system. It was intended to develop over time, and the critical theory of Horkheimer and Adorno is not identical to the works of later critical theorists, such as Jurgen Habermas.

Just as the theory has changed, so have the connotations of the term "critical" with regard to social work. Critical social work is no longer strictly aligned with critical theory. It now embraces the principles earlier associated with "radical," structural" or "progressive" approaches to social work.

A newer current, that of postmodern thought, has mingled with the structural, radical, progressive critical perspectives. The various strains of postmodern thought also question the separation of knowledge and power as did critical theory. Our grasp of both knowledge and power are contained within a narrative that informs the intellectual sensitivities of the period. Foucault suggests that the narrative may hide as much as it reveals, that there are many possible narratives, and it is the power relations that advance one or another narrative. The examination of the narrative is as important as an examination of the world the narrative attempts to define as natural, or objectify. Critical social work, regardless of its definition, is about power relations. Foucault suggests that these relations are enacted, though not exclusively, at a micro level. The practice of social work then becomes subject to examination in its role in recreating existing oppressive power relations.

There are several currents for understanding critical social work. None is necessarily more correct than any other, and all have merit. Within the range of themes presented by the four contributors are multiple paths to inform a critical social work perspective. With this foundation one should expect critical social work to be dynamic and fluid, linked to the social context and containing multiple possibilities. It is not the goal of critical social work to discover or establish the finite answers for "correct" social work theory or practice. Rather, the goal of critical social work is to identify the multiple possibilities of the present in order to contribute to the creation of a more just and satisfying social world.

Problematizing the Client-Worker Relation

A significant and contested issue for critical social work is the client-worker relation. This seems to be the focal point for a variety of issues, among them the nature of help, the role of the social worker, the nature of practice and the viability of social work "knowledge." These issues are mixed with highly complex questions concerning power and empowerment. Fook undertakes an analysis of the social control functions of social work and welfare. Ife addresses the power imbalances between worker and client by refusing to privilege professional knowledge. McBeath and Webb seek an examination of power and subsequent practice rooted in a far different approach. Rather than accepting differences (social worker-client; professional knowledge-vernacular; class, race and gender identities) as established and as a basis for analyzing/resisting/transforming power relations, they grasp power as "always-already" in our life world. From their perspective it is immanent, dispersed and inescapable. A suitable analysis is of the micro-physics of power within the processes of daily life. Within this volume, then, are widely varying views of power, from the existing institutions to the small interactions creating and maintaining the process of daily life. These views are at times complimentary and at times in conflict, illustrating again the range and diversity of critical social work.

Whatever its form, critical social work is concerned with the power imbalance that exists between workers and clients and seeks constructive methods for addressing it. This may look at the adoption of a self-reflexive and critical stance towards the often contradictory effects of social work practice and social policies (Healy). As stated earlier, McBeath and Webb see power as inescapable and are suspicious of strategies of service user empowerment and consciousness raising of providers.

Starting from a different vantage point, Todd attempts to understand, within community organizing, how white feminist organizers' ways of knowing, practices and self-recognitions are caught within specific histories and social relations tending to reproduce relations of power. With her deconstruction of community and unpacking of the narratives employed by feminist community organizing, she attempts to open a broader practice horizon. She believes that we must make visible the taken-for-granted ways in which our practice is historically and discursively situated, which in turn maintains certain social hierarchies and privilege. She believes however that we may be able to develop a more critically reflective practice that challenges us to seek out innovative ways of "unbecoming" social workers. This unbecoming entails a critical analysis of how practice is discursively situated.

In his analysis of human rights, Ife suggests a dual foundation for power. There is, on the one hand, the institutional framework supported by discourses that legitimate the power and perspective of the institution. In the case of human rights, it is the legal institutions that have achieved the prominent position. On the other hand, there is a *reflexive* construction, where rights are emerging from our own day-to-day interactions with friends, in families, the work place, communities and other public spheres. In the interaction, both parties, self and other, demonstrate through actions their conception of human rights. The inter-action between the parties is the acting out of these conceptions with another. While Ife acknowledges that the term "rights" is not acknowledged in these settings, the interactions are about right, power and responsibility. This perspec-tive brings the notion of right and power directly into the workplace with the client but it is not there alone. There is also the legitimating discourse of the institution; in this case perhaps the agency and even the very implementation of social policy.

Both as a strategy addressing the client-worker power imbalance and as an overall strategy, critical social work has often introduced the notion of empow-erment. It is frequently referred to in this volume. Empowerment, both as a concept and as a strategy, follows from the formulation of power. A clear under-standing of power and its interplay with social relations in society is required in order to conceptualize the endeavour of empowerment in social work practice. In much of the literature, empowerment is conceptualized as a process of the powerful giving power to the less powerful or powerless. It is treated as a commodity that is possessed and can be passed on. For example, you could empower members of a low-income community by helping them write a letter that would prepare a case for changes in their community. The concept is appealing as it often provides a ready-made solution to the issues of social control, self-determination and equality. However, if the term is to have any rele-vance to critical social work, it must be more carefully defined and delineated. How does empowerment differ from self-help or enablement? How can we conceptualize power in a way that captures its complexities?

Given the diversity of opinions on power within critical social work, it is not surprising that the approaches to empowerment are varied. These approaches range from interactions with clients to structural changes at a societal level. This is not to imply that these levels are necessarily mutually exclusive nor defined identically by the contributors. The concept of empowerment is often engaged as a potential solution to the power imbalance. For example, Ife discusses an accessible, dialogical form of practice, using the power of human rights to drive a program of empowerment. Broadening our focus a bit, we find Mullaly (1998, p.161), in an earlier work, referring to empowerment as a catalyst for social workers to continue to devise theory and strategies for working with oppressed groups. In his most recent text, Mullaly (2002, p.179) sees empowerment "as a process through which oppressed people reduce their alienation and sense of powerlessness and gain greater control over all aspects of their lives and their social environment. Again in an earlier work, empowerment-based social work at an operational level is spoken about as having three aspects: (1) explicated identified power elements in the client-worker relationship; (2) explicit experi-ence of control by clients; and (3) explicit support by social workers for the clients' efforts to gain greater control over their lives and promote change (Hick, 2002). Assuming a different starting point, Todd suggests a fuller recognition of the social worker in terms of privileging to allow for greater self-awareness, which has the potential to produce empowering practice. Noticeably, there are a variety of methods employed towards the goal of empowerment.

In this text, Fook and Morley challenge the notion of an empowering practice. The term "empowerment" as often used is steeped in a liberal tradition, rendering it of little use for a critical social work practice. They believe that the development of a practice of empowerment still needs to be accompanied by a broader postmodern and critical analysis if the intended empowerment is to be achieved. They maintain that the idea of empowerment is context-dependent and subject to changing theoretical perspectives. In some perspectives, the interpretation and usage of empowerment may provide a rationale for practices whose outcomes and political influence may be quite different than those embraced by even a loosely conceived critical social work. For Fook and Morley, the social work process itself is located within problematic discourses and relations. Even within critical social work at the theoretical level, there may be disparities; some are illustrated by McBeath and Webb. The practical distinction between how we intend to operate and how this is actually perceived and experienced by our service users is no less problematic. Critical social work should therefore offer glimpses into how we may be intentionally or unintentionally involved in reproducing the inequalities we seek to redress.

McBeath and Webb believe that critical social work's postmodernism is seriously flawed, particularly in its handling of power. They are correct in stating (in Chapter 11) that we cannot escape power. Using Foucault's notion of power, a society conceptualized without power can be only an abstraction. The client-worker power relation ("process" may be a better term) is only one element. There are the relations among workers, among administrators, the legitimating discourse at many levels, the location of the agency, as well as the extension of policy through agency actions and the organization of the social work profession itself. But does the limited attention given to the networks of power necessarily lead to the idea that social workers cannot analyze power relations within the social work relationship and work towards addressing them?

Perhaps this could be done in conjunction with clients. Can social workers recognize and analyze with clients the extent to which they are disempowered without relegating them to the status of the powerless? The oppositional politics of worker and client — one with power and the other powerless — suppresses similarity and shared commonality, which can be essential to the practice processes. Critical social work should recognize power, not try to escape it. Rather than focusing on eradicating power or transferring it from one place to another, we should analyze or transform how it is exercised.

Relevance to Direct Practice

A further challenge that is often raised is the applicability of critical social work to direct practice. Broad social theories and strategies for social change can seem disconnected from the day-to-day realties of clients. There remains some doubt about the usefulness of these theories and strategies for practice, particularly their applicability to direct practice. Healy discusses the danger inherent in defining critical social work in ways that exclude the majority of social worker workplaces. Rigid definitions of critical social work run the risk of denying the diversity of critical social work practices. According to Healy, many definitions of critical practice privilege practice strategies suited to small, collaborative organizational contexts, neglecting the potential for critical practice in many human service organizations and excluding most social workers. This reproduces the academic-practice split that has limited the development of critical knowledge development in social work.

According to Solomon, the challenge of critical social work is to demonstrate a critical approach (in our account of knowledge produced about critical social work) that avoids participating in a performance that is reductionist or a debate, a few speakers who occupy the most legitimizing social categories, an argument or fight, a single position, a final answer, a closed-off sense of the meanings of such words as *critical* and *good* (even as I use them here). A problem we face, particularly in this new borage of power, is to keep multiple ideas and standpoints (or ways we are made different from one another by power) visible as "we" talk, analyze and critique power together.

In part, at issue here is a distinction between "technique" and "practice." Practice is a broader term than technique. It is doing the stuff of the profession, in our case, of social work. Technique is the application of a set of procedures to a complex and often common task in order to achieve a particular result. It is relatively simple to conceptualize technique in terms of objects, perhaps in the repair of broken objects. There are ways, techniques, of fixing things, whereby the object is restored to a functioning state. For processes, the conceptualization of technique is more difficult. There is not an object to be fixed but a process to be continued. If the process is generative, one that creates, the conceptualization is more difficult in that the outcome is that which does not yet exist. Critical social work is a generative process intended to participate in the creation of a set of social relations that more adequately meet human need. There is no set of techniques to accomplish this. The level of conceptualizing the practice is within a different plane and is not reducible to technique.

Addressing the issue of practice, de Montigny suggests a reflexive practice, in particular, a *reflexive* materialist practice. This is a practice that is rooted in the concrete lives of clients. It is a practice that recognizes the specific and local in the lives of people while seeing these lives as interwoven with past and present realized courses of action. It considers more than a snapshot of the present. It sees the snapshot as a frozen moment in a trajectory moving from a past, through the present, to a future. The actions in the present, created in the present but with flavour of the local and specific, modify the trajectory. From this perspective, social work is about modifying the trajectory, not in the abstract but in relation to actual, lived experience; it is participation in an ongoing process.

Linking the Everyday and the Structural

One of the key challenges that is identified throughout this volume is that of drawing the link between the day-to-day lives of situated people (clients) and the macro-relations and structures in society, and of doing so without creating grand theories or dualisms that fail to account for multiple realties of oppression. It is the challenge of taking up both a materialist analysis that examines structures and a postmodern analysis that rejects starting with a grand theory.

The issue is further complicated in that, just as critical social work is not a unified perspective, the meaning of terms such as "structure" is not unanimously agreed upon by critical social workers. Some favour a linguistic approach; others, a symbolic approach; and still others, a materialist approach. The differences, sometimes in the level of analysis, sometimes in the focus and at times in the basic orientation, lends itself to constructive debate.

This mingling of critical social theory with post-modernist or post-structuralist theory is necessary today. Some authors have called for a mingling of critical social theory and post-structuralist theory. The possibility of doing this has been debated, both in social work literature and in other fields. If either critical theory or postmodern theory is rigidly defined, then such a mingling is not possible. Granted there are particular concepts, assumptions and general sensibilities within each, but both are continually emerging and diverging and should not be understood as closed, unanimous or finalized frameworks.

In conceptualizing critical social work, we need a theory that is rooted in practice and that helps us to organize our thinking about people's experience and struggles, their everyday in its specificity and localness. The theory needs to link us to larger social structures and deeper analysis without becoming more "real" than concrete experience.

In conceptualizing critical social work, we need a theory that begins with practice, people's experiences and struggles or the everyday world, but goes on to explore how these are connected to larger social structures or relations. Everyday experiences or activities, as people speak of them, should be the beginning point. Social workers and clients can then go on to discover the social organization of the client's experience and bring this discovery back to everyday life. In this way, perhaps we privilege both the knowledge of the client and that of the worker. We force abstraction, as found in theory, to find its life in the day-to-day world. Perhaps this will help address some of the issues raised in this volume.

The client's day-to-day activities and, indeed, the client-worker relationship itself are organized by and articulated to our relation to macro-relations. "Macro-relation" refers to national- and international-level social relations and social and economic processes. These are not purely abstractions but can be identified in particular social practices. When examining how the client's lived experience is socially organized, we should examine the social relations that link or knit the local setting or lived experience to the macro.

This notion sees the examination of the world of everyday life as a way to disclose how it is articulated to societal-level social relations. By beginning with a known situated in experience, it opens up the possibility of exploring macro-relations as they organize particular work processes. For example, the relations of class, state, gender, race and so forth are viewed as extended social relations organizing everyday activities of people in different settings unconnected with one another. Everyday activity is viewed as being locked into an underlying complex dynamic, for example, the relations of production or reproduction, and is organized by the powers thereby generated. By starting in the everyday world, we attempt to grasp the underlying macro-relations organizing the activities of a setting.

Conclusion

Critical social work is not without imperfections both in theory and practice. Trying to lay bare societal-level social relations and structures has never been a straightforward enterprise. Ignoring the social in social work and examining only individual issues does not seem to be a viable option for many social workers these days. The challenge arises when we start to speak about how we analyze structures and what structures are important. We also face the danger of creating totalizing theories that attempt to generalize oppression for all people based on some causal structural theory. At the other end, we face the risk of seeing everyone's lived reality as unique and without a material base, open always to interpretation depending on one's situated context. Neither of these seems appropriate for critical social work.

There can be little doubt that the the effects of new technologies and changes in global capitalism are creating major social transformations throughout the world — a change that some have called "post-modernism." However, we see these developments more as a shift than as a rupture or radical departure. We are taking the position that we should not reject theories of the modern era out-of-hand. Instead, we should retain certain visions, theories and practices from the modern era, seeing the post-modern as continuous with the modern. In other words, social work practice in the current era definitely requries a turn in our modes of thought, but perhaps not a complete overhaul. The subtitle "a critical turn" was chosen by the editors to acknowledge that there has been a turn or shift in society that has important implications for social work theory and practice. A critical turn is required if we as social workers are to understand how the dramatic changes that are occuriing in society are affecting the very people we are seeking to help.

This text aims to open up this debate and begin to explore ways that the personal and political, or the lived experience of situated people and the broader structures and social relations in society, are linked. It also tackles the issue of the role of social work in social control or in perpetuating existing privileges and social hierarchies. In many ways, this volume challenges us to "unbecome" social workers and then struggle with clients to uncover the contours of the world implicated in a shared, lived reality.

References

Fook, J. (1993). *Radical casework: A theory of practice.* St. Leonards, Australia: Allen & Unwin.

Hick, S. (2002). *Social work in Canada: An introduction.* Toronto: Thompson Educational Publishing.

Horkheimer, M. (1937). "Traditionelle und kritische theorie." *Zeitschrift fur Sozialforschung* 6(2).

Horkheimer, M. (1972). *Critical Theory.* New York: Herder and Herder.

Jay, M. (1973). *The dialectical imagination.* Boston: Beacon Press.

Marcuse, H. (1964). *One dimensional man.* Boston: Beacon Press.

Mullaly, R. (1998). *Structural social work: Ideology, theory and practice.* Toronto: Oxford University Press.

Mullaly, R. (2002). *Challenging oppression: A critical social work approach.* Toronto: Oxford University Press.

Reisch, M and J. Andrews (2001). *The road not taken: A history of radical social work in the United states.* Philadelphia, P.A.: Brunner-Routledge.

PART 1

Critical Perspectives on Social Work:
An Overview

1

Current Understandings of Critical Social Work

*Contributions from Jim Ife, Karen Healy, Trevor Spratt
and Brenda Solomon, with summaries by the editors.*

This chapter seeks to provide an overview of a few of the assorted understandings of critical social work. Four leading scholars who have identified themselves as critical social workers, and whom we thought might have dissimilar viewpoints, were asked to write a short essay on "what is critical social work." Each of the four contributors discusses the foundational grounding of their views, key elements that comprise a critical approach to social work and the dangers in producing such an account. Below are excerpts from their essays, followed by short commentaries.

The authors in the brief essays that follow have addressed the issue of critical social work from various entry points with differing foci and levels of complexity. Jim Ife, in the following brief essay, guides us through an historical account of the critical tradition in social work.

What Is Critical Social Work Today?

Jim Ife

Social work has had a tendency to follow the fashions of the day, and this is also true of the critical tradition within social work. In the late 1960s, critical social work adopted a social action model, Alinsky (1969, 1971) was studied, often uncritically, in social work schools and critical social work was out to change the world. In the 1970s and early 1980s, as it became clear that the revolution in Western societies was after all not imminent, "radical social work" turned to a more reflective study, being concerned with the contradictions of the welfare state, cultural hegemony, social work's role in social control and social work as an ideological state apparatus (Corrigan & Leonard, 1978; Skenridge & Lennie, 1978; Galper, 1980; Jones, 1983). In the 1980s, as Western governments, led by Mrs. Thatcher, started their love affair with privatization and smaller government, the critical stream within social work became concerned with mounting a strong defence of the welfare state. It also became heavily influenced in the 1980s and 1990s by feminist scholarship in its various forms (Dominelli & McLeod, 1989). The 1990s brought an interest in postmodernism and post-structuralism as the bankruptcy of economic rationalism and managerialism, with their modernist positivist foundations, became increasingly apparent, to practitioners, students and academics engaged in the ongoing search for a social work that not only helped people in their day-to-day lives, but also sought to challenge and change the social, economic and political order (Leonard, 1997; Ife, 1997; Pease & Fook, 1999; Healy, 2000; Powell, 2001). Anti-racist practice and post-colonialism also became important sources of critical theorizing. There was some interest in Green political theory and environmentalism as a consequence of increasing concern about the ecological crises facing the earth, though the influence on critical social work remained marginal. More recently, the impact of globalization has generated a concern for an alternative internationalism and a corresponding interest in human rights and the peace movement (Ife, 2001).

This following of trends has been evident across the whole spectrum of social work and not only in social work that might be described as "critical." The large numbers of American students specializing in community organization and social action in the late 1960s and early 1970s has been replaced by an apparently overwhelming interest in private practice, therapies and a reliance on the market—accurately reflecting the change that has occurred in American political norms over this period. And in Britain the radical social work of Bailey and Brake (1975) and Corrigan and Leonard (1978) (among others) has given way to a more pragmatic approach after the assault of years of Thatcherism and now New Labour. It is perhaps disappointing, though unsurprising, that social workers who self-define as "critical" or "radical" have shown themselves to be as adept at following the fashions of the day as their more "conservative" colleagues (though the distinction between "radical" and "conservative" social workers is, of course, highly problematic).

Despite these changes, I believe it is possible to discern an approach to critical social work that has grown significantly over the last fifty years, and that retains a continuity as well as following the intellectual and political fashions of the day. In the remainder of this paper, I will outline briefly what I believe constitutes such an approach to social work praxis.

A critical social work approach starts with the simple proposition, common to most if not all social work, that the problems of a person, group, family or community are not all their own fault, but are caused largely by factors outside their control and sometimes beyond their knowledge or understanding. This is hardly controversial: refusing to "blame the victim" is standard fare for social workers. What sets critical social work apart is its insistence that social work must therefore somehow address the causes of disadvantage, rather than only helping people to adapt, adjust and make the best they can of their lives. Critical social work does not imply ignoring or refusing to help the individual, family, group or community; critical social workers will of course offer such help, but they will at the same time insist that it is not enough and will seek somehow to change "the system" as well.

Views of what needs to be changed will of course vary, depending on the theoretical orientation of the social worker. It may be class divisions; it may be patriarchy; it may be colonialism; it may be a more generalized understanding of structures of oppression; it may, in post-structural terms, address discourses rather than structures and so on. But the common theme is an attempt to identify the causes or origins of disadvantage, and somehow to address those causes or origins as well as helping the disadvantaged themselves. And those causes or origins are addressed, not as some out-of-hours activity in a social worker's private capacity, but as a necessary part of social work practice itself.

From this simple definition, a number of important characteristics of critical social work emerge. First, critical social work is, by its very nature, critical of at least some aspects of the society within which it is practised. It refuses to accept the status quo, but rather seeks to effect some kind of social, economic, political or cultural change. The critical social worker will thus, inevitably, come up against entrenched power with interests in maintaining the system as it is. There will be some element of struggle, possibly, though not necessarily, in solidarity with the struggles of "client" groups, or in alliance with social movements. The critical social worker is likely to encounter resistance and opposition, especially within conservative and managerial environments, and sometimes also within professional bodies.

Critical social work inevitably involves linking the personal and the political. Some writers, myself included, have argued that this should be an essential component of all social work, but while such a view might be contested, it seems inconceivable that any "critical" social work could avoid the personal-political link. Indeed, it is precisely because critical social work makes that link, between personal suffering and wider political and social structures or discourses, that it takes on its critical perspective. A critical social work will seek to understand the personal in terms of the political, and the political in terms of the personal. It seeks knowledge, understanding and change in both domains, and indeed will question the traditional boundary between the personal and the political (the personal *is* political, and the political *is* personal).

This is not the only boundary that critical social work questions. The establishment and maintenance of boundaries is characteristic of dualistic Western thought, which a critical perspective seeks to overcome. The boundaries between professional and personal, between local and global, between theory and practice, between knowledge and action, between science and art, between macro and micro all come under scrutiny within a critical perspective, and various writers within the critical tradition have sought to reconceptualize social work by deconstructing these dualisms. Critical social work seeks at least to cross all these boundaries, if not to question their very validity.

Critical social work, because of its acknowledgement of the importance of power inequalities (however one might theoretically understand power), has always been concerned about the common power imbalance between worker and "client." This can be readily understood in terms of the privileging of the worker's professional knowledge over the client's personal knowledge. Hence a critical social work refuses to privilege professional knowledge in this way. The client has significant knowledge and wisdom that the worker does not, just as the worker has knowledge and wisdom that the client does not. If worker and client are able to acknowledge the validity and importance of the each other's knowledge, they can then enter a dialogue where each sets out to learn from the wisdom of the other. In that way both can learn, and they can join together in action based on wisdom and knowledge that is greater than the wisdom and knowledge of either in isolation. In wider practice settings involving more than the simple dyad of worker-client, the same principle applies; all actors—whether clients, professionals, community members, family members, supervisors or whoever—can contribute knowledge and wisdom, which can be pooled to achieve a desired result. This idea of dialogical change and consciousness raising has drawn heavily on the work of Paulo Freire whose *Pedagogy of the Oppressed* (1972) has been perhaps the most influential single source for critical social workers.

A strong value base is an essential component of critical social work. This is usually cast in terms of social justice, human rights or some vision of humanity. A critical social work realizes that practice can never be value-neutral, and if critical social work is to be successful in challenging an oppressive system, it must have a clearly articulated value base. Practice without values can lead to the instrumentality of managerialism and unquestioning obedience to rules and to "legitimate" authority. Some of the world's worst human rights abuses have been committed under such conditions; the implementation of the Holocaust was in many ways a triumph of efficiency, rationality and obedience to authority, and a denial of the validity of human values or the need to make moral choices.

The non-violent tradition is a common thread in much, though not all, critical social work. Some within the critical tradition, particularly more "hard-line Marxists," have articulated views that are hardly compatible with the Ghandian philosophy, espousing a militancy and a need to crystallize and promote conflict rather than consensus and dialogue. This perhaps reached its height in the 1970s, while in more recent times it appears that an approach based on dialogue and non-violent change is more preferred; certainly that is the case for this writer.

A variety of theoretical positions have informed, and continue to inform, critical social work. Among these are structural theories, post-structural perspectives, interpretive and phenomenological approaches, postmodernism, post-structuralism, feminism, post-colonialism and radical environmentalism. Space does not permit a critical evaluation of their respective contributions, except to assert that, for me at least, all these traditions have something to contribute, and it is in the interaction between them, the evaluation of one in terms of the other, that some of the most creative work can happen.

Because of the strength of conviction of many who advocate radical positions, critical social work, like other critical or radical formulations, has suffered from the impact of fundamentalism. In this context, fundamentalism means an insistence on seeing the world through a single lens and accepting only one theoretical or analytical framework as "fundamental" to an understanding of theory and practice. Sometimes this can be the insistence on the predominance of a single dimension of oppression, such as class (Marxist fundamentalism), gender (feminist fundamentalism) or race (anti-racist or post-colonialist fundamentalism). At other times it takes the form of advocating a single worldview or dimension of human activity, such as Green fundamentalism or even postmodernist fundamentalism, as well as other forms of fundamentalism often demonized by critical social work: religious fundamentalism, economic fundamentalism (also known as economic rationalism) or managerial fundamentalism. In each case, the characteristics of the fundamentalist are the insistence that she or he has the right answer or "truth" (hence the need to convert others to the one true way), that no other view can be tolerated, and that everything can be understood from within that single frame of reference. The truly critical social worker, however, knows that life—and social work practice—are not that simple. Critical social work can draw from many different traditions, realizing the importance and the richness of their interactions, and it is important for critical social workers to value the views of others and to dialogue as openly and constructively with colleagues as they do with clients.

An essential part of the critical practice perspective is the assertion that theorizing undertaken only by social workers, excluding those with whom we work, is unacceptable. Theories and knowledge must emerge, be constructed, critiqued, deconstructed, researched and implemented through the same dialogical process discussed above, involving workers, clients and any others engaged in the social work enterprise. A theory that is inaccessible, dressed up in words that most people cannot understand, is intimidating, exclusive and actually runs counter to the aim of critical practice. Indeed one of the major problems with many so-called "critical theorists" is that they write in language that excludes the very people they claim to be seeking to include and to liberate. Social workers cannot afford the luxury and the intellectual security of using obscure words; their language, like their practice, has to be grounded in the experiences of those with whom they work. This derives from the important linking of theory and practice, often characterized as praxis, which maintains that knowledge and action cannot be divorced from each other, but that they are two aspects of the same process: we know through what we do, we do through what we know, and so good praxis is a continuing process of learning-doing. This is not unique to critical social workers, but when placed alongside the linking of the personal and the political, the insistence on a partnership of learning-doing involving both worker and client(s), and the imperative to address oppressive structures and discourses, it is a powerful prescription for progressive social work.

Commentary

Ife identifies several elements of critical social work. The two most obvious are that critical social work embraces an emancipatory interest—its purpose is to improve the lives of real individuals—and that critical social work is critical to some aspects of current social practices. The latter can be viewed as social practices and institutional arrangements that do harm or at least have a greater potential to do harm.

Ife goes on to articulate the beginnings of a specific value system of critical social work. The approach generally falls within a non-violent tradition. Part of the foundation for this non-violent approach stems from a rejection of dualistic thinking common to contemporary Western thought. One form of dualistic thinking makes a distinction between means and ends. Means are actions or pathways while ends are goals. With this distinction, the argument can be made that ends may justify means.

If society is understood as resulting from the social interactions of concrete individuals and not as a object somehow distinct from the social activity of real people, this notion of ends justifying means becomes problematic. The means are real social interactions. If they are the stuff of society, then they are also the ends, perhaps the ends in progress. The method of achievement shapes the achievement itself. In a more practical sense, the way a social worker treats a client is part of the stuff of that client's life. A social worker cannot dominate a client and expect empowerment to result. Such domination reproduces relations of dominance. This may be physical dominance as in restricting activities or a kind of intellectual domination via inaccessible professional languages.

Ife address client and social worker relations. First there is an imbalance of power by virtue of position. Working with the client and creating knowledge with the client can lessen this imbalance. This becomes the foundation alternate social relations. It is from this personal experience with the social worker that alternate political possibilities may develop.

For Ife's critical social work, the personal and the political are linked. This is both seeing the political implications of one's action and understanding one's life within a political context. Trevor Spratt develops this theme as he offers his understanding of critical social work.

Critical Theory and Critical Social Work

Trevor Spratt

Before I venture into a discussion of what critical social work might be, I want to share the journey that got me there. Critical thinking started for me on a summer Saturday in 1974. The catalytic incident occurred on a building site near our home in Belfast. As I remember it, the afternoon was hot and the tracks of hard-baked rutted mud made my father's truck sway and lurch as he drove in low gear towards a flat dusty area at the centre of the site. Ahead, a group of "lads" (our local term for adolescent males) seated on concrete slabs tracked our progress with sun-squinted eyes. I knew them. We attended the same church but not the same school. Their fathers owned small- to medium-sized businesses (*petit bourgeois,* I would later learn to class them) and paid for their private education. I climbed from the cab and greeted them, and they lazily began to stir. Our communications were always a little strained, our age and stage granting commonality of experience, our differing social classes roughing our edges. We joked and jibed while my father unloaded the truck. Then one of the lads looked towards my father and called to him. "Hi, Jim (I always called their fathers "Mister," but such were the signifiers of class). Hot day for heavy work." My father, a good natured man with no thought for status, smiled and agreed. The lads began to elbow each other in the ribs, and to whisper and snigger. Their collective mood was changing. They rose to their feet and gathered at the back of the truck. My father closed the tailgate and got into the cab. I followed him. My father started the truck and engaged the gears. In the side mirror I watched one of the lads swing a nail-pierced club into the metal flanks of the truck. The sound was like gears failing to mesh. "What was that?" asked my father. "That was nothing, Dad," I replied.

In such circumstances my critical thinking was born. It started with anger, which begat analyses, which in turn begat understanding and led to action. But it was a long journey, and not without its share of wrong turns and blind alleys.

My anger burned for a while. I hated the "lads." I left their church and joined another. I made friends with the sons and daughters of the working and professional classes. But raw emotions only take you so far. I began to reflect upon and classify my experiences. How much were we exercising free will, how much were we influenced by our social groups? Moral agents or unconscious actors? I devoured a school course in sociology and spent time without a job. And propelled by this interlocking of thought and experience, I entered university. Like so many of my generation, I became infatuated with German intellectuals. The first of these was Karl Marx. His proposal, that our social performances were dictated by huge and largely unperceived economic forces, appealed to my hungry appetite for a radical philosophy. It also mollified my need for status, as I comforted myself that my total lack of power or wealth was easily compensated for by a sophisticated understanding of social processes that elevated me above the unconscious actor and placed me in the pantheon of those *who knew*. For a while I actually believed that social injustices could be addressed by revolution, this despite the evidence from around the planet as to what actually happened when such revolutions occurred (i.e., that power became appropriated by new elites). But Marx became unfashionable (how we hate to admit that such lofty notions are actually subject to such a flimsy concept as *fashion*) and became the preserve of college lecturers with beards and tweed jackets, and ageing trade unionists with peaked caps and badges who met together in scout halls on winter nights to subject the texts to endless revision and remember old battles, usually lost. Anyway, there was Max Weber to think about. Weber's theories were more subtle, and they allowed for the independence of ideas. They demonstrated how these ideas worked through history and expressed themselves in different ways in different places. These ideas were less doctrinaire, more grown up. And, as I thought of myself as maturing, they sat well with me. At this point I was a long distance from individualistic and personal accounts of human history. I rather had accepted that structural accounts offered the best basis upon which patterns of action on the part of individuals, families, communities and nations might be understood. Thus armed, I re-entered what my non university friends called the "real world."

This was the beginning point of my interest in social work. My anthropological explorations in the world of work (I had to give my purposes some kind of intellectual veneer as the jobs were invariably so badly paid) convinced me that a career in intellectual diversions could not be as satisfying as everyday human interaction. I was happy. Paradoxically, it was my wife, a pragmatist rather than a theoretician, who encouraged my return to university on the basis that a job in the real world was not the same thing as a real job. I duly enrolled in post-graduate social work. The teaching on this path represented individual problems in the collectivized form of social issues. This reflected a tradition in British social science of treating social ills by the application of social benefits. While such an approach did not pathologize individuals, neither did it theoretically address issues of causation, aside from a general understanding that the less access one had to resources the more likely one would be to suffer a range of social ills. Social work was less about challenging the political and economic structures that created social ills, through restricted access to social and economic capital, and more about offering casualties of such processes some protection against the effects. On becoming a social worker, the reasons for such emphasis became clear. Social workers were, in the main, employed by government agencies, and such agencies were not in the business of challenging the policies of their masters. Rather, they constructed social work as a remedial service for those in society who could not or would not service their own needs. And, as I found in my first job working with families and children, the emphasis was firmly on the "would nots."

Child care social work has for me represented an enduring battle site between those who primarily understand the problems of families and children as products of individual deficit and those who locate causation within the structures of society. While the British tradition of applying social benefits to social ills resulted in the benefits of the welfare state being targeted on the poorest in society, such an approach struggled to make sense of the emergence of child physical abuse in the 1960s and child sexual abuse in the 1970s. The colonization of "abuse" as a concept by initially medical and, later, legal interests influenced social workers to adopt theories of individual pathology as premises underlying their practice. So it was in my ten-year career in social work practice. We looked for "signs and symptoms" of child abuse. We forensically analyzed family histories and parental behaviours. We took people to clinics, and we took them to court. Occasionally we observed that our clients were socially homogenous, but we reassured ourselves with theories of working-class visibility and presumed equal prevalence hidden behind middle-class privet hedges. There was little German influence upon our thinking. Our saving grace was that we did realize something was wrong. By and large we had come into social work to help people and not to act as inquisitional agents of the state. The distance of contradiction between our aspirations and our actions generally made us unhappy. We needed some new ideas.

I went back to university again, to do some research and to do some thinking. Would it be possible to develop ways of understanding work with families and children that allowed for structural considerations of their problems yet offered ways to address these which eschewed paternalism in favour of partnership? Could I marry critical theory with the realities of practice? I wasn't sure. I turned to another German for help. My advice is not to try and read Jurgen Habermas's original texts as they are densely written and the arguments are complicated. They do, however, contain lots of good theory, which is more easily grasped by reading any one of a number of very fine Habermas readers—let someone else do the hard work for you. It was Habermas who offered a way of conceptualizing what was going on between state agents and families. His notions of *system* and *life world,* with the former seeking to colonize the latter with pathological consequences, did not require much refining in their application to the relationships between social workers and families. The more difficult task lay ahead: how to move beyond analysis to action. To add method to theory. Happily, synchronicity was to now to play a part. First, I met Stan Houston, a man with a mind immersed in theory and wanting to find a way to conceptualize his social work experiences with families. He proposed we delineate the ideological premises underpinning social work practice and suggested Habermas's theory of communicative reason as an ideological ideal type to which we might aspire. This we duly did. Second, we met Tom Magill, an actor with a method but lacking theory to support it. We introduced Habermas to Tom and he introduced Augusto Boal to us. And from this exotic fusion we evolved a methodology for consciousness raising and collective action described elsewhere in my chapter in this book (see Chapter 7). The methodology has now been tested in a number of educational and social work settings. The world has not been set on fire, but the results have been encouraging.

So that's the journey. Time now for a definition of what I think critical social work might be. But first, three things it is not. It is not an intellectual prop to justify personal anger, frustration or failure. In his novel *The Corrections*, Jonathan Franzen offers us the central character of Chip Lambert, the family failure and an untenured "critical theory" lecturer at a small college on the eastern seaboard. Chip teaches Veblen through to Habermas, encouraging his students to challenge the march of capitalism that has resulted in universal commodification. At least he does until a particularly insightful student observes that it is only angry people like him who see anything wrong with people making money and being happy. Critical theory should not be a Trojan horse for our own personal failures or frustrations. These things may start at the experiential equivalent of my building site, but they cannot end there. Nor should critical theory be an end in itself. The more potent the idea, the more likely a resulting intellectual intoxication. This is a short step to irrelevancy. The use of critical theory in social work must be harnessed to practice, otherwise it is of no practical use. It may satisfy an individual need for academic kudos but will leave the world unchanged. Lastly, it is not a totalizing theory. It will not explain everything, nor should it be stretched to do so. The road down which doctrine leads to oppression has been well travelled, and there is no need to go that way again. For example, critical theory offers a plausible rationale for the causes of child physical abuse but has less to say with regard to the causes of child sexual abuse. That leaves me with what critical theory should be. It should, I think, offer an understanding as to how structural processes produce inequalities. It should offer insights as to how we may be consciously or unconsciously involved in reproducing these inequalities. It should offer strategies for action aimed at challenging or resolving contradictions created by such structures of oppression.

One last thought: theory and social work have always been uneasy partners. We have borrowed ideas haphazardly and used them promiscuously. We have done this for the best of reasons, to make lives better. Yet we have seldom acted reflexively to examine our own position. Critical theory offers us the potential to identify our own tendency to shore up agencies of oppression as well as to create contradiction in our lives. Only when we have done that work may we move on to the business of other people's lives.

Commentary

Overall, Spratt is assuming a connection between critical theory, in this case the work of Jurgen Habermas, and critical social work. Not everyone who sees himself or herself connected in some fashion to critical social work shares the connection to critical theory. This is, though, a quite common connection. Critical, in Spratt's piece, has several meanings. It refers to a type of thinking that is focused and requires evidence and consideration before accepting typical commonsense explanations. This critical thinking is a key component to critical social work, as Spratt understand it. Critical in this sense refers to the application of a type of thinking to action, not that thought and action are that separable. There is also the suggestion that process be guided in some fashion. Spratt finds his guidance in critical theory, particularly the work of Habermas. Within this work, and this is significant to Spratt's approach, there is the application of critical thinking to your own thinking. The stance of the thinker/actor does not escape critical consideration.

Habermas, like the critical theorists before him, was concerned with the legitimating function of sets of ideas. A set of ideas, a theory if you like, often contains assumptions that rest upon an implicit political perspective. Spratt states that the British approach of treating social ills with the application of social benefits is a practice based on a theory of individual need and avoids questioning the structural components of social ills. In that sense it is inherently conservative, fostering the status quo. This level of analysis is consistent with critical theory and a significant part of Spratt's critical social work. He illustrates it again in referring to the colonization of the concept "abuse."

As with the critical theorist, it is true for Spratt that purposeful action, in this case the intent of social workers to help people, must be informed by theory. Two concepts proved useful for Spratt, *system* and *life world*. They are addressed in Chapter 7, which is authored by Spratt. For our purposes, we see that Spratt uses these concepts to develop a method for consciousness raising and collective action. Again, there is an emphasis on thought and action. This is a central theme in Spratt's approach.

Spratt leaves us with three negative definitions of critical social work, or what critical social work is not. These negative definitions leave open the possibilities of what critical social work is, is becoming or could be. The emphasis upon the potential resonates with Spratt's critical social work. His negative definitions are that critical social work is not (1) an intellectual prop to justify personal anger, frustration or failure; (2) an end in itself; and (3) a totalizing perspective. Critical social work is, as Spratt has illustrated, a wedding of the personal, political and the possible.

Given his abilities and fortunate circumstances, Spratt had the opportunity to develop a practice for his perspective. Most social workers do not have that flexibility in their work. Is there a place for critical social work in the context of traditional social work settings? Healy, below, addresses that issue in her understanding of critical social work. Her perspective blends context and theory within the confines of a traditional social work agency.

What Is Critical Social Work?

Karen Healy

The act of defining critical social work is both a necessary and dangerous one. It is necessary because to support and promote critical practices we must differentiate them from non-critical approaches. Yet, it is also dangerous for two reasons. First, such definition runs the risk of denying the diversity of critical social work practices. For example, many definitions of emancipatory practice privilege practice strategies suited to small, collaborative organizational contexts and, in so doing, neglect the actuality or potential for critical practice in many human service organizations. Narrow definitions of what counts as critical practices exclude most social workers from the critical canon, thus reproducing the academic-practice split that has limited the development of critical knowledge development in social work.

Second, defining critical social work is dangerous because it may compromise social workers' capacities for critical practice. As I have stated elsewhere, "acts of making social work processes visible should be approached with caution and with an ongoing reflexivity about the linkages between this project and the processes of governmentality to which social work practices in the post-modern era are increasingly subjected" (Healy, 2000, p.146). For instance, a social worker in deeply conservative organizational contexts, such as some hospital or welfare bureaucracies, must adopt highly strategic approaches to activism. Indeed, their activism may only be effective insofar as it is not recognized by others as transformative and therefore is not perceived a threat to the usual order of things. Paradoxically, then, the most effective critical social work practice, in some organizational contexts, is that which is not recognized as critical at all. While the illumination of these forms of activism may be useful for critical social work education, they may be less helpful and possibly counterproductive for the achievement of institutional transformation.

It is in full recognition of these risks that I outline my understanding of critical social work (see Healy, 2001b) as approaches characterized by

- a recognition that large-scale social processes, particularly those associated with class, gender and race, fundamentally contribute to the personal and social dislocation encountered by many service users;

- the adoption of a self-reflexive and critical stance towards the often contradictory effects of social work practice and social policies;

- a commitment to co-participatory rather than authoritarian practice relations. This involves workers and service users, as well as other stakeholders working together as co-participants in problem solving and social change, engaged with but still distinct from one another; and

- working with and for oppressed populations to achieve social change.

A broad range of theories of practice are contained under the umbrella of critical social work, including: radical, feminist, anti-oppressive, structural, radical community work and, more recently, critical postmodern approaches. Despite their diversity, these practice approaches draw at least some of their core assumptions from the critical social sciences. These assumptions are, first, that overarching social structures, such as the structures of capitalism, patriarchy and imperialism, fundamentally shape institutional and interpersonal relationships. Hence, from an analysis of an individual's location in the social structure, we can deduce their relation to institutions and also to other individuals.

Second, a critical social science analysis accords priority to the understanding of power relations among opposed categories of individuals, such as men/women, able bodied/disabled, white/non-white, as fundamentally conflictual. According to the conflict perspective, the power of individuals or groups reinforces and reflects structural inequities.

Third, the critical social science model promotes "consciousness raising" as key to personal and social transformation. In accordance with Marx's materialist dialectic, it is recognized that people's analysis of the world and their place in it is shaped by their structural location. The complicity of the oppressed in their oppression is secured by dominant ideologies that immobilize people's capacities to develop a rational and self-conscious understanding of the structural origins of their disadvantage. Consciousness raising is advocated as a process whereby oppressed individuals can discard false ideologies in favour of understanding their structural disadvantage and an orientation towards developing capacities for overcoming it.

Fourth, critical social science theories aim to empower their audience to transform the social order via participation in collective action (Fay, 1987, p.23). Critical social scientists argue that collective action offers the only viable path for oppressed individuals to transform the social order.

These core principles provide a useful, though partial, framework for defining critical social work practices in the twenty-first century. I contend that any contemporary definition of critical social work must also attend to the following dimensions.

First, contemporary definitions of critical social work must recognize how the institutional contexts of practice shapes activist possibilities. In defining critical practice, then, we should refer not only to a set of abstract critical social science principles, but also to the organizational and policy environment shaping practice. For instance, the definition of critical social work will be very different in one context of practice, such as a small advocacy organization, than a large bureaucratic organization, such as public welfare agency or a major hospital. In short, our definitions of critical practice must be sufficiently open-ended to allow recognition of the possibilities and constraints for critical practices within specific institutional contexts.

Second, our definitions of critical social work must recognize social workers and service users as embodied actors who bring different capacities to the goal of social transformation. Without this sensitivity to difference, critical social work practice theories potentially exclude forms of activism that differ from Eurocentric and masculinist norms of critical practice. For example, the Participatory Action Research tradition, often posited as a critical approach to social work research (see Finn, 1994), draws on a conflictual notion of power relations and approaches to social transformation. Although this approach is often characterized as an international model of social research, its conflict orientation means that it is unsuitable to cultures where the open expression of conflict is seen as inappropriate and disrespectful, such as many of the cultures in the Asia Pacific region (Healy, 2001a). In short, critical theories of practice must recognize activists as embodied actors.

Third, while new definitions of critical social work theories must incorporate analyses of social super-structures, we must also resist seeing disadvantaged people as victims of the social order (Crinnall, 1995). To be sure, many of the service users we meet in social work practice are subject to a myriad of social oppressions. Yet, we must also find ways of recognizing and supporting people's capacities for transformation in the context of these disadvantages. Furthermore, we must do so in ways that respect different perspectives on the world and an individual's position in it, rather than dismiss these views as evidence of false consciousness. For example, in my work with young homeless mothers, I am often struck by the capacity of young women to understand their situation and to develop strategies for "getting by" and eventually to "get ahead." I am also critical of the extent to which critical strategies, such as consciousness raising, can diminish young women's understanding and capacities for action.

In this paper I have offered some beginning pointers for contemporary definitions of critical social work practice. My approach draws on the rich tradition of critical social work practice models and yet seeks to move beyond them to recognize the institutional context of social work practices, social workers and service users as embodied actors, and finally, to value individuals' capacity to understand and act on their world in a myriad of ways. These suggestions are offered in the spirit of enriching and promoting critical social work practices.

Commentary

Healy addresses the task of defining critical social work with understandable caution. The intent of critical social work is social change achieved through inclusion. It is a praxis, a blending of theory and practice. Any theory that cannot inform practice or defines practice that is impossible within the current social conditions is irrelevant for critical social work. This then introduces the arduous task of defining a critical perspective that has the potential for being employed within a traditional setting. Later in the volume Webb addresses the same issue by examining the relationship between social worker and client. Healy suggests that a stringent definition of critical social work may eliminate the possibility of doing critical social work. As a minimum definition Healy sees critical social work as characterized by (1) a recognition that large-scale social processes contribute to the dislocation of service users, (2) a self-reflective and critical stance towards social work practice and social policy, (3) a commitment to co-participation, and (4) a working towards social change with and for oppressed populations.

Healy has addressed practice within the confines of the traditional social work context. Solomon addresses practice from a far different angle but within a critical social work perspective. Solomon reminds us of the importance of recognizing the power relations involved in producing knowledge about critical social work itself. In defining and discussing critical social work, we must not overlook and leave out the voices and ideas of those with the least access to power. An academic book such as this does run that danger.

Good Morning: Thinking about Critical Perspectives

Brenda Solomon

In a debate that I later learned was entitled "Justice Talking," Zinn argued that teachers should encourage students to critically explore United States history in public schools, while Gibbon asserted that teachers should be casting a positive light on U.S. history, exploring its "virtues, triumphs and glories" (National Public Radio, 2003, February 7, n.p.),

While many things struck me about the Zinn-Gibbon debate, what seemed most alarming was that it was familiar to me. This sort of challenge to critical inquiry was becoming more common, the questioning of questioning was gaining momentum, and the use of "good" or "a good light" to re-signify and overcast critical analysis was, indeed, forming a wake-up call.[1]

Up to the point of listening to the Zinn-Gibbon debate, I thought this paper should be concerned with the *expression* of critical analysis in social work — what is meant by it, what seems to be at play in the actions of those who are doing "critical social work," how the attention of critical inquiry has shifted, and what questions and concerns need to be addressed in the actualities of performing critical social work in texts, classroom discussions and practice situations. But after hearing this debate, my attention has been drawn to the knowledge produced *about* critical social work and the relations of power at play in the meanings made of it.

Certainly, taking a critical stance, like doing critical social work, is not easily summed up and explained. Yet it seems safe to say that traditionally (at least from where I write in the United States) taking a critical stance has been talked about and treated in ways that suggest its general value, linking with ideals of freedom, education, forming independent opinions, participating in the democratic process and democracy itself.[2]

Yet more recently (in and out of the United States), a critical stance in academic and professional work has at times, if not more so, been associated with and informed by social constructionist and postmodern methods of inquiry and interests in knowledge formation. Although, like critical social work, postmodern and social constructionist positions are not easily rendered and explained, most often a critical stance utilizing these ways of explicating lived experience in social work and other related areas of study is more concerned with taken-for-granted knowledge about freedom, independent thought, and

---

[1] Critical analysis of U.S. policy and academic and intellectual freedom in colleges and universities are subjects of reports in recent news and academic association and society publications. For instance, see Rogers, J., & Vanden Heuvel, K. (2001, November 25). What's left? A new life for progressivism. *The nation.* Online at <www.thenation.com/doc.mhtml?I=20011210&s=kvh20011125>;Glenn, D. (2001, December 3). The war on campus. *The nation.* Online at <www.thenation.com/doc.mhtml?I=2001203&s=glenn>; American Library Association. (last modified 2002, January 24). Resolution reaffirming the principles of intellectual freedom in the aftermath of terrorist attacks. Online at <www.ala.org/alaorg/oif/reaffirmifprinciples.html>; Miller, R. (2002, September 5). UC Berkeley: A safe harbor for hate. *Front Page Magazine.* Online at <www.FrontPageMagazine.com/articles/readarticle.asp?ID=2725>; Various Contributors. (2002, January 10). Tattletales for an open society. *The nation.* Online at <www.thenation.com/doc.mhtml?i=20020121&s=tattle20020110>; and Sherwin, M.J. (2002, January 9). Tattletales for an open society. *The nation.* Online at <www.thenation.com/doc.mhtml?i=20020121&s=sherwin20020109>.

[2] In the "Justice Talking" debate, Howard Zinn indicates a connection between thinking critically about U.S. history and democracy as follows: "I'm not suggesting we trash the past...I want to prepare young people to say 'no' to the government. There are times where you might say 'yes' to the government, but I'm suggesting patriotism means being true and loyal — not to the government, but to the principles which underlie democracy.

democracy and the power relations involved in producing what is taken for truth about these (and other) supposed ideals.[3]

For those of us who take a critical stance in social work that is informed by social constructionism and postmodernism, our critical thinking concerns taken-for-granted knowledge claims, the power relations involved in making those claims and the ways in which such claims produce subjects. With an interest particularly in the production of marginalized subjects, such approaches in social work highlight the ways social life is formed and interpreted to advantage some at the disadvantage of others.[4] As philosophers Linda Alcoff and Elizabeth Potter (1993) point out in their introduction to *Feminist Epistemologies*, to take this sort of stance is to

> raise a question about the adequacy of any account of knowledge that ignores the politics involved in knowledge...[to] attend to the complex ways in which social values influence knowledge, including the discernible social and political implications of its own analysis,...[and] to contribute to an emancipatory goal: the expansion of democracy in the production of knowledge. (pp. 13-14)

Those of us who articulate our work in terms of critical social work, or are implicated by association with it, are being strung along with other producers and supposed producers of critical work to find ourselves located at a freshly contested site of "power/knowledge" production—at the very site where we do critical work. Therefore, as knowledge is produced about taking a critical stance towards power relations and the production of knowledge, the focus of critical social work seems to require a shift to begin analysis in the knowledge produced about critical social work itself.

In order to keep our attention on power, we need to begin with the meanings made of our project of critical social work as we carry out that project in the many forms it takes. And, while this is not an entirely new area of awareness, at this point, the call for such a shift in focus seems to be increasingly urgent.

More so, in our response we have an opportunity to show how critical social work may produce more just power relations and consequences: that more people participate and have their say in negotiating social arrangements.[5]

---

[3] While I realize that postmodern, social constructionist and critical social work positions are not synonymous and may be taken at cross purposes, it seems, at this point, they commonly inform and extend social work analysis that may begin from any one of these positions. For more about these positions and their relation to one another in social work see L. Dominelli (1996), K. Healy (2001), G. Miller and J.A. Holstein (1993), N. Parton (1994), B. Pease and J. Fook (1999), and R.G. Sands and K. Nuccio (1992).

[4] My use of the term "power" to explicate relations is mostly informed by French philosopher Michel Foucault (1972, 1980) and Canadian sociologist Dorothy E. Smith (1987, 1990, 1996). Foucault talks about power as a complex relation rather than an essential feature of institutions or individuals. He is interested in how power works in consort with knowledge to produce subject positions. Smith, through her method of institutional ethnography, problematizes taken-for-granted everyday activities, connecting them to larger objectifying forms of organization and social relations. She also is interested in the ways text enter into the production of power.

[5] As Rhodes (1986) points out, justice itself is a negotiated concept that is not adequately sorted out for the purposes of ethical practice in social work. Similarly, Linda Briskman (2001) discusses the conceptual and ethical issues in articulating positions such as the social good in practice contexts.

To explain, I return to the Zinn-Gibbon debate. Among the things that struck me about it was how I temporarily accepted the performance of debate—two designated experts talking back and forth, two male, white, educated voices, one with a position for and the other with a position against, and that these together suggested a comprehensive representation of views and possible assertions and rebuttals. Of course, all of these features of debate hooked into and reinforced the dichotomizing of good and critical.

Yet, despite the overwhelming suggestion to the contrary, Howard Zinn and Peter Gibbon could not possibly know, speak about or be interested in all of what could be said about how to teach American history fairly, nor fully establish "critical" and "good" as essentially opposing approaches. Although I listened to two people debate good and critical and gladly felt lumped on to the side of Howard Zinn, I didn't hear all of what I have experienced and believed in what Howard had to say. While I was glad he said what he did, and that it was Howard talking, the format of debate itself necessitated a spokesperson and at least the idea of "our side." It made it possible for me to be grateful to Howard or someone like him for, after all, representing me. He brought legitimacy to something that seemed to be "our" position even though he did not say what I had to say and could not speak from my experience or what I imagined so many others of "us" would have wanted to express.

And herein lies our challenge: to demonstrate a critical approach (in our account of knowledge produced about critical social work) that avoids participating in a performance that is reductionistic, that is, a debate, a few speakers that occupy the most legitimizing social categories, an argument or fight, a single position, a final answer, a closed off sense of the meanings of such words as critical and good (even as I use them here).

A format that reduces "us" to our most common and therefore narrowest ideas and experiences renders the complexity of ideas and experiences of too many of us invisible. This is a problem we face, particularly in this new barrage of power, to keep multiple ideas and standpoints (or ways we are made different from one another by power) visible as "we" talk, analyze and critique power together. We may and perhaps should enjoy the ways we have been brought together, yet remain cautious of a strength formed out of being lumped into one so as not to reduce our positions.[6] To act from such commonness, we inadvertently will overlook and leave out the voices and ideas of those with least access to power, and therefore resemble and sound like those closest to and most comfortable with it. And, of course, these ways of power (that produce too few speakers and create devastating ideological and material consequences for so many) are why our project has such relevance.

Even so, considering recent positions with regard to war with Iraq, whereby power and resistance seem obvious and in full view, I am concerned about ways

---

[6] In the way that French philosopher Collette Guillaumin (1995) talks about difference and dominance, I wish to acknowledge and be aware of the ways that we have been made different from one another through power relations in order to raise concern about a fuller array of consequences made to our lives.

to form analysis and take action without further dichotomizing positions, engaging in a "battle" of constructions and being drawn into a chorus of good versus evil.

I wonder how to form a dialogue that values complexity and an array of standpoints in a context wrought with contest, debate and argument.

I wonder how we may form responses that reveal not only the many ways we think but the methods by which we form our ideas—a dialogue among us that necessitates our many voices, bodies, lives, locations and reveals a use of ourselves as speakers—not to talk back to—but peacefully with—in the threat or wake of being blasted.[7]

I wonder how we may participate in dialogue so that those who are most colonized and have the least control of the ideas and resources involved in what may constitute "their say" in any matter will be able to enter dialogue and benefit from it.

At this time when power appears unquestionably pronounced, in view and most vulnerable, work critical of its use may be seen as a threat to it in ways it has not in the recent past, and those concerned with keeping power may be taking a sweeping motion of retribution, denouncing any and all critiques of power.

It seems that as critical is being recast and produced, named and articulated within governmental projects of promoting goodness (such as my example of United States), our critique of power and power relations might best shift to accommodate the historical, socio-political economic times in which we find our critical working selves embedded. Such study holds promise. As Foucault explains:

> The critical ontology of ourselves has to be considered not, certainly, as a theory, a doctrine, nor even as a permanent body of knowledge that is accumulating; it has to be conceived as an attitude, an ethos, a philosophical life in which the critique of what we are is at one and the same time the historical analysis of the limits that are imposed on us and an experiment with the possibility of going beyond them. (1986, p.50)

In this way, as we make visible what is at play in our subjectivity, we make visible the potential service of our methods – a way beyond good and evil.

Commentary

Solomon weaves together several themes and embraces a set of assumptions familiar to many critical social work practitioners. Among these are the guiding values of self-determination, participation and democratic process. There is a recognition of inequitable power relations and restricted lives that result from

---

[7] I rely heavily on a complex of feminist writers involved in analyzing connections between speaking, listening and use of power. For instance see Belenky et al. (1986), Collins (1991), DeVault (1990, 1995), Minh-ha (1989), Reinharz (1992) and Riessman (1997).

those relations. As is common within critical social work, there is also a recognition of a relationship between power and knowledge. In fact, Solomon prefers to speak of "power/knowledge" production.

Solomon suggests that form in the production of knowledge and power influences the possible results. The debate form poses spokesperson against spokesperson in a conflictual process to achieve a single answer. A single answer is not a legitimate quest for critical social work, and Solomon points out that given the power-knowledge nexus, single answers are an illustration of power. The less powerful become excluded from the expression of their experience.

Critical social work or the knowledge foundation of critical social work does not escape the knowledge-power nexus. It too will, to a greater or lesser extent, privilege some over others. To the extent that we consider the knowledge of critical social work to be true, permanent and fixed, the privileging will be to a greater extent. From this perspective, Solomon ponders a method that favours dialogue, that values complexity over contest, debate and argument, responses that reveal many ways of thinking as well as the way by which we form our ideas, and how to include the least privileged in the construction of knowledge and hence power. In many ways, Solomon's definition is a very elaborate and articulate integration of theory and practice.

Conclusion

The "understandings" presented above provide an excellent entry point for further discussion about the theory and practice of critical social work. All would agree that an enterprise such as this will undoubtedly contain multiple perspectives and standpoints. But the diverse understandings are not without their commonalities. The following common features emerge from the contributions of Ife, Healy, Spratt and Solomon:

- larger social relations, whether we call them social structures, large scale social processes or society, contribute to personal and social dislocation or personal problems;
- a self-reflexive and critical analysis of the social control functions of social work practice and social policies;
- working with and for oppressed populations to achieve personal liberation and social change;
- participatory rather than authoritarian practice relations between "worker" and "client"; and
- a recognition that critical social work knowledge itself is socially produced and may exclude the voices of those with the least power.

Critical social work therefore seems to be concerned with developing theory and practice in an inclusive and participatory manner that challenges social relations and structures, as well as social work itself.

References

Alcoff, L. & Potter, E. (Eds.). (1993). *Feminist epistemologies.* NY: Routledge.

Alinsky, S. (1969). *Reveille for radicals.* Random House: New York.

Alinsky, S. (1971). *Rules for radicals: A practical primer for realistic radicals.* Random House: New York.

Bailey, R., & Brake, M. (Eds.). (1975). *Radical social work.* London: Edward Arnold.

Belenky, M.F., Clinchy, B.M., Goldberger, N.G., & Tarule, J.M. (1986). *Women's ways of knowing.* NY: Basic Books, Inc.

Briskman, L. (2001). A moral crisis for social work: Critical practice & code of ethics. *Critical Social Work, 2*(1), n.p. (electronic version).

Collins, P.H. (1991). *Black feminist thought.* NY: Routledge.

Corrigan, P., & Leonard, P. (1978). *Social work practice under capitalism: A Marxist approach.* London: Macmillan.

Crinnall, K. (1995). The search for a feminism that could accommodate homeless young women. *Youth Studies Australia, 14*(3), 42-47.

DeVault, M.L. (1990). Talking and listening from women's standpoint: Feminist strategies for interviewing and analysis. *Social Problems, 37*(1), 96-116.

DeVault, M.L. (1995). Ethnicity and expertise: Racial-ethnic knowledge in sociological research. *Gender & Society, 9*(5), 612-631.

Dominelli, L., & McLeod, E. (1989). *Feminist social work.* Macmillan: London.

Dominelli, L. (1996). Deprofessionalising social work: Anti-oppressive practice, competencies and post-modernism. *British Journal of Social Work, 26*(2), 153-175.

Fay, B. (1987). *Critical social science: Liberation and its limits.* Cornell University Press: Ithaca.

Finn, J. (1994). The promise of participatory action research. *Journal of Progressive Human Services, 5*(2).

Foucault, M. (1972). *The archaeology of knowledge.* NY: Pantheon Books.

Foucault, M. (1980). *Power/knowledge: Selected interviews & other writings 1972-1977* (C. Gordon, Ed.). NY: Pantheon Books.

Foucault, M. (1986). What is enlightenment? In P. Rabinow (Ed.), *The Foucault reader.* Harmondsworth: Penguin.

Freire, P. (1972). *Pedagogy of the oppressed.* Penguin: Harmondsworth.

Galper, J. (1980). *Social work practice: A radical perspective.* Englewood Cliffs, NJ: Prentice Hall.

Gibbon, P.H. (2002). *A call to heroism: Renewing America's vision of greatness.* NY: Atlantic Monthly Press.

Guillaumin, C. (1995). *Racism, sexism, power and ideology.* NY: Routledge.

Healy, K. (2000). *Social work practices: Contemporary perspectives on change.* London: Sage.

Healy, K. (2001). Reinventing critical social work: Challenges from practice, context and postmodernism. *Critical Social Work, 2*(1), n.p. (electronic version).

Healy, K. (2001a). Participatory action research and social work: A critical appraisal. *International Social Work, 44*(1), 93-105.

Healy, K. (2001b). Reinventing critical social work: Challenges from practice, context and postmodernism. *Critical Social Work, 2*(1). Online at www.criticalsocialwork.com.

Ife, J. (1997). *Rethinking social work: Towards critical practice.* Longman: Melbourne.

Ife, J. (2001). *Human rights and social work: Towards rights-based practice.* Cambridge: Cambridge University Press.

Jones, C. (1983). *State social work and the working class.* London: Macmillan.

Leonard, P. (1997). *Postmodern welfare: Reconstructing an emancipatory project.* London: Sage.

Miller, G., & Holstein, J.A. (Eds.). (1993). *Constructionist controversies: Issues in social problems theory.* Hawthorne, NY: Aldine de Gruyter.

Minh-ha, T.T. (1989). *Woman, native, other.* Indianapolis: Indiana University Press.

National Public Radio (2003, February 7). Justice talking/citizen student: Teaching patriotism in time of war. *Morning edition.* Online at <discover.npr.org/features/feature.jhtml?wfId=957688>.

Parton, N. (1994). The nature of social work under conditions of (post)modernity. *Social Work and Social Sciences Review, 5*(2), 93-112.

Pease, B., & Fook, J. (Eds.). (1999). *Transforming social work practice: Postmodern critical perspectives.* St. Leonards, NSW: Allen & Unwin.

Powell, F. (2001). *The politics of social work.* London: Sage.

Reinharz, S. (1992). *Feminist methods in social research.* NY: Oxford University Press.

Rhodes, M.L. (1986). *Ethical dilemmas in social work practice.* London: Routledge and Kegan Paul.

Riessman, C.K. (1987). When gender is not enough: Women interviewing women. *Gender & Society, 1,* 172-207.

Sands, R.G., & Nuccio, K. (1992). Postmodern feminist theory and social work. *Social Work, 37*(6), 489-494.

Skenridge, P., & Lennie, I. (1978). Social work: The wolf in sheep's clothing. *Arena, 51,* 47-92

Smith, D.E. (1987). *The everyday world as problematic.* Boston, MA: Northeastern University Press.

Smith, D.E. (1990). *Texts, facts, and femininity: Exploring the relations of ruling.* NY: Routledge.

Smith, D.E. (1996). Telling the truth after postmodernism. *Symbolic Interaction, 19*(3), 171-202.

Zinn, H. (2003). *A people's history of the United States.* NY: New Press.

2

Therapeutic Critique: Traditional versus Critical Perspectives

Richard Pozzuto, G. Brent Angell and Paul K. Dezendorf

Social workers use a variety of practice approaches with individual clients. Over the past thirty years, these approaches have increased in number and diversified in technique. Underlying these various individual practice approaches, however, is a fundamental division between those based on a traditional foundation versus those built on a critical foundation. The use of the terms traditional and critical is guided by the distinction articulated by Max Horkheimer (1972) in his essay "Traditional and Critical Theory." This perspective has been extended by Habermas (1972) in his work entitled *Knowledge and Human Interests*. Here, Habermas suggests a technical interest, which is consistent with but not identical to Horkheimer's traditional theory, that substitutes technique for reflexive action (p. 316). In the former, technique is applicable regardless of context. The increased emphasis on technique in social work illustrates a movement towards practice founded on this traditional underpinning.

A "traditional" foundation rests on the assumption that social work is nestled within mainstream society, accepting directives for the maintenance and functioning of that society within traditional social work's technical requirements. This traditional approach views the proper place for solving individual problems as within the mechanisms of the current social order. This is not necessarily a position consciously adopted by the profession or the practitioner. This position flows from the perspective assumed as a result of the knowledge base of the field. A "critical" foundation rests on the belief that the "givens" of any particular society should be viewed with suspicion, and critical social work seeks opportunities to uncover the possibility for alternative and better social forms. This critical approach fosters self-directed emancipatory practice for both individual and social transformation.

This discussion describes the underlying basis for both approaches using the concept of the "deep stories." For traditional social work, such stories include those of the autonomous individual created by Adam Smith, Thomas Hobbes and John Locke. Critical social work's deep stories lie in the relationships described by the models and perspectives of writers such as George Herbert Mead, Cooley and Gergen. The difference between traditional and critical approaches is illustrated in practice by an examination of what the authors term "narrative therapy." Narrative therapy questions the fundamental concepts that each individual utilizes to understand and create their world. Narrative therapy attempts to remove the "naturalness" of present social relations and reveal their future possibility. As a result, the "necessity" of a particular action is replaced by contingency and choice, thus facilitating human agency.

Traditional Social Work Perspective

A social work organization's mission reflects their history. The dominant professional group in the United States, primarily composed of practitioners, is the National Association of Social Workers (NASW). The dominant educational group, primarily composed of educators, is the Council on Social Work Education (CSWE). CSWE recognizes and defers to NASW regarding ethical practice and incorporates the NASW Code of Ethics into social work education. For CSWE and NASW, the mission of social work is contained in the preamble of the NASW Code of Ethics:

> The primary mission of the social work profession is to enhance human well-being and help meet the basic human needs of all people, with particular attention to the needs and empowerment of people who are vulnerable, oppressed, and living in poverty. A historic and defining feature of social work is the profession's focus on individual well-being in a social context and the well-being of society. Fundamental to social work is attention to the environmental forces that create, contribute to, and address problems in living. (NASW, 1999)

Two international organizations, the International Federation of Social Workers (IFSW) and the International Association of Schools of Social Work (IASSW) perform functions analogous to the NASW and the CSWE. The IFSW in conjunction with the IASSW defines the mission of social work as follows:

> The social work profession promotes social change, problem solving in human relationships and the empowerment and liberation of people to enhance well-being. Utilizing theories of human behaviors and social systems, social work intervenes at the points where people interact with their environments. Principles of human rights and social justice are fundamental to social work. (IASSW, 2001)

Both mission statements call on social work to enhance human well-being and to recognize the connections between people and their environment; both statements highlight empowerment and advocate social change. The differences between them, however, suggest ideological perspectives that in turn reflect different intellectual perspectives. NASW's wording highlights the well-being of the individual and society; the statement suggests that there is little conflict expected with society on the part of the individual. Rather, the individual will seek improvement within the social order. The international organization's statement emphasizes human rights, social justice and social change; the statement suggests that there is inherent conflict with society when seeking to improve the lot of individuals.

The international statement appears compatible with perspectives that recognize conflictual relations between and among groups, perhaps centered around distribution of scarce goods, competing religious or political beliefs, or claims to authority, as a common aspect of society. These conflicts, in turn, impact human rights and social justice, thus creating a need for social change. Such conflict perspectives have not been well received in the U.S. The NASW statement appears in keeping with a functional rather than conflict perspective, and, in fact, functional models such as those by Parsons (1951) or Putnam (1993) have been better received in the U.S. than models based on conflict.

Those differing perspectives date back to the beginnings of social work. At that time, the technological innovations of the Industrial Revolution and the intellectual currents of the Enlightenment were bringing about a new type of society. Whose interests should be represented by the new common good? The propertied class, the developing industrialists or the newly emerging working class? Social work was born out of these issues and the tumultuous conditions created by the growth of a market economy (Lewis, 1998; Pozzuto, 2001). Polanyi (1957) captures the spirit of "the great transformation" in his book by that name:

> At the heart of the Industrial Revolution of the eighteenth century there was an almost miraculous improvement in the tool of production, which was accompanied by a catastrophic dislocation of the lives of the common people. We will attempt to disentangle the factors that determined the forms of this dislocation, as it appeared at its worst in England about a century ago. What "satanic mill" ground men into masses? How much was caused by the new physical conditions? How much by the economic dependencies, operating under new conditions? And what was the mechanism through which the old social tissue was destroyed and a new integration of man and nature so unsuccessfully attempted? (p. 33)

The destruction of what Polanyi aptly called the "social tissue" and the resulting fear, anxiety and physical deprivation (suffered in proportion to one's position in the new social order) stimulated the growth of social work's progenitors — the Charity Organization Society (COS) and the Settlement House Movement (SHM). COS and SHM were motivated by fear and by compassion: fear that the "respectable" members of society would be overrun by the emerging working classes (Jones, 1971; Pumphrey, 1959) and compassion for the working classes' deteriorating social conditions. In order to resist the "pauperization of the poor," the COS sought to adjust the needy, primarily by moral approaches, to the needs and ethos of the new social order (Camilleri, 1996). The poor (and their affinity for socialism as they saw it) presented a threat to the COS and all it stood for (Bosanquet, 1997).

The SHM was more accepting of some forms of socialist thought and more flexible in its attempts to adjust society to the needs of the poor (Seigfried, 1999) while assisting the individual. The COS-SHM split — between adjusting the individual to society or society to the individual — remains embedded in social work (Chanbon, Irving, & Epstein, 1999). Over time, much of social work accepted a dichotomy between the individual and society; in turn, the profession emphasized work with individuals and small groups in order to adjust the individual to society. In doing so, social work passed up the opportunity for a broader vision of a common good, perhaps transcending the individual-society dichotomy. This dichotomy is quite functional to a traditional approach in that it maintains separate, distinct categories for analysis and issue resolution.

The dichotomy is illustrated by the development of social work in the U.S. The COS/SHM period was followed by the development of three schools of social work theory: the New York Freudian or diagnostic school, the Pennsylvanian Rankian or functional school, and the Chicago school of public welfare. Each school had doctrinaire adherents while many other social workers simply "practised" social work. Social work further split into various groups and subgroups such as medical, psychiatric, public assistance and so forth. While each grouping might have merit regarding practice knowledge, all of these groupings had made the transition from "cause" to "function" articulated by Porter Lee.

Porter Lee, the director of the New York School of Social Work, argued that social work changed from a cause, social reform, to a function, the organized provision of casework and help to individuals in need (Lee, 1939). Lee showcased that argument in a famous speech following the Milford Conference in 1928. Lee argued that social work had positioned itself within mainstream society and that the profession had taken responsibility for the maintenance and functioning of that society.

Social work has a long and varied history mixed with strands of compassion, protection and reform. As social work professionalized, seeking legitimacy and protection for its practitioners, social work built selectively on this history. It is beyond our scope to address the fit between the institutional location of social work, which has varied over time, and the preferred practice perspectives. Suffice it to say that there were alternate paths for social work and, in fact, there are alternate futures. These futures depend on actions in the present. In the following sections we will provide elements of a foundation for a future steeped within an alternate perspective of social work. Our goal is not to recreate the past in the future but to learn from our past and draw on the yet unrealized potential.

Critical Social Work Perspective

With the advantage of hindsight, it appears that the preferred practice perspective of social work and the primacy of casework were in sharp contrast to the need for addressing social problems brought about by the massive changes from Polanyi's great transformation (Jones, 1971). Social work in the U.S. even seemed unable to recognize the "great transformation" and lost sight of the need for another transformation to offset the problems of the first (Watson, 1971). In part, this approach follows from the "traditional" perspective with its objectified view of the social world. In contrast, we are suggesting a "critical" perspective for social work and active participation in the creation of the future.

As stated earlier, the use of the terms "traditional" and "critical" is based in the distinction articulated in 1970 by Max Horkheimer in his essay "Traditional and Critical Theory" (1972):

> The traditional idea of theory is based on scientific activity as carried on within the division of labor at a particular stage in the latter's development. It corresponds to the activity of the scholar which takes place alongside all the other activities of a society but in no immediate clear connection with them. In this view of theory, therefore, the real function of science is not made manifest; it speaks not of what theory means in human life, but only of what it means in the isolated sphere in which for historical reasons it comes into existence. (p. 197)

Traditional social work takes place alongside all the other types of labour that maintain society. Traditional social work is focused on "individuals in need" and operates within a limited sphere despite the widespread problems, individual and social, present at the time of social work's creation in the late eighteen hundreds up to the present. Traditional social work does not recognize responsibility for constructing the social world. Indeed, traditional social work remains unaware of its contribution to increasing the burden of need placed on individuals, its relationship with the structure of market economies and its foundation in the transformation of society.

The instrumental or technical approach used by traditional social work, again in the sense adapted from Horkheimer, does not question the organization of society. Perhaps the obvious example is the psychologizing and individualizing of problems, thus conceptually rendering them amenable to psychotherapy (Chanbon, Iriving, & Epstein, 1999). With this conceptualization the focus of the intervention emphasizes adaptation at the micro level. From this perspective, society appears to be the way things "naturally" occur and current society, as the "natural" order of things. However, the concept of "natural" does not flow from the world itself but rather is a social construction. The social form is a function of the thoughts and practices, including intentional thoughts and practices, of humans as they engage in the various aspects of their lives. As such, the natural occurrences within the thoughts and practices of life are specific to both historical conditions and intentional acts.

A perspective that questions such "naturalness" is informed by what Horkheimer (1972) described as a critical attitude:

> [T]he critical attitude of which we are speaking is wholly distrustful of the rules of conduct with which society as presently constructed provides each member. The separation between individual and society in virtue of which the individual accepts as natural the limits presented for his activity is relativized in critical theory. The latter considers the overall framework which is conditioned by the blind interaction of individual activities (that is, the existent division of labor and the class distinctions) to be a function which originates in human action and therefore is a possible object of planful decision and rational determination of goals. (p. 207)

Restated simply, the "givens" of any particular society must be viewed with suspicion. Mindless adherence to such givens simply reproduces the society without an opportunity to uncover the possibilities for alternate and better forms of organization. The active role that humans play in constructing the social world is hidden by the apparent naturalness of the world. Thus, humans disempower themselves and do not engage in the creation of a more just social world. The individual is blinded to the active role that he or she may play in recreating life in a more satisfying form. Such a lack of critical perspective towards the structure of society is equally applicable regarding the meaning of structures of individual lives. In conceptualizing "society" and "individuals" without a critical attitude, the recognition of the influence of a particular social form is minimized and the role of the individual in the creations of social forms is obscured. Planful decisions for the purpose of emancipatory actions are hidden.

Critical theory fosters self-directed emancipatory practice at the level of individual or social transformation. While much of the effort in traditional social work is directed towards immediate need, we may find traditional social work perpetuating the production of immediate need. In contrast, critical social work addresses immediate need without turning a blind eye to larger social issues. Mills (1967) highlighted that contrast:

> Know that many personal troubles cannot be solved merely as troubles, but must be understood in terms of public issues — and in terms of the problems of history making. Know that the human meaning of public issues must be revealed by relating them to personal troubles — and to the problems of the individual life. (p. 226)

Returning to Habermas and his idea of cognitive interests, we see two different orientations provided by a traditional versus a critical perspective. The traditional perspective assumes a fixedness to the focus of study. That may be appropriate to the natural sciences (although not without argument; see Husserl, 1970, or Latour, 1979), but when applied to the social world, such fixedness becomes an active force in the creation of a reified, objectified world. The social world is, in part, a reflection of the assumptions and subsequent actions taken to study it (Rorty, 1979). The focus of a critical perspective is, in part, an examination of the actions, both in thought and deed, that contribute to the apparent naturalness of the social world and an expansion of possible alternatives for the future.

Discourse and Social Work

A clearer understanding of traditional social work may be found by comparing the differences between traditional theories of practice and the embedded theories of action and their critical theory counterparts. Theories of practice are found in practice approaches and techniques; these theories are stated in texts and protocols. Theories of practice are manifestations of theories of action, though the theories of actions are often unstated and unrecognized by the practitioner (see Schon, 1983).

The theories of action tap into the deep stories underneath theories of practice, thus providing a coherence for the theories of practice and supporting a naturalness of the social world for the practitioner. Taken most broadly, these deep stories are what Foucault (1977) refers to as discourses or systematic ways of thinking and carving out reality:

> Discursive practices are characterized by the delimitation of a field of objects, the definition of a legitimate perspective for the agent of knowledge, and the fixing of

norms for the elaboration of concepts and theories. Thus, each discursive practice implies a play of prescriptions that designate its exclusions and choices. (p. 199)

Discourses create the parameters for the social processes that define reality; discourses are also a function of the processes themselves without being a mere reflection of them. Discourses occur not as tangible products but as moments in continuing social practices. Such social practices within the parameters of varying discourses give the social world meaning: distinctions between good and bad, legal and illegal, deserving and undeserving, or us and them. Foucault's (1978) work on what he termed "discursive practices" provides a seminal example of identity construction through social practices.

Discourses are dependent on continual maintenance, creation and re-creation through social practices. Like a stream, their continued existence is dependent on continued replenishment. Discourse and streams exist as processes, not as objects, and, as processes, discourses (and streams) are open to modification. In turn, changes in the process (in this case of discourses, the social practices) result in changes to the discourse itself. A simple illustration in terms of practice can be found in regards to mental health workers. Analytically trained workers tend to emphasize, among other things, psychosexual development and defense mechanisms. Mental health workers with an existential perspective tend to emphasize meaning, responsibility and awareness of death, again, among other things. The significant components of the world for an analytically trained worker and an existential worker are not the same. The resulting talk within the therapeutic sessions reflects this difference, and that talk becomes part of the social world.

The deep stories for traditional social work rest on the idea of an autonomous individual (O'Brian & Penna, 1998). This Enlightenment idea was carried forward by Smith (1937), Hobbes (1969), Locke (1924) and others. Such thinkers did not recognize the inherent social nature of human life as they worked to pry society loose from the grip of church and king. One example is Adam Smith's "invisible hand" guiding the new industrial economy; the invisible hand was assumed to be the manifestation of the aggregated self-interested acts of society's individuals. From a different perspective, Hobbes saw the natural state of humans as a war of all against all; a condition that required at least tacit mutual agreement so that a social unit could be formed. Locke posited the independent individual, through contract of consent, as the foundation of society. These deep stories form the theory of action supporting the overt theories of social work practice in traditional social work. This is the liberal underpinning of social work (O'Brian & Penna 1998).

Our point is that traditional social work's practice reflects a discourse relying on the idea of an autonomous individual. Traditional practice has emphasized individual therapy and small group work within an established social order. As in the preamble of the NASW Code of Ethics discussed initially, the "primary mission of the social work profession is to enhance human well-being and meet the basic human needs of all people" (NASW, 1999). Current social work practice is largely traditional practice based on work with individuals within an accepted social order.

Underlying Basis for Critical Social Work

Deep stories also exist that present an alternative to traditional social work. Critical social work can be understood by using a relational model to describe individuals and society (Mcnamee & Gergen, 1998).[1] A starting point for understanding relational models is the work of George Herbert Mead, whose approach is summarized in "The Sociological Implication of the Thought of George Herbert Mead" in Blumer (1969).

For Mead, and the symbolic interactionists that followed, the self is "first and foremost" a reflexive process of social interactions (Callero, 2003). From this perspective the self results from the human capability of self-reflection. In self-reflection, the person is both acting and being acted on, both subject and object of the action. In Mead's view, the self initiates all actions — physical, contemplative or otherwise. These acts are the ways in which the person copes and participates in the world. The actions themselves are constructions intended to achieve some purpose, whether grand or trivial. The resulting social interactions are actions with other selves engaged in the same process. Each self initiates, interprets, assesses and again initiates throughout the exchange. The selves are not identical, and each self needs to find ways to successfully interpret the intention of others.

Accordingly, self-knowledge requires other selves. Cooley's "looking-glass self" provides a well-known illustration (Cooley, 1992). Cooley states that we know ourselves through the responses we perceive in others; we know who we are by how others respond to us. But, the responses of others are not automatically understood by us: they must be interpreted. Therefore, our self-knowledge is achieved through the processes of interaction and interpretation; that is, our reflection on the interaction.

Mead's and Cooley's works are consistent with Gergen's (1999) perspective of the individual as a "relational self." Gergen views the individual as existing in relationship with others within a cultural context. Gergen suggests that we are born into an already ongoing social world with already formed customs, meaning and language. In our own ongoing social world, we learn to interact, to communicate and to speak. This ongoing social world includes discursive practices that focus on some elements, exclude others and weave the chosen elements into a coherent-enough ongoing account of our lives. Our language, using the term very broadly, always carries the stamp of the specific ongoing world.

---

[1] For our purposes we have collapsed Habermas' categories of cognitive interests (technical, practical and emancipatory) by combining practical and emancipatory. The technical interest correlates most closely with the perspective of traditional social work while the combined category of practical and emancipatory interests correlates most closely with critical social work.

However, our communication, our talk, is not always that of the others in our group. Our utterances in the present, in attempted coordination with the others of the present, always carry elements of the past. We are double voiced (Bakhtin, 1981) as the messages of the past are always in the current interaction. Irving and Young (2002) elaborated on this point and its specific relation to social work practice. For others to grasp our utterances (or for us to grasp theirs), a dialogic process occurs in which the possible meanings are selected and prioritized depending on intent (Gergen, 1999). This double-voiced quality provides for social continuity by bringing the past into the present while the dialogic process ensures that the past is not simply replicated.

For Gergen, communication both conveys meaning and performs action in relationships. These social relationships, acts of communication in their varied forms, are the stuff of society. The conveyance of meaning requires a dialogical process due to the double-voiced quality of speech and because all messages have the potential of multiple meanings. The meaning is established in the dialogic process. It is not reducible to the utterance, language, sign or gesture. Gergen's perspective includes both individual and society as process and not as object. The individual requires an "other" to become a "self" while society results from social interactions among selves and others at the level of both individuals and groups.

From a critical perspective, the link between the actual individual and the active social interaction involving that individual cannot be ruptured; it is impossible to speak meaningfully of the individual without addressing the context of actual social relations. And, the social relations of society lose much of their abstractness when they are recognized as results of ongoing, tangible human interactions. From this perspective one must speak of social processes constituting both the individual and society. Since the individual and the society are inseparable, the therapy of the individual then necessarily involves the broader social relations. The critique of the social order necessarily involves the concrete action of real people before our eyes. Therapy of the individual and critique of the social order are part of the same process.

With all that has been said, we need to recognize that the categories of traditional and critical are human creations that help organize our grasp of the world. They are not qualities of the world itself and, they do not purport to be so. All practice does not necessarily neatly fit into one category or the other. Our discussion is a schema for viewing the world, and it is only one of the many possible ways of organizing the world. It is, though, a way that the authors find useful in analyzing the current practices of social work.

Critical Social Work Example: Narrative Therapy

Given the suppositions regarding traditional and critical social work and the underlying differences as described above, what therapeutic approach might be used to illustrate a critical social work approach in therapeutic practice? In other words, what would be appropriate approaches to treatment that acknowledge both the person in the society as well as the society in the person?

First, the notion of working solely with an individual must be discarded. Individual and social context are inseparable. Further, the individual, recognized as an actual entity within a specific field of social relations, may not be in need of change. It may be the social environment, the continually reproduced network of social relations, that needs modification. Increased coping skills for the individual may be in order but not to alleviate the strain within a social environment. An oppressive set of social relations requires a change in the relations and not increased coping skills of the individual. Increased coping skills, however, may be in order to enable the individual to function while they change their environment.

A necessary step for the practitioner is to take a stance that critiques the social order. This critique, simply put, involves asking two questions: "Can it be otherwise?" and "Can we do better?" For this the naturalness of the social order requires closer examination. The traditional approach, with an individual-society dichotomy, only allows for the critique to be done separately. A critical approach, however, provides a foundation for conducting a unifying critique of both the individual and the society. Viewing both individual and society as processes that are mutually influencing eliminates the dichotomy. Thus the function of "helping" the individual includes a critique of the social. That is not simply viewing the person-in-environment as if one or the other is a stable entity, but seeing the individual and the social as non-identical, inseparable entities.

A next step is to adopt a narrative approach in working with a client (Freeman & Coombs, 1996; Mcnamee & Gergen, 1992; White, 1992). From the perspective we have developed, narratives are an essential part of understanding individuals and societies. At the individual level, there are narratives that provide coherence to our self-understanding. These narratives, like discursive practices, focus on some elements while excluding others, then weave the included into a meaningful whole. Discursive practices perform much the same function at the level of society.

These individual narratives are not held in a vacuum. They continually interact with various discursive practices and other narratives. This process, the interaction with other discourses, is a narrative re-figuring of the self-other relation. Narrative therapy, given its conceptualization of the social world, has the capability to focus on narratives or discursive practices at various levels. The focus could be the life story of an individual, or the family narratives often conveyed in family myths (Stone, 1988) or social practices (Bruner, 1986).

Narrative therapy addresses not just the individual narrative but the cultural narratives as well. The social worker joins with the client in a process that explores the individual's narrative and the influence the cultural narrative has on the individual. For example, one element of the examination focuses on the "naturalness" of a concept, belief or relationship. Is it natural? Has it always been that way? Is it that way in every case? How did you learn it was natural? Does this naturalness benefit some people more than others? If it weren't natural, what would happen? Perhaps it is natural in relation to the cultural narrative, but the cultural narrative is not assumed to be neutral. Rather, it is seen as having a vested interest in ensuring its continuation through shaping individual behaviour and communication patterns.

The articulation of these interests is part of the therapeutic process. Narrative therapy does not locate the problem within the individual nor does it isolate it in the social structure. Both the individual and the social are understood as processes. The problem rests in the processes that necessarily include the individual and the social since they are mutually influencing. As individual behaviours change so do social processes. At the same time, as social processes are modified, so is the stuff of the social contexts. Narrative therapy, because of its critical, deconstructive elements, has the possibility of modifying the continued reproduction of social relations.

From another perspective, narrative therapy may be said to be a critical examination of the life world of the client that recreates the object of its examination. The therapist becomes a participant as the client examines and creates opportunities at directing his or her life. As the client is embedded within an ongoing social order, these opportunities must necessarily correspond to the socially available possibilities but are not limited to previously taken or identified possibilities. There is space for created alternatives. The client-worker relationship is this seeking or creating of alternatives.

Narrative therapy questions the fundamental concepts each individual utilizes to understand and create his or her world. Narrative therapy seeks to remove the "naturalness" of present social relations and reveal their possibility. In this sense, it is a critique; in the sense that it assists in creating opportunity and alternate human actions facilitating growth and development, it is therapy.

The critique is destabilizing. Necessity is replaced by contingency and choice. A pattern of interaction continues if enough people participate in recreating it. New patterns develop though participation, conscious or otherwise. This is not to imply that individual or social change is easy. To problematize the natural is not an easy task, particularly since power relations and systems of knowledge support it (Foucault, 1980, 1988). It is not, however, an impossible task.

Conclusion

In the body of this chapter, we have developed a story that, in our opinion, provides a coherent summary of the current needs of social work and the history that led to these needs. We also have provided glimpses at a possible future. Ours is not the only possible story, and like all stories, we have emphasized some aspects and minimized others. We have not commented on things we thought of less relevance and, most likely, have missed elements that lie beyond the limits of our horizon.

Our account started in the middle then moved in both directions. The starting point was the mandate for social work provided by documents from NASW and IASSW. These are not identical documents and reflect somewhat different systems of thought. Our focus was around the issue of conflict as understood from a social theory perspective. Of particular interest is the conceptualization of society. Is it a relatively harmonious whole or various groups of individuals contesting ranges of issues? The NASW document, consistent with a U.S. perspective, seems to assume a consensus model for society, relegating conflict to a limited, perhaps aberrant, role. The IASSW document seems to acknowledge a conflict model. The importance of this difference has to do with the role of social work. To what degree does social work as a profession act in the interest of the society as a whole, and to what degree does it act in the interest of particular social groups potentially challenging the current social order? This is an issue that we believe is obscured by much of the current practice of social work.

We presented a transformation point of Western society as the founding period of the profession of social work. This was a period of great upheaval, uneasiness and conflict between various social groups. In the initial period, the progenitors of social work had diverse perspectives regarding their goals and strategies for achieving them. Their motives as well as their thinking reflected the social conditions of the time. The Enlightenment issues were working their way into the structure of daily life. For our purposes, the redefinition with an emphasis on the individual was the most significant aspect. Hand-in-hand with this was the increased emphasis on rational thought in the production and validation of knowledge. We have not suggested an ordering of elements, but we have relied on the belief that theory, action and knowledge are all interrelated with the temper of their particular historical location. The notion of discursive practices provides a venue for examining this interrelation.

Horkheimer's distinction between "traditional" and "critical" theory provided a perspective for examining the conceptual foundation of social work and of viewing the intellectual principles of the Enlightenment in action, though only in relation to social work and human agency. The dichotomy between individual and society contributes to the current dilemma for social work practice. This dichotomy for social work stifles a critique of the social order by hiding the inescapable social network with which we all are necessarily and always surrounded. We attempted to "problematize" what had been "naturalized" by, as we are calling it, a traditionally founded social work. In order both to illustrate the issue and to begin to show an alternate future, we developed, briefly, a relational model and demonstrated the fit between a narrative therapy approach and such a model. This model sees individual and society as non-identical but inseparably linked. A society devoid of concrete actors is an empty abstraction. Any conceptualization of concrete individuals without recognition of the "always and already" social environment that is necessary for their existence is also an empty abstraction.

Social work practice as we view it is not the application of a set of techniques. The practice is created in the interaction between worker and client, individual or other, to promote change. Exactly what is to be done is constructed by the worker and the client. We have tried to provide a perspective, a place for the worker to stand, to begin to construct his or her practice. We have articulated some of the "hidden" issues that we believe have influenced practice. At this point we are content to end our story in hope that it can be used by others as they construct their practice.

References

Bakhtin, M. (1981). *The dialectical imagination: Four essays.* Austin: University of Texas, Press.

Blumer, H. (1969). *Symbolic interactionism.* Englewood Cliffs, NJ: Prentice-Hall.

Bosanquet, B. (1997). Socialism and natural selection. In D. Boucher, *The British Idealist.* Cambridge: Cambridge University Press, 50-67.

Bruner, J. (1986). *Actual minds, possible worlds.* Cambridge: Harvard University Press.

Callero, P. (2003). The sociology of the self. *Annual Review of Sociology 29*(1), 115-133.

Camilleri, P. (1996). *(Re) constructing socialwork.* Aldershot: Avebury.

Chanbon, A., Irving, A., & Epstein, L. (1999). *Reading Foucault for social work.* New York: Columbia University Press.

Coleman, J.S. (1990). *Foundations of social theory.* Cambridge: Belknap Press.

Cooley, C.H. (1992). *Human nature and the social order.* Transaction Social Science Classic Series. New Brunswick, NJ: Transactions Publishers.

de Saussure, F. (1996). *Course in general linguistics* (W. Baskin, Trans.). New York: McGraw-Hill.

Ellis, A. (1999). *How to make yourself happy and remarkably less disturbable.* San Louis Obispo: Impact.

Foucault, M. (1965). *Madness and civilization: A history of insanity in the age of reason* (R. Howard, Trans.). New York: Random House.

Foucault, M. (1977). What is an author? In D.F. Bouchard (Ed.), *Language, countermemory, practice: Selected essays and interviews.* Ithaca, NY: Cornell University Press.

Foucault, M. (1978). *The History of sexuality.* New York: Pantheon.

Foucault, M. (1980). *Power/knowledge: Selected interviews and other writings.* New York: Pantheon Press.

Foucault, M. (1988). *Politics, philosophy, culture: Interviews and other writings, 1977-1984.* (L. Kritzman, Ed.). London: Routledge.

Freeman, J., & Coombs, G. (1996). *Narrative therapy: The social construction of preferred realities.* New York: Norton.

Gambrill, E. (1995). Behavioral social work: Past, present, and future. *Research on Social Work Practice, 5*(4), 460-484.

Gergen, K.J. (1999). *An invitation to social construction.* Thousand Oaks: Sage.

Glasser, W. (1998). *Choice therapy: A new psychology of personal freedom.* New York: HarperCollins.

Glasser, W. (2000). *Reality therapy in action.* New York: HarperCollins.

Habermas, J. (1972). *Knowledge and human interests.* Boston: Beacon Press.

Hobbes, T. (1969). *Leviathan.* Menston: Scholar Press.

Homans, G. (1961). *Social behavior.* New York: Harcourt, Brace & World.

Horkheimer, M. (1972). *Critical theory.* New York: Herder and Herder.

Husserl, E. (1970). *The crisis of European sciences and transcendental phenomenology: An introduction to phenomenological philosophy.* Evanston, IL: Northwestern University Press.

IASSW. (2001). *International definition of social work.* Retrieved May 6, 2004, from <http://www.iassw.soton.ac.uk/Generic/DefinitionOfSocialWork.asp?lang=en>.

Irving, A., & Young, T. (2002). Paradigm for pluralism: Mikhail Bakunin and social work practice. *Social Work, 47*(1), 19-21.

Jones, G.S. (1971). *Outcast London: A study in the relationships between classes in Victorian society.* London: Clarendon Press.

Latour, L. (1979). *Laboratory life: The social construction of scientific facts.* Beverly Hills: Sage Publications.

Lee, P. (1939). Social work: Cause and function. In F. Lowry (Ed.), *Readings in social case work 1920-1938.* New York: Columbia University Press.

Lewis, G. (1998). *Forming nation, framing welfare.* London: Routledge in association with the Open University.

Locke, J. (1924). *An essay concerning human understanding.* Oxford: Clarendon Press.

Mcnamee, S., & Gergen, K.J. (1998). *Relational responsibility.* Thousand Oaks, CA: Sage Publications.

Meichenbaum, D. (1977). *Cognitive behavior modification: An integrated approach.* New York: Plenum.

Mills, C.W. (1967). *The sociological imagination.* London: Oxford University Press.

NASW. (1999). *Code of ethics of the National Association of Social Workers.* Retrieved May 6, 2004, from <http://www.socialworkers.org>.

O'Brian, M. and S. Penna, (1998). *Theorizing welfare: Enlightenment and modern society.* London: Sage.

Parsons, T. (1951). *The social system.* Glencoe, IL: Free Press.

Polanyi, K. (1957). *The great transformation.* Boston: Beacon Press.

Polkinghorne, D. (1988). *Narrative knowing and the human sciences.* Albany, NY: State University of New York Press.

Pozzuto, R. (2001). Lessons in continuation and transformation: The United States and South Africa. *SocialWork/Masstskaplike Werk, 37*(2), 154-164.

Pumphrey, R.E. (1959). Compassion and protection: Dual motivations in social welfare. *Social Service Review, 33*, 21-29.

Putnam, R. (1993). *Making democracy work.* Princeton: Princeton University Press.

Rorty, R. (1979). *Philosophy and the mirror of nature.* Princeton: Princeton University Press.

Schon, D.A. (1983). *The reflective practitioner.* New York: Basic Books.

Scott, M., & Dryden, W. (1996). The cognitive-behavioral paradigm. In R. Woolfe & W. Dryden (Eds.), *Handbook of Counseling Psychology.* London: Sage.

Seigfried, C.H. (1999). Socializing democracy: Jane Addams and John Dewey. *Philosophy of the Social Sciences, 29*(2), 207-231.

Smith, A. (1937). *The wealth of nations.* New York: Modern Library.

Stone, E. (1988). *Black sheep and kissing cousins: How our family stories shape us.* New York: Times Books.

Watson, F.D. (1971). *The charity organization movement in the United States.* New York: Arno Press.

Weber, M. (1976). *The protestant ethic and the spirit of capitalism* (T. Parsons, Trans.). New York: Scribner.

White, M. (1992). Deconstruction and therapy. In *Selected papers of David Epston and Michael White, 1989-1991.* Adelaide, South Australia: Dulwich Center Publications

Wittgenstein, L. (1978), *Philosophical investigations.* Oxford: Blackwell.

3

Reconceptualizing Critical Social Work

Steven Hick

This chapter aims to take some of the major debates raised in the critical social work research and move forward to reconceptualize and reformulate a critical approach to practice. It draws together common themes and endeavours to reconcile key debates. Recurring themes emerge, such as power, empowerment, difference, reflection, social change, personal liberation and location, which are scattered throughout the critical social work literature. Doubts and challenges from various theoretical perspectives, particularity postmodern social theory, frequently arise. This chapter is not an attempt to give definitive answers or solve theoretical issues once and for all. The critical social work project will never be complete, and analysis will shift over time and place. I simple want to add my voice to the mix and move the project forward.

In this chapter, I seek to take what I see as the fundamental parameters of critical social work and interrogate them with postmodern social theory and reflexive inquiry. To accomplish this, I first outline some key aspects of critical social work and postmodern theory. Next, I examine how some constituent features can be made useful to the critical social work program. I reject the notion often made that critical social work is fundamentally different from postmodern theory and therefore cannot be combined or mixed in any fundamental way. Further, the suggestion that critical theory, as a purely modernist analysis, is no longer useful in a postmodern era is not taken up here. At the same time, I do not believe that we can take theory of the nineteenth century into today's world without significant interpretation and reformulation. I will take critical theory and explore how this can be strengthened by key postmodern and reflexive ideas. The chapter is based on the premise that postmodern social theory has much to offer critical perspectives on social work.

Postmodern Turn of Critical Social Work

The term "postmodern" is perhaps one of the most misunderstood. It cannot really be defined, but we can explore its meaning in a broad sense before we look at its usefulness for critical social work. It is more than a buzzword for pop culture or an excuse for unclear writing. It must be taken seriously, and be analyzed and interrogated. There is often heated debate between critical theorists and postmodern social theorists. Frequently, each side reifies the other, creating a straw model and dismissing their opponents. There are, in fact, many different versions of postmodern and critical social theory. It is inaccurate to discuss a "postmodern theory" or a "critical theory" in the singular. There is a diversity of theories on both sides. Therefore, we can only speak of postmodern theories and critical theories. With regard to postmodern theories, there exists a wide variety of positions and politics with a large degree of complexity and often conflicting viewpoints. There are vast differences between writers such as Derrida, Foucault, Lyotard, Agger and Jameson, just as there are enormous differences between critical thinkers such as Adorno, Horkheimer, Marcuse, Habermas and Lukacs. And each theorist shifts and moves their ideas over time. The objective should be how to specify the postmodern challenges and make use of them to supplement critical social work theory.

First, it is useful to speak of a postmodern turn, rather than a break or shift from modernity to postmodernity. Best and Kellner (1997, p.31) argue that we are living between a modern era and an emerging postmodern era that remains to be adequately conceptualized. They believe that we are currently living in a borderland between the modern and postmodern with tension, confusion and significant risks and dangers, as well as the hope of new possibilities. A paradigm shift, in the sense that Kuhn used the term, is currently in progress. But, as Foucault observed, it is impossible to completely describe a new paradigm until after it has fully taken shape. Therefore, according to Best and Kellner, it would be a mistake to discount postmodern social theory as an ephemeral fashion or the theoretical equivalent of the hula hoop. In this situation of being between, it is necessary to engage the discourse of the postmodern.

Postmodern social theory is difficult to define. Even Foucault, who is often referenced as one of the foremost postmodern thinkers, professed not to know what the word "postmodern" meant. He believed that it is an emerging paradigm that is something we glimpse only as a thin line on the horizon (1973, p.384). I do not believe that a strict and definitive definition of postmodern is possible. It is not an essence that can be defined, but rather a constellation of discursive constructs. Best and Kellner (1997, p.254) summarize it as a postmodern "research program" that reworks key aspects of modern thought and culture in a plurality of ways, that generates new theories and concepts and whose outcome is indeterminate.

Difficulties also emerge when definition of "critical social work" is attempted. But generally social work theorists and practitioners by and large understand what is meant by the term. Discussion of critical or radical perspectives on social work began with theorists such as Bailey and Brake (1975), Corrigan and Leonard (1978), and Galper (1975, 1980). They largely based their perspectives on Marxist analysis with a strong emphasis on examining socio-economic structures as a source of people's problems rather than looking solely to intrapsychic or interpersonal explanations.

More recently, academics around the world are rallying around the term "critical" as the descriptor for alternative social work with authors such as Healy (2000), Ife (1997, 1999), Pease and Fook (1999) and Rossiter (1996, 2001). The term is increasingly being used to capture a range of perspectives on practice, including structural, feminist and radical. For example, Bob Mullaly in his most recent book (2002) examines the "critical social work approach," whereas his earlier (1993) publication explores "structural social work." Jan Fook has used the phrase "radical casework" (1993) and "critical theory and practice" (2002) in her titles. Titles aside, the discussions and approaches discussed have a similar core. This chapter uses the term with the intention of capturing that broad-spectrum core.

The notion of reflexive inquiry used here draws from the method of institutional ethnography of Dorothy Smith (1983, 1987, 1990, 1999). Critiques of dominant social science research in terms of its social organization have emerged from a variety of sources, but Smith is the one taken up here. Smith sees knowledge itself as organized by what she calls "extralocal relations or apparatuses of ruling." Smith (1987, p.69) sees "sociology as a constituent of a consciousness organized by the abstracted, extralocal relations of ruling." Here, Smith draws from Alfred Schutz's (1962, p.207) notions of a number of various orders of reality, each with its own type of existence and the organization of consciousness associated with a shift from one province of meaning to another. In short, according to Smith, the world of scientific theory organizes consciousness in the abstracted objectified mode detached from daily life. This is what Schutz (1962, p.245) similarly refers to as "scientific attitude." On the other hand, Schutz refers to "wide-awake man" [*sic*] within the "natural attitude." Here consciousness is organized by the world of everyday life, or the world of our working, of bodily movements, of manipulating objects and handling things and men [*sic*] (ibid., pp. 222-223). It is this "plane of consciousness" that Smith defines as her "locus for the sociological problematic."

With reflexive inquiry one explicates or unfolds the social processes and practices organizing people's daily lives from the standpoint of direct experience. But the social relations organizing the everyday or experienced world are not revealed simply in the perceptions and views of those situated there. Analysis of the description of "need" or oppression is required to show the link with national and international social relations. The social organization or complex of social relations is present in the ordinary talk of people describing their particular lived reality and setting. The categories and terms used express social organization as they depend on larger social relations for their meaning.

Now, let us explore the parameters of a renewed critical social work theory.

Structures of Oppression: Situated "Client" and Social Worker

Critical social work tends to focus on the dialectical connections between everyday life and social structures. It rejects economic determinism or theories that see the superstructures (culture) as determined by the base (economics). Instead, people's everyday lives are seen in a dialectical relationship with structures, or are organized by and articulated to structures. But fundamentally critical social work considers structures and social relations as they affect individuals. It does not isolate the individual and direct energy predominately at changing the individual in some way. It emphasizes a close look at society, and does not take what appears as natural or given.

An updated critical social work theory follows from a view of the social worker as a situated knower and discoverer. It views the cover of neutrality as an inappropriate measure of validity. The myth of scientific neutrality justifies the status quo as inevitable and knowledge of it as universal truths. Because established knowledge and methodology is grounded in particular interests, it is not something that can be taken over. It must be reformulated and reconstructed. Critical social work, then, should be concerned with the organization or the material conditions and practices upon which consciousness depends.

The practice method of the critical social work proposed here goes beyond mere descriptions of experience to an explication of the larger social relations of society underlying the descriptions. I am not concerned with describing a local setting in and of itself. Nor does the beginning in everyday experience mean that experience is somehow more real or that one person's experience is more authentic than another's. The intent is not to understand experience subjectively, but rather reflexively. It would aim to uncover the social relations organizing people's everyday experience. Both the social worker and the client are viewed as situated. The methods used are similar to Smith's institutional ethnography, which aims to explicate or unfold the social processes and practices organizing people's daily lives from the standpoint of direct experience (Smith, 1987, p.151). It draws from Gouldner's (1971) notion of "reflexive" inquiry.

For example, the notion of an "unemployable" person, a term used by welfare workers to describe someone who can receive social assistance without having to look for a paying job, presupposes certain productive relations. The definition and use of the term is taken for granted by welfare workers and people who know welfare work. An unemployable person, however, comes into existence due to a determinate set of social relations. Such a person arises out of a capitalist social organization where wage labour has a use only if it can be productive and produce a surplus value to the owner of the means of production. If the labour power cannot produce surplus value at minimum-wage levels, then the person is unemployable. The person is not reducible to the object we could create in our imagination of a person who is unemployable. It does not mean the person cannot function or perform work. The term "unemployable" is rooted in and depends upon the presupposed social relations of a capitalist labour market for its meaning. Without this context, this aspect of welfare work would not exist or would take a very different form.

A key task for critical social workers is to lay out the logic of everyday life. The original conceptualization of the Frankfurt school's critical theory extended Marx's concept of the alienation of labour into the large notion of domination. The second generation of Frankfurt school theorists examined how "fast capi talism" (Agger, 1989]) or late capitalism entangles productive and reproductive labour. The third generation of critical thinkers are looking at ways to locate or uncover the relations of domination or ruling in commonplace forms in language, discourse and institutional processes or, as Marcuse (1964) called it, "one-dimensional" everyday life. Constituting the social organization and determinations of our lived experience can be used as a method of guiding and focusing social work practice. This method involves returning to the social relations that produce the named phenomena. Rather than delving into the individual in order to change the individual, the social worker examines the practical activity of particular persons in order to uncover the social phenomena that are affecting their lives. The best interests of the client remain paramount as most social work codes of ethics dictate, but their interests are pursued in relation to factors outside their internal psyche or behaviour to uncover discourses, language games and social structures that constitute them as needing help, organize a lived reality of oppression or define them as "other" or outside "normidity." Inquiry begins with a knower situated within society and not separate or remote of it.

This method of critical social work is concerned with social organization or how social happenings are assembled and coordinated socially. Here, social phenomena exist only as they are instituted by people's activities and therefore are observable only to the extent that the actions that bring them into being as social objects are available for examination. Thus, according to deMontigny 1988, it is precisely because our lives are shaped by forms of social organization that are not immediately visible that it is incumbent on social workers to work with clients to help explicate, unfold and name the social contours and forces of the world". In deMontigny's reflexive materialist social work practice, social workers struggle with clients to try to bring into view the contours of a world worked on and shared in common.

Explicating or uncovering the social organization of oppression for critical social work practice can draw on the Derridean notion of the multiplicity of oppressions. A common tension in critical social work revolves around discussions about which oppression is primary or most important. Derrida's ideas around difference theory are potential contributions to critical social work. Derrida (1976) explores how language conceals secret hierarchies. He sees language as a system of signifiers or symbols that acquire their meaning not from their connection to the lived reality that they purport to represent but only in terms of their internal relations of "difference." Difference refers to the idea that words and signifiers only acquire meaning in relation to their difference from other terms. For example, "man" is defined in terms of what he is not or what is "other" to him. Therefore, attempts to understand the multiplicity of oppression must recognize that there are a variety of undecidable narratives, with none being the final word or most authoritative. No one narrative is privileged over another. All must be deconstructed.

Derridean notions of difference have given rise to a variety of trends including identity politics and multiculturalism. It can provide useful arguments for critical social work theory. A critical social work theory rooted in the appreciation of difference can view many discourses as important and no one discourse as more primary than another. Theoretical discourses, professional discourses and everyday life discourses are all equally valid. Discourses examining class, race, gender or sexuality should all be equally compelling. According to Derrida, we must learn to speak many "polyvocal" discourses. This rejects the notion that there is one overriding theory of oppression that is somehow primary. People occupy different subjective positions, and acknowledging and validating this may assist in the critical social work project. This postmodern theoretical perspective helps critical social work resist "grand narratives" of oppression. It presents the possibility of identifying and critiquing ideologies using a deconstructive discourse theory.

Ideological Processes: Constructing and Understanding the World

Integral to the coordination of institutional processes are ideologies. Postmodern theorists would generally use the term "discourse" to describe the ways that we make sense of and construct the world through language. Discourses, following Foucault's use, are the historically variable ways of specifying knowledge and truth. Ideologies mediate by providing categories and concepts that express the relation of work practices to institutional functions. Ideology is a practice or method of organizing relations between people's everyday activities and the social relations of society in general. It substitutes discursively organized relations for the actual relations of daily life.

The concept of ideology being used here to inform critical social work is different from some current usages in the social sciences that refer to the notion of a political Weltanschauung or a general system of values, beliefs and feelings. Lukacs (1973, p.262), for example, conceives of ideologies as expressions of different class interests, which is very different from Marx and Engels' usage in *The German Ideology*. Mannheim's (1972, p.26) sociology of knowledge frames his conception of ideology as biased knowledge tainted by class interests.

Ideology splits concepts from practices, thereby becoming a substitute for relations as experienced by the participants. To think ideologically is to remain in the realm of imagination or in the conceptual mode. Smith discusses the three tricks of ideological representation. Ideological method first separates ideas from material conditions. Next, mystical connections between the ideas are (re)presented as natural relationships. The ideas are then attributed back to actual people. For example, deMontigny (1988) outlines how social workers make "mystical connections" when they reorganize the particular "facts" of a situation according to the frames and models of an institutional discourse. Social workers transform the experienced realities of clients into the organizational relevancies of the state agency. It is in this way that ideological practices are grounded in larger social relations of power and control and operate to legitimize and sustain exploitative social relations.

This concept of ideology is useful for critical social work in identifying ideas or concepts that conceal and therefore reproduce social contradictions. Mannheim and Lukacs's definition tends to reduce consciousness and class struggle to economic deterministic levels. Social reality is therefore compartmentalized into static levels (base-superstructure). Ideology is certainly socially determined itself. But contrary to Mannheim's view that social determination makes all ideas invalid as partial positions, the critical social work proposed here views the social determination of ideas as having a detrimental affect on the validity of ideas only when this is not acknowledged and incorporated into the analysis. Therefore, knowledge that is developed with social determination preserved is viewed as valid and non-ideological. Ideology, then, refers to a specific kind of idea or concept that conceals social relations of exploitation and therefore organizes and sustains them.

More specifically, ideological practices construct reality through concerted and intended activity according to the relevances of ruling organizations. The activity or work processes involve creating, abstracting and universalizing concepts as social or psychological processes not anchored in material conditions. According to Walker, these work processes or the social relations in which they arise are not visible in the concept itself, but are dropped out or disappear (1986, p.37). The concept becomes a substitute for reality.

This does not mean that there should not be concepts. I am referring to the process where researchers take for granted the legitimacy or accuracy of existing concepts that may categorize and define phenomenon according to the needs of ruling classes or groups rather than according to the relevances of ruled people and with the goal of revealing the aspects producing the phenomenon. For example, concepts such as "single-parent family," "family violence" and "work" hide more of reality than they reveal. For example, the concept "work" hides the reality of housework as work. There is, however, nothing inherently wrong with using concepts. The issue is that the concept must be based on the relevances, interests and concerns of the people experiencing the phenomenon under investigation rather than on institutional categories and functions.

Ideology refers to the use of concepts or abstractions that do not represent or are not anchored in people's experiences. This ideological process is circular in that the categories set up to explain the phenomenon operate to select and assemble it as "facts." The ideological circle is a process described by Dorothy Smith, which provides the means of accounting for the "actual" (read: people's experienced reality) in terms of a schema or of the formal categories that coordinate objectively and rationally a ruling apparatus or macro-relations (1983, p.322). The process remains circular because the schema for organizing the particulars is not questioned.

Critiques of Dominant Social Science

Social work research in the past twenty years has been criticized for being based predominately on functionalist theories and positivist assumptions and methods. The critique argues that the functionalist-positivist approach proceeds from several basic assumptions. These assumptions include the notion that human thought and behaviour can be explained by objective enquiry to find unchanging laws that regulate the nature of human affairs. Further, the social world is ordered and regular, governed by immutable laws that can be captured as a system. Such a framework is within the functionalist paradigm, which is characterized by a view of the social world that regards society as ontologically prior to people and activities. Social work research is also dominated by positivist epistemology, which seeks to explain and predict what happens in the social world by searching for causal relationships. Positivism assumes that an external world exists and that this world itself determines only one correct view of it, independent of the process or context of viewing. Few researchers seriously defend such an ontology, but much of the social work research makes sense only in terms of such unexamined positivist assumptions.

Alternative critical social work research practice stems primarily from the critique of the core assumptions of dominant social science, commonly referred to as positivism. This notion draws heavily from critical social theory. The critique here is not directed only at positivism, for that can end in a debate about terms and their definitions. Rather, the critique addresses what is seen as the core assumptions or epistemological presuppositions underlying or characterizing dominant social work research.

Positivism in the social sciences is the view of the world that sees the social world as a distinct observable variable, independent of the knower. I define positivism as a way of seeing and constructing the world, claiming that the social and physical world are in all essentials the same. Social reality is viewed as "objectivity constituted," which is discernable if researchers can remove themselves from involvement in what they study. Positivism is not synonymous with scientific inquiry. Because positivist social science is the contemporary dominant paradigm, it has unfortunately been put forward by its advocates as science itself, synonymous with scientific inquiry. The view taken here is that empirical-analytical research methods can be scientific without being positivist.

A close examination of the core epistemological presuppositions of dominant social science, whether we call it positivist or not, raises several serious questions about its approach to science and research. The core presuppositions include the notions that society and all its phenomena can be measured with quantification, then predicted and controlled by objective scientists. The premises and the rules for this are borrowed from the natural sciences. We can therefore begin by questioning the likelihood that assumptions and techniques of the natural sciences can be borrowed and adapted appropriately in investigating a social world. Transference is not the only problem as natural scientists are increasingly questioning the basis of these assumptions for the study of natural phenomena.

Critical social work questions the epistemological presuppositions of dominant science as practised on several grounds. First, without doubting the desirability of isolating social phenomena to be objectively measured free from human bias (although this can be questioned in that it objectifies and controls human beings), critical social work questions the likelihood of such an occurrence. Social phenomena cannot be put in a test tube. They cannot be considered separate from the researcher when the researcher is a part of the society in which the social phenomena occurs. Researchers must live and act in the society they are researching and therefore cannot detach themselves from the object of study as laboratory researchers isolate themselves from a phenomenon in a test tube.

Second, critical social work questions the notion that a causal model of a slice or single phenomenon of society can be isolated and controlled. This is an oversimplification of a society that is complex and socially organized. Generally the method makes no attempt to place the social phenomenon into the larger social context to see how it is socially organized. Based on this critique, critical social work takes the notion of beginning research with the lived reality or practical activity of situated people and puts both the researcher and the object of research in its social context.

Participating in Social Change: Empowerment as Process

With this conception of critical social work, power is not seen as some objective commodity out there to be taken and passed on. This modernist notion of power has been critiqued, and the problems it presents have been discussed in numerous recent texts on social work theory (see Fook, 2002, p.50; Mullaly, 2002, p.179). Postmodernist and post-structuralist theoretical discussion have examined how such conceptions of power spilt the world into binary opposites or oppositional groups — the powerful and the powerless. McBeath and Webb do not hesitate to discredit this approach when they state that there is no place for critical social work's humanistic ethics resting, as it does, on a "power/non-power" distinction. This logic of "difference," of dominant and subordinate, fails according to McBeath and Webb because it wants to escape power via strategies of service user empowerment and consciousness-raising of providers while using ideas from Foucault that depend on the argument that power is inescapable (Beath and Webb, 2005, p.179).

But empowerment does not have to resolve power. Social workers and clients can co-participate, albeit in a relation of differential power, to deconstruct or explicate the power relations in society that impact their lives. In many cases these very power relations will affect both the worker and client, although in different ways. It is not a dualist choice between seeing power as an object relation versus a subjective relation. In this regard, much can be learned from the old debate of Marx and Engels (1970, p.62) when they critique the old materialism of Feuerbach who failed to see material reality as actual human activity. They also critique the idealism of Hegel, who failed to see the external character of the object to the subject (ibid., p.181). They used Feuerbach's ideas to criticize Hegel, and Hegel's ideas to criticize Feuerbach.

In short, I believe that Marx and Engels were arguing that we cannot separate individuals and their consciousness. They were consistent with their assertion that consciousness is neither independent of material conditions nor a mere function of it. Consciousness is determined by the reality of society originating in basic human necessities; therefore we cannot also separate individuals and their consciousness.

The treatment of commodities in capitalist societies is an example of the separation of subject from object. The subject, labour, appears as an independent entity separate from its object, commodity. The object appears not as something socially produced but as a naturally separate thing. Marx (1954) refers to this as the fetishism of commodities. An object whose value seems to be independent of a subject presents itself as a fetish. For Marx, the economic relations that appear as relations between things are really relations between people.

Marx's analysis of the commodity in *Capital* (1954) details the social relations of a capitalist economy whereby individual activity, labour, is hidden in the commodity. It is this invisibility that organizes the relations of exploitation, where surplus value is extracted as unpaid labour. Power can be conceptualized similarly. It is reproduced as relations between people. It should not be conceptualized as an objective commodity that can be transferred from one person to another. Nor should power be conceptualized as a subjective stance dependent on "revolution through consciousness." DeMontigny (1995, p.219) details how power is enacted in child protection work, finding that power is realized through organizational practices as social workers construct accounts of their client's lives.

Central to governmentality, to use Foucault's words, is "the conduct of our conduct" (1980). Foucault provides a useful analysis of the modern state, recognizing that it is not a singular omnipotent entity (Dean, 1999), but rather yielding power through a network of rules, relations and processes. Sovereignty has given way to governmentality. Examining disability policy, Price (2004, p.63) finds that rules and practices governing individuals operate in and through various state and non-state institutions, organizations, tactics and procedures. With bio-politics, the state becomes "governmentalized," and power is exercised by inducing people to seek self-improvement and advancement and by the use of countless categories and subcategories.

By reconceptualizing power as something that is assembled and coordinated socially rather than simply possessed, we can begin to consider empowerment strategies. Since social phenomena exist only as they are instituted by people's activities and therefore are observable only to the extent that the actions that bring them into being as social objects are available for examination, we can begin to explore with clients how power is acted out in their lives. In fact, we can use the client-worker phenomena as a set of activities to be deconstructed. By laying bare the mechanisms of power that influence people's lives, it could be said that empowerment takes place. There is no power transferred, but the knowledge of how power is exercised can be empowering.

Conclusion

Postmodern social theory and reflexivity ideas offer several useful insights to the critical social work project. The exploration of this points towards a renewed and updated critical or structural social work theory with the following components:

- Critical social work examines how *structures of oppression* are reproduced in the everyday lived reality of people. Fundamentally, oppression is seen as structural. Viewing power reflexively, as something that is assembled and coordinated socially rather than simply possessed, critical social work can begin to consider empowerment strategies.
- Critical social work argues that structures of oppression are reproduced through *ideological processes*. Ideology separates concepts from practices, thereby becoming a substitute for relations as experienced by the participants.
- Critical social work *critiques dominant social science*, commonly referred to as positivism. Positivism in the social sciences is the view of the world that sees the social world as a distinct, observable variable, independent of the knower, like the natural world.
- Critical social work is political in that it believes that people can *participate in social change*. It endorses the view that society can move towards a possible future free of domination and oppression.

These parameters are not exhaustive or conclusive. They are merely contours I have drawn from my practice and readings of critical social work theoretical literature. The components of critical social work presented above draw from my multiple readings of postmodern social theory. I do not claim to represent a conclusive reading of this either. There is not one singular reading of any postmodern perspective, but instead a multiplicity of readings and writings that shift and transform over time. To critique my understanding of postmodern as I apply it to critical social work theory would be to critique my reading and life experience.

References

Agger Ben (1989). *Fast capitalism: A Critical theory of significance*. Urbana: University of Illinois Press.

Bailey, R., & Brake, M. (Eds.). (1975). *Radical social work*. London: Edward Arnold.

Beath, Graham, & Webb, Stephen (2005). Post-Critical Social Work Analytics. In S. Hick, J. Fook, and R. Pozzuto, *Social Work: A Critical Turn*. Toronto: Thompson Educational Publishing.

Best, S., & Kellner, D. (1997). *The postmodern turn*. New York: The Guilford Press.

Campbell, M., & Manicom, A. (1995). *Knowledge, experience, and ruling relations*. Toronto: University of Toronto Press.

Campbell, M.L. (1988). Management as "ruling": A class phenomenon in nursing. *Studies in Political Economy, 27.*

Corrigan, P., & Leonard, P. (1978). *Social work practice under capitalism: A Marxist approach.* London: Macmillan.

Dean, M. (1999). *Governmentality: Power and rule in modern society.* London: Sage.

Derrida, Jacques. (1976). *Of Grammatology.* Baltimore: Johns Hopkins University Press.

deMontigny, G. (1988). *Accomplishing professional reality: An ethnography of social workers' practice.* Unpublished doctoral dissertation, University of Toronto.

deMontigny, G. (1995). The power of being professional. In M. Campbell and A. Manicom (Eds.), *Knowledge, experience, and ruling relations.* Toronto: University of Toronto Press.

Fals Borda, O. (1980). Science and the common people. In F. Dubell (Ed.), *Research for the people/research by the people.* Linkoping, Sweden: Linkoping University.

Fook, J. (1993). *Radical casework: A theory of practice.* St. Leonard's, Australia: Allen & Unwin.

Fook, J. (2002). *Social work: Critical theory and practice.* London: Sage.

Foucault, M. (1973). *The order of things.* New York: Vintage Books.

Foucault, M. (1980). *Power/knowledge.* New York: Pantheon.

Galper, J. (1975) *Politics of the social services.* Englewood Cliffs, NJ: Prentice-Hall.

Galper, J. (1980) *Social work: A radical perspective.* Englewood Cliffs, NJ: Prentice-Hall.

Gouldner, A.W. (1971). *The coming crisis of Western sociology.* London: Heinemann.

Healy, K. (2000). *Social work practices.* London: Sage.

Ife, J. (1997). *Rethinking social work: Towards critical practice.* Melbourne: Addison Longman Wesley.

Ife, J. (1999). Postmodernism, critical theory and social work. In B. Pease & J. Fook (Eds.), *Transforming social work practice: Postmodern critical perspectives* (pp. 211-223). London: Routledge.

Leonard, P. (1997). *Postmodern welfare.* London: Sage.

Larrain, J. (1979).*The concept of ideology.* London: Hutchinson.

Lukacs, G. (1973). History and class consciousness. London: Merlin. (Original work published 1923)

Mannheim, K. (1972). *Ideology and utopia* (L. Wirth & E. Shils, Trans.). London: Routledge & Kegan Paul.

Marcuse, H. (1964). *One-dimensional man.* Boston: Beacon Press.

Marx, K, (1954). *Capital: A critical analysis of capitalistic production* (Vol. 1). Moscow: Progress Publishers.

Marx, K., & Engels, F. (1970). Preface to a contribution to the critique of political economy. In *Selected Works Vol. 1.* London: Lawrence and Wishart.

Mullaly, B. (1993).*Structural social work: Ideology, theory and practice.* Toronto: McClelland and Stewart.

Mullaly, B. (2002). *Challenging oppression: A critical social work approach.* Toronto: Oxford University Press.

Pease, B., & Fook, J. (Eds.). (1999). *Transforming social work practice: Postmodern critical perspectives.* London: Routledge.

Prince, M.J. (2004). Canadian disability policy: Still a hit-and-miss affair. *Canadian Journal of Sociology/Cahiers canadiens de sociologie, 29*(1), 59-82.

Rossiter, A. (1996). A perspective on critical social work. *Journal of Progressive Human Services, 7*(2), 23-41.

Rossiter, A. (2001). Innocence lost and suspicion found; do we educate for or against social work? Retrieved May 20, 2004, from <www.criticalsocial work.com/CSW_2001_1.html>.

Schutz, A. (1962). On multiple realities. In *Collected papers* (Vol. 1). The Hague: Martinus Nijhoff.

Smith, D.E. (1983). No one commits suicide: Textual analysis of ideological practices. *Human Studies, 6.*

Smith, D.E. (1987). *The everyday world as problematic: A feminist sociology.* Toronto: University of Toronto Press.

Smith, D.E. (1990). *The conceptual practices of power.* Toronto: University of Toronto Press.

Smith, D.E. (1999). *Writing the social: Critique, theory, and investigations.* Toronto: University of Toronto Press.

Swift, K. (1986). *Knowledge about neglect: A critical review of the literature.* Unpublished comprehensive paper, Faculty of Social Work, University of Toronto.

Walker, G.A. (1986). Burnout: From metaphor to ideology. *Canadian Journal of Sociology, 11.*

PART 2
The Practice of Critical Social Work

4

Human Rights and Critical Social Work

Jim Ife

This chapter will examine the idea of human rights as providing an important framework for conceptualizing critical social work in terms of both theory and practice. An approach to critical social work must satisfy a number of criteria. These are:

- It must be accessible. The ideas of praxis, and the language in which they are expressed, must be accessible not only to social workers but to those with whom they are working to ensure dialogical action can take place.
- It must connect the macro and the micro, drawing clear links between the private experiences and suffering of individuals and families and the socio-political context in which those experiences are located. This link applies both to theoretical understandings and also to ideas of action. It can be expressed as linking the personal and the political, as linking private troubles and public issues (Mills, 1970) and also as linking "macro" practice and "micro" practice.
- It must link theory and practice, in some notion of praxis that engages both worker and "client."
- It must facilitate genuine dialogue between worker and client towards dialogical action.
- It must lead to some form of action for change or transformation in a way that addresses structures and discourses of disadvantage and/or oppression.

It is the contention of this chapter that a social work built around human rights praxis meets all these criteria. However it is more than just a case of social workers looking to human rights to provide a framework for practice; social workers also have a significant contribution to make to the understanding of human rights. This can occur across the four domains of social work practice — individual, community, national and global — which will be discussed later in the chapter.

The way in which human rights are commonly understood is largely within a legal discourse. Rights are usually defined in legal terms, and protected and guaranteed by laws, legal conventions, constitutions, human rights instruments and courts. While robust legal guarantees and processes for realizing human rights are important, human rights need to be understood more broadly if they are to become central to social work theory and practice. Law has come to be seen as the dominant human rights profession, and this effectively limits the construction of human rights. It favours rights that are readily justiciable (i.e., that can be protected by laws) and thereby marginalizes rights that do not so easily lend themselves to legal interpretation and protection. This construction also emphasizes human rights in the civil and political arena, and marginalizes the protection of rights in other contexts. For example, freedom of speech within the family cannot be readily protected by laws, so our idea of "the right to freedom of speech" is understood largely within the public domain of addressing public meetings and publishing written work rather than in the private domain of the family where the arm of the law cannot easily reach. Yet for many — especially children, women and the aged — the denial of a right to freedom of expression within the family is far more important than the denial of the right to freedom of expression in the public domain, even though it cannot readily be protected by laws or conventions.

This is just one example of the limitations of legal constructions of human rights, but an example that is of particular interest to social workers. Human rights rest on a foundation more encompassing than the legal system; they touch every aspect of our humanity and our interaction with other humans, often in contexts well beyond the reach of the law. While human rights remain primarily a legal construct, and are seen as principally the concern of the legal profession, their relevance for critical social work will remain marginal, and legal mechanisms will continue to be sought as the primary means for human rights protection. However, human rights can be understood in other ways that can become a powerful basis for critical social work and incorporate a broader range of rights than can readily be understood within the traditional legally dominated human rights discourse.

Rights and Obligations

Exploring the necessary connections between rights and obligations, or responsibilities, is a first step towards such an understanding. If a person is said to have a right, there is a corresponding obligation on others to allow that person to exercise that right. Thus my rights become another's responsibility, and another's rights become my responsibility. Rights, therefore, make no sense if understood only individually; they tie people to one another through a network of mutual obligations. In this sense, "rights" imply some construction of human community in which these obligations can be met. Even in this fairly narrow liberal context, the power of rights discourse to imply some notion of collective responsibility is strong, but the notion of obligation or responsibility can be extended much further. It is not only individuals who have a responsibility for the meeting or protection of people's rights, it is also the state and the organs of civil society. This is particularly important when considering such rights as the right to education, to health, to public safety, to housing and to an adequate material standard of living. These cannot fully be met simply by other individuals but require some form of collective provision of basic (and perhaps not so basic) services, and make a claim on both state and non-state actors. Thus, claims of rights can be seen as implying responsibility on the part of governments, corporations, non-governmental organizations (NGOs), civil society and so on. Such a discussion cannot be dealt with in more detail here, although it has been developed by other writers (Gewirth, 1996). The important point is that it moves rights away from an individualism into the domain of collectivism, and moves human rights work beyond individual advocacy to also include community and policy development.

Obligations, however, do not extend only to others. There is also a responsibility, by those who claim a right, to exercise it. What is the point, one might ask, of a society where the right of freedom of speech is protected if no one chooses to exercise that right? This could also be asked of the right to vote, the right to education, the right to join a union and many others. Implied in the idea of rights is therefore the idea of an active participatory society, and from this perspective, the passive, individualist consumer-based society is not particularly conducive to the attainment and protection of human rights. This suggests that there may be a contradiction between the idea of human rights and the "rugged individualism" implied by some of the more extreme advocates of free-market ideology. In the world of Margaret Thatcher, where "there is no such thing as society" (only individuals acting in self-interest), there is also no room for human rights and their corresponding social obligations. Human rights require human interdependence rather than naïve independence.

The Construction of Rights

Rights cannot be said to exist in a positivist[1] or objective sense. One cannot go out and discover or measure rights. There has been a tendency to regard statements of rights (for example, the Universal Declaration of Human Rights, The Convention on the Rights of the Child and so on) as somehow being holy writ, laid down on tablets of stone, and thereby unalterable. Yet this is, clearly, inappropriate. Statements of rights, even such powerful ones as the Universal Declaration, are products of their time and take place in historical, political and cultural contexts. Therefore we need to understand rights as constructed, and this construction occurs in two ways. The *discursive* construction of rights identifies the way in which our understanding of our rights (and corresponding obligations) are affected by dominant discourses of power. Most people would not be able to quote the Universal Declaration, yet when asked about their human rights, would be able to come up with a number of rights statements on which they would assume general agreement (not always consistent with the Universal Declaration, of course). These rights claims, such as freedom of speech,

---

[1] A positivist world view sees social phenomena, such as rights, needs, community, alienation and so forth, as existing in an objective sense, as able to be measured in a value-free way and as being connected through causal relationships. Hence it applies the same scientific approach as is applied in the physical sciences, with a view to objective measurement, establishing causal relationships and prediction.

freedom of religion, the right to vote and so on — though they would vary somewhat from one culture to another — would be derived from dominant discourses about what constitutes rights and citizenship. To understand how we come to "own" these rights, we therefore need to deconstruct these dominant discourses.

The other form of construction of rights is the *reflexive* construction, where we can understand rights as emerging from our own attempts to make sense of the world and from our day-to-day negotiations with other people with whom we interact in families, workplaces, communities, public spaces or wherever. The way I treat other people every day is a product of my personal construction of their rights, and the way they treat me is a product of their construction of my rights. We may not use the word "rights" in thinking about these everyday inter-personal transactions, but we can readily understand human rights in these terms. In waiting in a queue in a bank, I recognize the right of those in front of me to be served first, so I do not push past them, and those behind me recognize my right in the same way. However, when an elderly woman using a walker enters the bank, I invite her to take a place in front of me at the head of the queue, because of my understanding of her rights arising out of her physical needs. No one complains, because we all share this understanding. When I reach the teller, he recognizes my right to receive efficient service, which he provides. I exchange a few friendly remarks with him, recognizing his right to be treated with dignity and politeness, but I keep these brief, recognizing the right of those in the queue behind me not to be kept waiting. My trip to the bank is therefore full of assumptions about rights (mine and others) and the obligations that go with them. If I make assumptions about those rights and responsibilities that conflict with the assumptions of other people in the bank, there is likely to be conflict; the successful "operation" of the bank depends on its clients sharing more or less common understandings about our respective rights and responsibilities in this context.

This might seem like a trivial example and far removed from "human rights" as they are often understood. But by seeing rights as something that we work with every day, and that govern how we behave towards each other in our day-to-day lives, we are starting with an idea of human rights that is at the opposite extreme from the Universal Declaration of Human Rights and its various conventions and treaties. Rather than the discursive idea of human rights "from above," the reflexive idea of human rights is human rights "from below." It can be a powerful way to think about human rights for a social worker engaging in dialogue with clients or community groups.

This approach to the construction of human rights can be extended to families (think of all the interlocking rights and responsibilities when a family sits down to a meal together), workplaces (rights and mutual responsibilities of managers, supervisors, employees, trainees and customers) and so on. We are constructing and reconstructing networks of rights and obligations all the time. To think of rights in this way is quite radical: we are used to thinking, for example, of the right to adequate income only in the context of the workplace and the wider society, but to ensure this right we also need to understand income distribution within families where this right can be frequently violated. Thus all things we might claim to be human rights need to be understood as operating at all levels where human beings interact; not only as *applying* at all those levels, but as actually being *defined, constructed* and *reconstructed* at all those levels.

Understanding human rights as both discursively and reflexively constructed opens up the possibility of a social work, based on rights, that links both the personal/reflexive and the political/discursive and that can focus on how we go about this constant understanding and negotiation of the rights and obligations of ourselves and of others. Social work can focus on an exploration of how people in any situation define and understand their own rights and the rights of others, and how they see this as translating into responsibilities or obligations (not only of the individual, but also of the community or the state). Framing such dialogue around human rights is a powerful way in which human rights can become accessible to people rather than being an essentially privileged legal discourse.

The point about *human* rights is that we are understanding these rights, constructed in the interplay between the discursive and the reflexive, as some kind of definition of our common humanity. They are not rights we wish to ascribe only to particular groups but are rights that we believe all people should be able to claim, simply because they are human beings. Such constructions will, inevitably, vary with cultural and political context, but nonetheless they are constructions that the person or group concerned would wish to ascribe to all of humanity. Some people in Asia, for example, may wish to emphasize collective understandings of rights rather more than the mainly individualist formulations of Western liberalism (Bauer & Bell, 1999; Bell, Nathan, & Peleg, 2002; Meijer, 2001; Van Ness, 1999). Some people may ascribe different responsibilities to a particular right. For example, the right to health may be seen by some as obligating governments to provide comprehensive heath services, while to others it may imply an obligation on the individual to exercise daily and eat a balanced diet, while to still others it may imply an obligation on the family to care for the individual in times of ill health. These different constructions of rights do not negate their essential universalism; the advocates of health as a human right would argue that the right to health belongs to all people in all societies and cultures.

The implication of a "common humanity" at the core of human rights may be dismissed by some as hopelessly modernist and therefore outdated in the era of postmodernity (Campbell, Ewing, & Tomkins, 2001). But if rights are understood as discursively and reflexively constructed, this allows a diversity of constructions rather than a necessary attempt to impose uniformity. This diversity can then open up the possibility of dialogue about human rights and what our "common humanity" might mean in an increasingly globalized world (Gaita, 1999). It should be noted that this does not negate the idea of the "universality" of human rights, though it does open it up for reinterpretation. Human rights will always be universal in the sense that they are what the definer of rights would wish to apply to all of humanity; when we claim something as a human right, we are claiming it for all members of the human race and hence it is a universal claim. But such universal claims will be constructed in different ways in different contexts, and this diversity creates a space for dialogue across cultural and other boundaries about how we see our common humanity.

We also need to question the consequences of doing away with a discourse of human rights, as some postmodernists might advocate; it could readily lead to an amoral philosophy of "anything goes," where lack of concern for standards of humanity would allow untrammelled human rights violations. Rather, human rights represent one of the most currently acceptable alternative discourses to the dominant paradigm of economic rationalism and managerialism with which social workers are all too familiar. As such, a discourse of human rights can create an important space for the development of critical social work approaches that challenge the dominant structures and discourses of oppression.

Four Domains of Social Work

We can identify four domains within which social workers work. These are the individual/family domain, the community domain, the national domain and the global domain (for a fuller discussion, see Ife & Morley, 2002). Social work within the individual/family domain involves personal development, counselling, support, "casework," couple and family therapy and so on. In the community domain, social work involves community development, strengthening community resources and other aspects of community work. Social work in the national domain involves social policy development, and the management and administration of the welfare state. At this level, in the era of privatization, it is important to include not only government/state bodies as the concern of social workers, but also private sector and NGO sector organizations. While not "the state," these organizations tend to operate co-operatively with it through funding and tendering arrangements, and are an important location for social work administration, and social policy development and advocacy. And at the global level, relatively small numbers of social workers are engaged with international organizations, NGOs, UN agencies and so on.

Social work not only operates within each of these four domains, but it also mediates between them. For critical social work, it is imperative to work across these four domains, consistent with the criterion stated at the beginning of this chapter regarding linking the macro and micro, and private and public. Social workers frequently will work with the interaction between the individual/family domain and the national domain (for example, in securing government benefits or other services), between the individual/family domain and the community domain (for example, integrating people into a community, generating community supports for people, encouraging participation in community life) and between the community domain and the national domain (for example, securing state funding for a community organization, making representations to government on behalf of a community group and so forth). The interactions between these three domains and the global domain are not as well developed in social work theorizing, but ideas such as "globalization from below" (community-global) or linking the individual with global resources through the Internet represent a beginning definition of social work roles in this context, brought about by the imperatives of globalization.

This way of understanding social work could be developed further (Ife & Morley, 2002), but such development is not the purpose of this chapter. For present purposes, it is sufficient to note that critical social work practice must be located within and between these four domains, and hence any approach to critical social work theory or the conceptualization of social work praxis needs to encompass all four. The aim of the remainder of this chapter is to show that human rights represent an ideal framework for such a conceptualization, and to indicate how human rights can thereby be applied to the development of a critical social work.

Human Rights and the Four Domains

The idea of human rights, when carefully examined, is necessarily located in and between each of the four domains described above.

The individual/family domain may initially seem to be an unlikely arena for a human rights discourse. However, in one sense human rights are deeply and profoundly personal. Human rights, after all, are about our constructions of our essential humanity, and understanding our essential humanity requires a degree of introspection as well as engagement with others. Indeed, an existential understanding of human rights would require that I look deep within myself in order to seek that essential humanness that I have in common with others, the sharing of which becomes the basis of human rights (Morley & Ife, 2002; Ife & Morley, 2002).

Understanding human rights at this deeply personal level leads naturally to an approach to social work with individuals that starts with their construction of their own and others' humanity, and works from there. But in reality, most social work at the micro level is about more than this. It is concerned not just with one person or client, but with the interactions between that person and one or more significant others: parent, child, partner, sibling, friend, supervisor, other relative, teacher and so on. Here, a human rights perspective can be particularly important for social work. As we saw above, rights involve responsibilities, and our day-to-day lives become a web of interlocking sets of rights and corresponding responsibilities that we are continually reconstructing. Thus human rights, and our understanding of them, can be a focus for discussion with a client about how they interact with others around them, how they deal with interpersonal conflict and so on. And it can be particularly useful where more than one person is involved, for example, in couple counselling or family therapy. This can lead to the development of a counselling or even therapy based on human rights. The power of assisting people to construct their own understandings of rights (their own rights and those of others with whom they interact), and then to explore the multi-layered responsibilities that are associated with those rights, can produce significant changes in self-esteem, empowerment and action, and provides a basis for dialogue. Such an approach is fully consistent with the idea of critical social work, because it inevitably leads to a consideration of rights and obligations in the wider context (for example, the obligations of the state, the rights of other members of the community and so on). Linking the personal and the political is a natural consequence of such a rights-based approach to counselling, and it should be emphasized that this is more than the conventional "welfare rights" perspective on practice, where the emphasis is on identifying the client's rights and then helping them, through advocacy, to attain them.

Traditional "welfare rights" is but one element of the human rights perspective on micro social work described here. As with the human rights perspective we are also required to consider the responsibilities that go with those rights, including the responsibilities of the client. So-called "radical social work" has tended not to consider the responsibilities of clients, seeing them solely as victims. They thereby, ironically, become passive recipients of social work "help" in order to attain their rights. This has done radical social work a disservice, as it fails to take account of the fact that clients too are human beings with responsibilities as well as rights; these responsibilities need not be the oppressive "blame-the-victim" obligations so often imposed on the poor and disadvantaged by neo-conservatives. Social workers need not be coy about the fact that individual responsibilities are tied to rights, but rather they can use the connection between them as a way to develop a more inclusive and empowering practice. There are three important components to this: One is to understand the client's responsibilities within an analysis of structures and discourses of power, ensuring that the responsibilities of the client are reasonable and able to be defined and owned by the client, and not merely a form of punishment imposed by a powerful and coercive system. The second is to ensure that such individual responsibilities are seen only as part of a larger network of responsibilities, including, for example, the responsibility of the state, of the employer, of the manager, of the community, of the government department, of other family members and so on. The third is to ensure that the client is able (often in dialogue with others) to construct those responsibilities for himself or herself, rather than have to accept their imposition by authoritarian, patriarchal or paternalistic politicians, managers, bureaucrats or community leaders.

We move now to human rights and the community domain of practice. Earlier, the connection between human rights and community was identified. Human rights, because of the reciprocal obligations that go with them, imply some form of community, as they must be collectively shared and collectively constructed. Thus community becomes a necessary condition for the realization of human rights, a very different notion from the idea of human rights as belonging only to the individual. They are "our" rights as much as "my" rights Hence community development work becomes synonymous with human rights work. By developing communities, we are creating the context within which human rights can be constructed and effectively realized. Similarly, by promoting human rights, we are also promoting the idea of community — the community of rights (Gewirth, 1996). Human rights workers commonly describe their work as seeking our *common humanity*, while community workers are traditionally concerned with *human community*. The two phrases are the same, as the words "common" and "community" have the same origin, and this highlights the parallels between community development and human rights work.

Thus human rights lead naturally to a concern for community practice, or community development, the aspect of social work concerned with strengthening communities, establishing programs at community level and organizing or facilitating community-based programs (Ife, 2002). Critical social work that is concerned with human rights is as naturally "at home" in the community domain as it is in the domain of working with individuals and families. And the critical perspective requires that this not be conservative "blame-the-community" practice, or practice that reinforces gender, class or race inequalities within a community, but rather practice that addresses the discourses and structures of oppression.

The connections between human rights and the national and global domains are more readily understood, as this is part of the dominant discourse of human rights. The nation state is commonly regarded as being responsible for preventing human rights abuses in the case of negative rights (rights that need *protection*, for example, rights to free speech, free assembly, fair trial, security and so on) and also is held responsible for the realization of many positive rights (rights that need *provision,* for example, the rights to education, health, housing, employment, social security and so forth). It is nation states that enter into human rights agreements, at the regional or global level, and are parties to the various human rights conventions. This is in realization of the fact that the state can have a major role to play both in protecting human rights through the provision of adequate court and justice systems, an effective and incorrupt police force, legislation to ensure freedom of speech, assembly and so on, and also in ensuring the attainment of human rights through the programs and services of the welfare state: health, housing, education, social security, and so forth. Hence the promotion of human rights becomes a matter of social policy, and progressive social policy is a prerequisite for human rights. Social policy development and advocacy have long been seen as essential for social work praxis and form an important part of social work education — a human rights perspective therefore readily facilitates the incorporation of policy analysis, advocacy and development.

At the global level, again, the relevance of human rights discourse is clear: human rights are generally understood as universal, applying to all of humanity and therefore, by nature, a global discourse. Human rights have been part of the internationalist movement, seeking to understand what it means to "live in one world" in terms of issues such as peace, social justice and environmental protection, rather than in terms of open markets and freedom for global capital. The relationship to social work, however, is somewhat more tenuous than is the case with the other three domains. International social work has occupied a marginal position in the social work profession (when compared with individual/family work, community work and policy development). However, there have always been some social workers seeking to practise in an international context, whether in UN agencies, NGOs, or in fields such as refugee resettlement and inter-country adoption. All such work, of course, readily lends itself to a human rights framework, and indeed the power of the global human rights discourse can influence more social workers either to work in the international field or to see global issues as an essential component of their practice.

There is, therefore, a clear connection of human rights with the four domains of social work practice. This connection can be further emphasized by thinking about human rights as forming the basis of critical social work *between* the four domains. In working across the individual-state boundary, social workers are really concerned about the rights of individuals and the responsibility of the state to provide the structures and programs to enable those rights (for example, to health care, income security and so on) to be attained. Working across the individual-community boundary, social work is characteristically concerned with the community's responsibility to respect the individual's rights, and the responsibility of the individual to contribute to the community through an understanding of the rights that reside collectively within the community and the corresponding obligations these bestow on individuals. Working across the community-state boundary, social work has a concern for the rights of communities, and of the individuals within them, to the resources of the state, and also the rights and responsibilities of communities to contribute to policy determination. Similarly, connecting the global domain and the other three domains also involves human rights: the ratification of human rights conventions by governments, communities joining in global movements for a just share of resources and individuals being able to participate in global campaigns.

In summary, then, a human rights framework readily relates to social work practice within and between the four domains of practice and enables connections between them to be made. The view of human rights as constructed — discursively and reflexively — means that human rights-based social work is not simply the application of set principles, but rather requires the active participation both of a social worker and also of those with whom a social worker interacts, whether as clients, colleagues or community members.

Conclusion

At the beginning of this chapter, five criteria were asserted for a critical social work. In conclusion, we will briefly examine how well human rights-based social work meets these criteria.

The first criterion is accessibility. Human rights is an idea with which people can easily engage, and ideas of my rights, our rights, your rights, and my responsibilities, our responsibilities, your responsibilities, are certainly accessible — they are, after all, the basis for human interaction. Those working with human rights education programs find that it is very easy to engage in a discussion with people about human rights, and even quite young children have clear ideas about what is fair and how people should treat one another. There are many techniques that have been developed by human rights educators for making human rights accessible, including theatre, art, games and other exercises, as well as more traditional classes and discussions. Ideas of rights are close to people's hearts, and they generally need little encouragement to talk about them.

The second criterion is that critical social work should link the personal and the political, or the macro and the micro. This is clearly inherent in the human rights approach above, especially if the idea of responsibilities is seen as incorporating, not only individual responsibilities, but the responsibilities of the state and other structures. Asking questions about human rights leads naturally and inevitably to analysis and critique of the political system, and the exploration of alternatives.

Linking theory and practice is the third criterion. By encouraging people to define the rights and responsibilities of themselves and others (whether individually or collectively) as the "theoretical" basis for practice, the link between understanding and action, or theory and practice, is clearly made. One cannot talk about a "theory" of rights, in the sense described above, without it also leading to a "practice" of rights.

The fourth criterion is that critical social work should facilitate dialogue. There is a necessary connection between the human rights approach as described above and dialogue. A claim of right also requires the claim of responsibility by one or more others, and rights can be realized only if both parties are able to reach a shared understanding of the nature and limitations of both the right and the responsibility. This can be achieved only through dialogue and genuine exchange, and this becomes the basis for social work practice using a human rights perspective.

Finally, the last criterion is that the critical analysis must open up the possibility of action, as a major aim of a critical theory perspective is the achievement of change in challenging structures and discourses of oppression. A human rights approach has the potential to challenge the established order, partly because of the power of the human rights discourse (it is something many people can readily relate to and feel passionate about), and partly because a human rights analysis leaves it very clear what has to happen and who should be responsible by spelling out the necessary obligations (whether individual or collective) that go with human rights. It requires that institutions, processes, structures and discourses be critiqued from the point of view of humanity, and that human values and interests take precedence over economic, managerial and political interests.

There has not been the space in this chapter to spell out the full implications of a human rights approach to critical social work. Indeed, it would be wrong to develop too prescriptive a "model" for human rights-based social work, as that would deny the people concerned the opportunity to construct the understandings of rights and obligations themselves. There has also not been space to explore the various debates about human rights, for example, around universality, cultural relativism, individual and collective rights, the gendered nature of much human rights discourse, the hegemony of Western Enlightenment worldviews and so on. The field of human rights is complex and contested, and any social worker wishing to develop praxis from a human rights perspective will need to understand the issues at far greater depth (see, for example, Ife, 2001; Reichert, 2003; Hayden, 2001; O'Byrne, 2003; Leiser & Campbell, 2001). However it is not difficult to transfer this understanding to an accessible, dialogical form of practice, using the power of human rights to drive a program of empowerment.

References

Bauer, J., & Bell, D. (Eds.). (1999). *The East Asian challenge for human rights.* Cambridge: Cambridge University Press.

Bell, L., Nathan, A., & Peleg, I. (2001). *Negotiating culture and human rights.* NY: Columbia University Press.

Campbell, T., Ewing, K.D., & Tomkins, A. (Eds.). (2001). *Sceptical essays on human rights.* Oxford: Oxford University Press.

Gaita, R. (1999). *A common humanity: Thinking about love, truth and justice.* Melbourne: Text Publishing.

Gewirth, A. (1996). *The community of rights.* Chicago: University of Chicago Press.

Hayden, P. (Ed.). (2001). *The philosophy of human rights.* St. Paul: Paragon.

Ife, J. (2001). *Human rights and social work: Towards rights-based practice.* Cambridge: Cambridge University Press.

Ife, J. (2002). *Community development: Community-based alternatives in an age of globalisation.* Sydney: Pearson.

Ife, J., & Morley, L. (2002). *Integrating local and global practice using a human rights framework.* IASSW Conference, Montpellier.

Leiser, B., & Campbell, T. (Eds.). (2001). *Human rights in philosophy and practice.* Dartmouth: Ashgate.

Meijer, M. (Ed.). (2001). *Dealing with human rights: Asian and Western views on the value of human rights.* HOM, Utrecht.

Mills, C.W. (1970). *The sociological imagination.* Harmondsworth: Penguin.

Morley, L., & Ife, J. (2002). Social work and a love of humanity. *Australian Social Work 55*(1), 69–77.

O'Byrne, D. (2003). *Human rights: An introduction.* Harlow: Pearson.

Reichert, E. (2003). *Social work and human rights: A foundation for policy and practice.* NY: Columbia University Press.

Van Ness, P. (Ed.). (1999). *Debating human rights: Critical essays from the United States and Asia.* London: Routledge.

5

Empowerment: A Contextual Perspective

Jan Fook and Christine Morley

The concept of empowerment has been popular for the last two decades in social work literature and practice, and in many ways seems more widely used than ever. Yet because of its popularity, it is an idea open to misinterpretation and indeed co-option by ruling interests (Baistow, 1994/1995). It has possibly also been seen, at times, as a substitute for theoretical approaches to social work that are more explicitly "critical," such as structural social work (Furlong, 1987). It is timely to examine the broad usefulness of such a concept, since many of the universal assumptions of a more "modernist" version of social work are coming under question (Parton, 1994; Leonard, 1997). We therefore revisit the idea of empowerment in this chapter. How much is it possible to generalize about the concept of empowerment? How much does its meaning, interpretation and practice change according to context? And, is such a "single concept" idea a useful substitute for the more theoretically coherent "critical" social work approaches?

These are the questions that motivate this chapter. We aim to contribute to the ongoing debate about empowerment by examining and, to some extent reworking, its meaning with reference to a specific context, the Australian context. We believe the choice of Australian context is useful in that Australian social work is becoming recognized for its contribution to the area of critical social work more generally (Fook, 2003), and there is a solid body of Australian literature in this progressive vein (for example, Rees, 1991). It is argued that Australian social work relies strongly on a social justice foundation (Ife, 1997). Australia is also a younger nation, struggling to find an identity and place in a rapidly changing world. Its current conflicts thus epitomize many of the current global struggles.

This chapter is organized in the following way. After a brief outline of the Australian social work context, we review the usage of the term "empowerment" in Australian social work literature. Based on this discussion, the main body of the chapter takes the form of a case study of the practice of empowerment in a casework (sexual assault) situation. The practice in the case is theorized using this analysis of empowerment, and is then examined using a critical reflective approach to identify some of the complex ways in which empowerment is used, experienced, and needs developing. In the conclusion we relate these issues to general questions about the meaning of empowerment and compare these to the broader approach of critical social work.

Social Work in Australia

Australians have long prided themselves on having a welfare state and egalitarian values within it. Yet it has been more recently argued that it is among the weakest of welfare states (along with countries such as the United States, New Zealand, Canada and the United Kingdom) because of its low levels of welfare expenditure (Jones, 1996, p.36) and is often compared unfavourably with the Swedish model.

The place of human service professionals, particularly social work professionals, is also significant. Australian social workers are primarily employed in areas of welfare that have less universal scope than might be ideally envisioned by the mission of the profession. As well, the context in which Australian social workers practise is a culture and structure that has traditionally valued equality, but that in practice has not been as tolerant of differences or supported disadvantage to the extent it is often believed.

Social workers in Australia have historically been employed in casework or direct service positions (Franklin & Eu, 1996; Laragy, 1997) and generally enjoy high employment levels. High employment, however, does not necessarily translate into an empowered position for the profession, as there is some evidence to suggest that many social workers may in fact be employed in jobs requiring a lower level of qualification, and that in fact there is a downgrading of professional expertise (Murray et al., 1998). Australian social workers also face threats to professionalism through globalization, similar to that experienced in much of the Western world (O'Connor, Smyth, & Warburton, 2000).

With the Australian self-image of relative progressiveness in welfare matters, as well as the growing national and international interest in Australian social work literature, Australia is well placed to take some lead in empowerment practice in social work. However, it is ironic, as we noted earlier, that the peculiarities of the position of social work within Australia mean that, as a profession, Australian social workers are not well placed to influence structures or current economic changes. The theory of empowerment is well accepted as part of the Australian social work context. How it is played out in practice by practitioners might be a more complicated story.

The Theory of Empowerment in Australian Social Work

Evolution of the idea

Empowerment, as an idea and term, was probably first associated with the radical tradition in social work writing, which in Australia broadly paralleled, if a little behind, similar writings in the U.K. and the U.S. Any review of the concept therefore must incorporate a review of theories and practice models that have followed the emancipatory ideals of the early radical critiques of social work. In Australia, these critiques first appeared in the early 1970s (Pemberton & Locke, 1971; Throssell, 1975; Skenridge & Lennie, 1978). As with radical literature from the U.S. (Galper, 1980) and the U.K. (Bailey & Brake, 1975; Corrigan & Leonard, 1978), these early critiques were based primarily on Marxist analysis. It was the anti-oppressive stance, coupled with a specific emphasis on personal liberation (Fook, 1993b), which particularly lent fuel to the call for empowerment. The work of the liberatory educationalists, such as Freire (1972), was heavily used, and so continues to the present day (Rees, 1995; Mullaly, 1998). For example, the process of empowerment has been likened to a dialogical relationship in which those becoming empowered engage in a staged process of changing consciousness in relation to their social world, and their ability to act within it.

However, by and large, this early Australian radical writing remained at the level of critique and ignored applications to everyday practice. Although there were some significant practice alternatives developed in Australia at this time, born out of a variety of social movements (Healy, 1993), they did not generally make their way into the social work practice literature. According to Healy (1993) these developments included the rediscovery of poverty (Benn, 1981), the struggle for Aboriginal land rights (Camilleri, 1974; Tomlinson, 1977), and the Women's Movement (Nichols, 1973; Summers, 1975). The Family Centre Project of the Brotherhood of St Laurence (Liffman, 1978) represented a major early empowerment project. The emergence of the concept of empowerment can be seen in the statement of its basic goal:

> ...the redistribution of resources and power in the community by attempting to demonstrate with a small group of poor families that changes in their economic and social condition are a precondition to changes in their family and societal relationships. (p. 33)

In the 1980s, with the influx of feminist thinking into social work (Weeks, 1980; Marchant & Wearing, 1986), the imperative for empowerment was strengthened, linking personal liberation with political and social change. In social work education, the radical approach, with its feet set firmly in structural analyses of personal problems (Fook, 1993b), became recognized as an alternative approach and several social work programs (for example, the University of Sydney, and the then Preston Institute of Technology) clearly taught from this perspective.

Ironically, as the radical or structural approaches became better developed as theoretical models, there remained some doubt about their usefulness for practice, particularly their applicability to direct practice (Furlong, 1987; Crawley, 1989), which, as we noted earlier, is still the dominant practice form for Australian social workers. This theme, of the tensions between structural critique and individualized practice, has been one that recurs for practitioners committed to empowerment in Australia. Indeed, Furlong (1987) went so far as to argue that the concept of empowerment was more applicable to casework practice than a structural approach to practice (which is an idea that has been refuted several times (Fook, 1987, 1993b). We would argue that empowerment cannot properly be practised without a structural analysis, that is, an understanding of how social structures and political processes operate at the personal and individual level. The danger with a single concept such as empowerment is that the bigger questions of empowerment for what and for whom are still left unanswered without a broader theoretical and critical analysis (Fook, 1993a). It is this relationship of empowerment theory and practice to broader-based systems of theorizing, such as feminism, critical theory or postmodernism, that is one of the contested and developing areas in Australian social work. It has been regarded as easier, by many, to employ concepts of empowerment when working at direct and interpersonal levels, and to associate more critical systems of thinking with more collective modes of practice. We take this issue up later, particularly in relation to our in-depth practice example.

In further writings by Australian authors, such as Petruchenia and Thorpe (1990) and Fook (1993b), however, the idea of empowerment and its practice became better developed in relation to radical, anti-oppressive and structural approaches to practice. For instance, Benn (1991) characterizes social work approaches as either "ameliorative or empowerment." Rees (1991, 1995) develops a theory and practice of empowerment based on a sophisticated understanding of power. In some writings, empowerment has been incorporated into the broader approach as a set of techniques or strategies (for example, Fook, 1990, 1993b), rather than as an entire approach in its own right. Other writers associated the idea of empowerment with participation (Peers, 1990) and collaboration (Pease, 1990).

Mullaly (1998) (although originating from Canada, he spent some years working in Australia) is another key author in the area of structural social work. He includes empowerment practice as part of a suite of strategies used in a structural approach, particularly developing the links with anti-oppressive practice. De Maria (1992, 1993) also made a significant contribution, especially in terms of teaching practices. For other writers, the problem of empowerment is also the problem of social justice: both are terms too often uncritically and perhaps meaninglessly used (Liddell, 1997), which gets us caught in splitting individual and collective action.

Most recently, critical and postmodern theories (Ife, 1997; Pease & Fook, 1999) are being developed for their emancipatory potential in social work practice.

From these latter perspectives, the concept of power, and therefore the concept of empowerment, has been deconstructed and therefore criticized for its modernist and often disempowering functions (Fook & Pease, 1999). These include the notion of fixed identities (Healy, 1999), powerful groups often labelling disadvantaged groups in fixed, "powerless" ways (Crinall, 1999) and perpetuating a notion of difference that can be experienced as disempowering (Parker, Fook, & Pease, 1999). The modernist commodification of power, whereby it is assumed that power has a material presence and therefore the act of empowerment involves the "giving" of power to another, can also function to disempower workers. This more critical and reflexive understanding of empowerment is at the heart of postmodern and critical perspectives on social work practice (Leonard, 1997; Fook, 2000, 2002).

Other recent writing, which would probably be characterized as in the critical rather than postmodern tradition, places the emancipatory project squarely in the communitarian camp. Ife (1997, 2000), for instance, argues that this is the appropriate site and discourse for the long-espoused social work values of social justice. Using Ife's paradigms, Tesoriero (1999) argues that, if social work is to contribute effectively to social development, to develop community participation in ways that are inclusive, then a deconstructive analysis as well as critical and reflective relationships based on negotiation are needed.

Current uses and differences

This tracing of the evolving uses of the concept of empowerment in Australian social work literature also involves the tracing of differing and associated discourses. For instance, the term is used differently depending on the theoretical perspective taken by the author or practitioner. Conceptions of empowerment range from relatively simple notions such as the sharing or giving of power (Fook, 1993a, p.102), or having choice or control in one's life (Jackson & Dilger, 1995). These understandings and practices of empowerment will clearly depend to a great extent on the type of analyses and understandings of power. Mullaly's conception, for instance (1998, p.167), is clearly based on an inclusive understanding of oppression and the state of powerlessness this engenders for many different types of oppressed peoples. Rees's (1991, 1995) understanding of empowerment is also based on quite complex conceptions of power, on its personal, structural and processual dimensions.

> Empowerment refers to a process of treating people equitably and to a socially just outcome, as in achieving liberation which enhances the quality of life of more than one person, and does not interfere with others' struggles to achieve similar goals. (1995, pp. 12-13)

On the other hand, some notions of empowerment do not seem to include the notion of power at all. Furlong (1987) defines empowerment (in casework) as follows:

> [E]mpowerment as a goal in direct service provision involves the worker's practice being oriented by the attitude that particular client problems will arise, and be maintained, unless the client has attained a minimal degree of self-management... As such, the worker's tasks is to provide a context within which the client can experience, or have restored, a level of self management competence, equal to coping with the client's current life stage demands. (p. 25)

Because of its association with more progressive traditions in social work, its presence may be more commonly found in the discourse of community development and social action (for example, Regan & Lee, 1992) and associated with collectivist traditions (Ife, 2000). Unfortunately, in Australian social work, these traditions have often been constructed as opposed to casework and therefore in a sense to mainstream social work, so that discourses of empowerment and the practice of it may have been less developed in mainstream social work practice as a result.

As well, of course, the practice and understanding of empowerment varies between contexts. For example, empowerment in the Family Court workplace may involve motivating staff through the use of validation, information and participation (Gibson, 1995), or, in youth work, understood as a process of activating youth to speak out more loudly (Flowers, 1998). Empowerment issues for indigenous peoples may involve "pausing to understand" (Mundine, 1993) and the attainment of reconciliation. In the disability area, it may involve the recognition of the organic reality of disability and an analysis of its social construction (Hallahan, 1997). Rees (1995) argues that, in youth work, sometimes personal and social justice issues need to be separated in the actual practice of empowerment, so that personal meanings of power need to be addressed in young people's biographies as part of an empowering process. Herbert (1998) notes that, in rural development in Australia, the rhetoric of empowerment is based on notions of self-help, individual and community responsibility, and "bottom-up" techniques, all of which assume community rather than governmental initiative. Harley (1999) argues that empowerment of workers is a myth in the contemporary Australian workplace: supposedly empowering forms of work organization (such as total quality management, team-based work and consultative committees) have not resulted in employee autonomy.

How do we account for these variations? For adults with intellectual disabilities, the experience of social change may be too removed from their personal experiences. For Rees, this entails acknowledging the experience of empowerment of young people, and that no choice means powerlessness. For Harley, autonomy has not resulted because employees still lack access to structural power. In the case of rural communities, there is still a lack of resources and facilities. The suggestion is that, for empowering outcomes to be achieved, certain conditions need to be created. Empowerment is not simply a matter of the social worker giving the service user power.

An additional issue is that taken for granted theories of empowerment may not in fact be enacted, or experienced, in intended ways. The idea of empowerment, then, is perhaps context-dependent, subject to changing understandings and theoretical viewpoints. Its many different usages and interpretations may provide rationale for practices whose outcomes and political influence may be widely variant.

These are the theoretical challenges involved in the practice of empowerment. Integrated with the broader contextual issues facing Australian social work, there are further questions about what empowerment practice possibilities exist for a profession whose identity and boundaries are being eroded in the current workplace. What hope is there of empowerment practice for a profession whose influence is broadly confined to the more "Band-Aid" areas of welfare, in a country whose welfare system and culture is being gradually eroded?

In the following section we describe and analyze a specific program and practices within it from this standpoint on empowerment.

Case Study: The Theory and Practice of Empowerment in Sexual Assault

The following case analysis is developed from a practice research project that I (Christine) undertook at a Centre Against Sexual Assault (CASA). The project was specifically interested in empowering victim/survivors of sexual assault who had been assigned a psychiatric label. The empowerment took the form of exploring how critical mental health discourses could be applied to practice with this group. I used a reflective approach (Millstein, 1993; Fook, 1996, 2002; Pease & Fook, 1999) to critically deconstruct my practice and evaluate it in terms of its theoretical content. Using this analysis of specific practice experiences, I reconceptualized my notion of empowerment. What became apparent from my research is that empowerment is a very difficult concept to enact and measure. It is a highly subjective and relative phenomenon that shifts in form and definition depending on the context and perspective from which it is seen.

I will first describe the theoretical underpinnings of the practice. I will then describe my practice with a woman named Suzanne, and then offer my reflections and reworked theory about empowerment.

The theory

My initial thinking about empowerment was firmly grounded in radical and/or structural (Fook, 1993b; Mullaly, 1998) and feminist (Marchant & Wearing, 1986) social work literature. This involved the assumption that empowerment and personal liberation must be connected with broader social change in order to redress structural inequities. More recently, with exposure to critical postmodern perspectives (Ife, 1997; Leonard, 1997; Pease & Fook, 1999; Fook 2002), I had developed an awareness of the critiques levelled at modernist theories (such as structural and/or radical and feminist approaches) for being too universal regarding the experiences of oppression. I struggled with the dilemma of maintaining a strong commitment to the values of radical and/or structural and feminist perspectives, yet at the same time being aware of the limitations of these theories. I believed I could retain a structural and/or feminist analysis to understand the institutional dimensions of power (Fook, 1993a; Mullaly, 1998) while combining this with postmodernism to recognize that institutional power might additionally be maintained through accepting various dominant discourses. By acknowledging that these discourses can be changed (through rejection of the particular assumptions, beliefs and actions that hold them in place), I believed that social workers could facilitate empowerment and redress structural disadvantage by challenging and changing their own internal constructions of reality that are experienced as disempowering (Pease & Fook, 1999), and also fostering this reflective capacity in their clients.

This conceptualization of empowerment practice in social work, situated within a critical analysis of mental health discourses, has a number of direct implications for providing counselling to survivors of sexual assault who had been diagnosed with a psychiatric disorder. I therefore approached practice with this group informed by several assumptions, which are also reflected by some of the literature in this area (see, for example, Matthews, 1984; Robertson, 1990; Hurst, 1995; McLellan, 1995; Rummery, 1996; Astbury, 1996; Hodges, 1997). Briefly, some of these assumptions included

- that however a victim/survivor responds to sexual assault is legitimate, and that applying a medical label to behavioural and/or emotional responses of victim/survivors of sexual assault is pathologizing, stigmatizing, and therefore disempowering;
- that psychiatrically labelling, medicating or institutionalizing a victim/survivor individualizes the issue of sexual assault by depoliticizing the social causes that should be contextualized and acknowledged as a societal responsibility;
- that this process blames the survivor by emphasizing the individual's responses;
- that this conceals the need for social change by shifting the focus away from the perpetrator, and social arrangements that condone and conceal abuse; and
- that when a bio-medical analysis becomes the dominant paradigm from which victim/survivors and others understand their experience, social inequities are maintained by reproducing the broader social denial that exists around sexual violence (since the patriarchal conditions that sanction sexual assault remain unquestioned).

In concrete terms, these assumptions equated with a pivotal idea — that service users essentially must reject the medical model as the dominant discourse in order to become empowered. From a critical perspective, the medical model seemed fundamentally problematic to me at a number of levels. Psychiatry, for example, arguably operates to maintain the status quo in multiple ways. One of these ways is to assist women in particular to conform to socially prescribed gender roles. As Bainbridge (1999) explains,

> Women continue to be bombarded with a startling array of highly addictive tranquil-
> lizing drugs to help them maintain their subservient role. By labelling their distress
> as a clinical problem rather than an understandable reaction to role stresses, psychia-
> try serves the interests of patriarchal capitalism. (p. 187)

Using a critical analysis I actively aimed to challenge these processes in my practice by validating and contextualizing service users' experiences rather than pathologizing their responses, and by raising awareness of the patriarchal conditions that create sexual assault and medicalize victim/survivors' responses. This will be discussed further in the next section.

Work with Suzanne

Suzanne was a single mother of two children, in her late twenties. Suzanne initially contacted the agency in crisis, after being sexually assaulted by a close family member. She believed that if she did not seek counselling immediately, she would have a relapse of mental illness and be re-institutionalized (she had been diagnosed with post-natal depression and subsequently hospitalized for five weeks after the birth of her second child). She had been told by psychiatrists that she had a genetic predisposition to psychiatric illness and was informed that she would not cope with any events that caused stress. She indicated that she was feeling distressed, nervous, anxious and depressed and believed these responses could constitute the onset of a psychotic episode.

I perceived this interpretation as incredibly disempowering for Suzanne. Given the critical analysis informing my thinking, I felt that Suzanne's belief in her capacity to cope with the sexual assault had been undermined by medical professionals who had constructed her future and ability to cope with challenging circumstances in pathological terms. From my perspective, Suzanne had in fact coped with an event that was potentially extremely stressful, and had displayed enormous courage in contacting the service and speaking about her experience. I felt that these factors should be acknowledged and valued, rather than ignored. This guided me to assist Suzanne in recognizing the strengths that she had demonstrated and explore how these attributes constitute the foundations of empowerment. For Suzanne to feel empowered by this process, I believed she needed to be able to dismiss the deterministic implications of the medical perspective, which I judged to have denied her personal agency to cope with and respond to her experience. This became a significant goal of our work together.

In practice, this took the form of exploring and questioning Suzanne's unarticulated values and assumptions. We focused on these because they reinforced a cycle of thinking that supported the belief that the medical perspective constituted the only "truth" and that she was merely a passive vessel, powerless in the face of accepting her fate as medical "experts" had defined it. Reflecting on my practice showed that examining the contradictions inherent in Suzanne's account was one of the ways I attempted to explore and name the functions of particular medical and self-blaming beliefs that I believed were operating contrary to her interests. My intention was to assist Suzanne in analyzing the way her own beliefs, assumptions and social practices influence a situation to either maintain or challenge inequitable social arrangements, with a view to changing these ideas if they were potentially disempowering for her.

Inherent within this approach were many basic feminist counselling principles. This included normalizing, validating and universalizing common reactions to trauma, which are often dominantly defined as symptoms of psychiatric illnesses (Robertson, 1990; Hurst, 1995; McLellan, 1995; Rummery, 1996; Hodges, 1997). I also perceived that a major part of my role was to raise consciousness about the socially constructed constraints that maintain social control. This included generating possibilities that did not necessarily maintain the status quo or conform to socially prescribed gender roles (Hurst, 1995).

On initial reflection of our interactions, the goals of empowerment seemed to be achieved. The structural and/or feminist understanding of the issues appeared to have a clear influence in shaping the construction of our shared reality. This construction did in fact de-legitimize the dominant medical discourse, thus allowing for other discourses, such as the critical perspective, to emerge. When Suzanne had approached the service, she had defined her options in terms of either suffering in silence and slowly going mad or accepting the medical definition of her experience and taking medication to manage her psychiatric disorder. In this sense, counselling had provided an opportunity for Suzanne to develop other understandings of her situation that offered her different choices about how she wanted to see and respond to her experiences. At the end of our work, Suzanne indicated that she no longer saw her experience in pathological or medical terms. She rejected the notion that how she had coped with being sexually assaulted constituted a psychiatric disorder, and she developed a good understanding of how psychiatry as an institution is heavily implicated in the maintenance of social control. She decided to stop taking her medication. Identifying herself as feeling much more empowered, she was coping well without it. On one level, this model appeared to facilitate empowerment. A critical deconstruction of this practice, however, provides other interpretations from which to evaluate the outcomes. My critical intentions to empower Suzanne, for example, may have in fact *not* resulted in her empowerment, and indeed may have potentially resulted in some unintended disempowering outcomes for Suzanne. The implications of this will be more fully explored in the next section.

A closer look

As discussed earlier, the concept and practice of empowerment varies radically, depending on the theoretical perspective in which it is located. The implications of this relativity for practice with Suzanne involved recognizing that my attempts to empower may have actually evoked a number of inadvertent, disempowering consequences that I was unaware of at the time.

For example, in the process of exploring non-medical conceptualizations of Suzanne's experience, I raised the possibility that Suzanne's depressive symptoms might be a legitimate response to being sexually assaulted, rather than a psychiatric disorder. I acted on the belief that challenging the medical construction of her experience would be empowering by normalizing her responses and locating what had happened to her in a broader structural context. However, instead of freeing Suzanne from the dominant medical interpretation of her experience, her responding comment of "Yeah, you're probably right. I do believe it's stress-related and you can just talk yourself into having a problem" possibly indicated that she felt I was minimizing her feelings. Despite undermining the psychiatric construction of her experience, which I perceived was disempowering, Suzanne's commentary indicated she had retained an equally self-blaming, individualized and pathological analysis but without the medical justification for her feelings.

Other inadequacies were highlighted when I acknowledged that I was operating on the assumption that simply applying empowering theories to practice would automatically have the capacity to empower Suzanne. As discussed earlier, I was aware of the limitations of applying modernist theories to practice when trying to empower others. I thought, however, that combining this with a postmodernist framework would overcome these pitfalls. I initially thought my work was being guided by the postmodern contention that names the illegitimacy of privileging one version of reality as the dominant truth (Fook, 1995; Wood, 1997; Pease & Fook, 1999). Reflecting on the ways I facilitated the discussion of the other possible realities, however, forces me to acknowledge that I presented this, not in a way that would open up the possibility of multiple discourses in the postmodern sense, but with the implicit intention of inverting the perceived hierarchy between psychiatry and social work (Healy, 1995). Reflecting on my perception of this has enabled me to see that I actually constructed another hierarchical relationship where the medical and social were seen as diametrically opposed. In constructing these perspectives as polarized categories, I had de-legitimized the critical perspective by defining it as a marginalized alternative; presenting it not in its own right, but by virtue of its difference to the dominant medical model. In a way I had "othered" it. In practice, my attempts to facilitate change, and enact the empowerment of a perspective that is often rendered silent by the dominant discourse, ironically functioned to reinstate the dominance of the medical discourse. Additionally, in attempting to set an agenda that challenged medical dominance, I was unconsciously embracing the notion that the dominant psychiatric discourse might be superior. This unearths how my own values, assumptions and beliefs impacted on our interactions in ways I did not intend. Reflecting on our interaction in this way shows that I had unintentionally projected my own sense of disempowerment that I was struggling with both professionally and personally. My sense of disillusionment at how ingrained the dominance of the medical model appeared to be resulted in my internally constructing this as a barrier to the possibility of producing change, which potentially had a powerful influence on my ultimate ability to facilitate change at any level.

Having unconsciously internalized this structural perception, which is characterized by the dichotomous split of being either powerful or powerless, dominant or marginalized (Baistow, 1994/1995), not only undermined my intentions to promote the critical perspective, it also arguably subverted my intentions to empower Suzanne. Reflecting on our interactions from a critical postmodern perspective suggests that the very aim of attempting to empower someone is potentially problematic. Ironically, detecting people whom we assume need to be empowered is an exercise of power (ibid.). Within a modernist framework, and without critical insight, this process cannot escape the notion of commodifying power that evokes the condescending gesture of giving someone power (ibid.) or contributing to the "dilemma of difference"

(Minow, 1985, cited in Parker, Fook, & Pease, 1999, p.151). This is the unintended disempowering outcome of identifying and resourcing particular groups, who will consequently become stigmatized and constructed in binary oppositional terms.

Rossiter (1996, p.26) also discusses the limitations of the modernist conceptions of empowerment, which she suggests involves the undermining notion of constructing the service user as "a blank slate, awaiting inscription by a politically aware social worker." In assuming that service users can be empowered only if they accept certain beliefs that workers have defined as empowering, an unequal and devaluing relationship dynamic is established, whereby the worker is constructed as the expert and the service user as the learner. This contravenes all espoused tenets of the critical perspective that value and respect peoples' experiences, and acknowledge that surviving their experiences positions the service users as the expert on their own situations. Additionally, involving the notion that empowerment can be obtained only if certain beliefs are embraced (Fook, 1995) neglects to acknowledge Foucault's assertion that power is exercised rather than possessed (Foucault, 1975, cited in Parker, Fook, & Pease, 1999). Goodman (1998) similarly refers to the dilemmas inherent in attempting to empower others or conduct emancipatory practice or research, conceding that this places workers in an insidious paradox. He refers to the hazards of the Marxist notion of "false consciousness," for example, stating that "it suggests that people do not understand reality as Marx did suffer from *deficient* thinking, rather than merely having an alternative understanding of life experiences" (p. 56).

Deconstruction of my practice suggests this dilemma imposed a number of limitations on my hopes to empower Suzanne. My intention to privilege the critical perspective may have prevented me from hearing Suzanne's experiences and perceptions that did not fit with my analysis. Her assertion that medication temporarily dulled her pain, for example, was met with my response that this was pathologizing and medicalizing her reactions, which from my perspective individualized a problem that I perceived was a societal issue and responsibility. This position, while informed by a critical analysis that I believed would be empowering, possibly resulted in my inability to acknowledge the positive attributes she was gaining from the dominant discourse and in my potential minimization of the legitimacy of her perspective. This highlights the illegitimacy of privileging any theoretical perspective, particularly in the context of a counselling relationship where a strong potential exists for an hierarchical power relationship to develop between worker and service user (Goodman, 1998).

Another difficulty with my practice was that Suzanne's account of being diagnosed and treated in a psychiatric hospital indicated that she had experienced very real abuses of institutional power. My implicit suggestion that changing her thinking and interpretations of her experiences to reconstruct a different perception of herself could resist the impact of the structural realities she endured possibly seemed quite nonsensical to her, particularly given the way I had inadvertently framed the situation. In constructing medical and social perspectives in mutually exclusive terms, I thereby limited my intention to create the possibility of multiple discourses to two opposing perspectives only. I arguably operated to affirm Suzanne's participation in the medical discourse, thus defeating my purpose.

Although I tried to facilitate Suzanne's empowerment by locating the means of social change with her, my reflection on this work demonstrated that my unintentional positioning of Suzanne's experience in a modernist, structural framework constructed a reality in which abstract structures perpetrate a particular experience over which she could have no control or influence. While from one perspective Suzanne indicated that she had rejected the disempowering aspects of the dominant discourse, from another perspective, her interactions suggested that she had not repositioned herself in the discourse to reconstruct herself as a more empowered identity. As Suzanne stated, "When the doctor said I should go on anti-depressants, I didn't really want to, but if I told her I didn't want to go on them, she might have called in the CAT [crisis, assessment and treatment] team, and they do all sorts of stuff to you." It could be interpreted that she identified herself as a powerless individual, albeit one with a strong and clear philosophical understanding of why she was in opposition to a large, powerful system and resisting the dominant medical construction of her experience. Given that I had facilitated her resistance to the dominant medical discourse in modernist terms, potentially retained is the disempowering notion that she is ultimately powerless and limited to affect change in her own situation, due to being determined by external constraints and structures.

While it was an unproblematic process for me to deconstruct Suzanne's beliefs and assumptions, my neglect to scrutinize my own values, beliefs and subjective constructions of our shared meaning arguably neutralized many of the potentially liberating and empowering intentions informing my practice. Given the limitations inherent in this practice that aimed, and initially seemed, to transcend the potential paradoxes of empowerment, what are the possibilities for practicing social work in an empowering way? Is empowerment an elusive concept?

Empowerment and the Need for Critical Self-Reflection

Reflecting on and evaluating my work has enabled me to explore other possibilities for applying a critical perspective, with the intention of empowerment, to practice. Given the outcomes, does working to empower others necessarily involve a rejection of the critical values and beliefs that we normally aspire to in practice? In the context of trying to work in ways that are empowering to our service users, if we take an active role in shaping the interaction, is this necessarily bad, inappropriate or disempowering? If conscious of the repressive elements of power, isn't it possible to use the power we have as social workers in a productive way? What are the implications for practice if we refrain from presenting an opinion and strive to achieve neutrality? Wouldn't being neutral simply maintain the status quo? Is it therefore possible to be neutral? We would argue that every facet of social work by its very nature is highly political. What emerges, then, is perhaps not the need to deny our theoretical orientations, values and ethics, but to give emphasis to the process of how we apply critical perspectives to practice.

My inability to explore the contradictions inherent in my own assumptions and my failure to examine the impact of my own inadvertent values, beliefs and subjective constructions allowed for the rigid imposition of another discourse that replaced many of the disempowering and dominating functions of the medical discourse. In light of this, perhaps the potential for social workers to engage in practice that is empowering for our service users lies in our responsibility to continually scrutinize and critically evaluate our practice, constantly extending the "deconstructive gaze" (Fook, 1996, p.198) to the disparities between how we intend to operate and how this is actually perceived and experienced by our service users. Perhaps one of the most ironic factors about the empowerment literature is the apparent invisibility of service users' views and experiences of empowerment. Of paramount importance in the pursuit of empowerment is the need to locate ourselves in the discourse and evaluate our impact on the construction of the discourse in relation to the service user, thus emphasizing the importance of ongoing critical self reflection (Fook, 1996; Rossiter, 1996).

This may involve acknowledging the role of flexibility, diversity, complexity and contradiction, and developing an awareness of the modernist assumptions that potentially exist within the critical values we hold that can undermine the intention of empowerment. Perhaps a view of empowerment that draws upon both critical and postmodern perspectives maintains the core values of the critical perspective while ultimately respecting service users' internal constructions of their experiences. Rather than positioning the critical paradigm as the only perspective, the postmodern influence enables the acknowledgment and respect of the realities and experiences of service users, which is more consistent with the espoused social justice mission of the social work perspective.

In this work with Suzanne, this may have meant accepting that she derived some benefit from the medication she was taking, even if I did not see this as a long-term solution. A critical perspective of mental health would therefore not constitute an overt challenge to other frameworks, but it would provide another perspective in which Suzanne could legitimately choose to locate her experience. In this way, the potential for her to challenge individualized, pathological constructions of her experience would be made highly accessible, but it would remain her choice to enact this change. Our purpose as social workers, in terms of empowerment, may not ultimately be to resolve social problems but rather to reconstruct the problems in ways that avoid the paradoxes and dilemmas inherent in modernist conceptualizations of power and empowerment. As Parker, Pease, and Fook (1999, p.153) state, " The implication for practice therefore, is not to eliminate contingency, but to create the conditions that will enable people to exercise self determination in the face of contingency."

What this position also offers me as a practitioner is an opportunity to rethink how I have internally constructed barriers to facilitating change. Working through this process with service users in a "dialogical consciousness raising relationship" (Ife, 1997) reflects a partnership in which both parties are enabled to develop a sense of empowerment.

Conclusion

As we have argued in this chapter, the idea and practice of empowerment may take many forms and meanings in different contexts. Within the Australian social work context, with its high value on social justice but its limited access to structural change, it seems meaningful to pay attention to the ways in which empowerment might be practiced within direct service contexts.

In this chapter we have illustrated and analyzed an example of empowerment practice (informed by postmodern and critical thinking) within a sexual assault context. In so doing, we have deconstructed the ways in which an intended empowering practice may still function in ways to preserve dominant thinking. In this sense, we have illustrated how a practice of empowerment still needs to be accompanied by a broader postmodern and critical analysis if the intended empowering goals are to be achieved in ways that are appropriate to the specific needs of the individual in question. In this sense, we have contributed to developing a theory of empowerment practice that is more related to context.

References

Aberdeen, L. (1996). The politics of settlement. In A. Kellehear (Ed.), *Social self, global culture* (pp. 189-200). Melbourne: Oxford University Press.

Astbury, J. (1996). *Crazy for you: The making of women's madness*. Melbourne: Oxford University Press.

Bailey, R., & Brake, M. (Eds.). (1975). *Radical social work*. London: Edward Arnold.

Bainbridge, L. (1999). "Competing paradigms in mental health practice and education. In B. Pease and J. Fook (Eds.), *Transforming Social Work Practice: Postmodern critical perspectives* (pp.179-194). Sydney: Allen and Unwin.

Baistow, K. (1994/1995). Liberation or regulation? Some paradoxes of empowerment. *Critical Social Policy, 42,* 34-46.

Beilharz, P. (1996). Economy and government. In A. Kellehear (Ed.), *Social self, global culture* (pp.200-210). Melbourne: Oxford University Press.

Benn, C. (1981). *Attacking poverty through participation*. Bundoora: Pit Publishing.

Benn, C. (1991). Social justice, social policy and social work. *Australian Social Work, 44*(4), 33-39.

Bennet, S. (1999). *White politics and black Australians*. Sydney: Allen & Unwin.

Bryson, L. (1992). *Welfare and the state*. London: Macmillan.

Bulbeck, C. (1990). *Social sciences in Australia*. Sydney: Harcourt, Brace Jovanovich.

Camilleri, J. (1974). Under Labour: Aboriginal land rights. *Arena, 36,* 5-11.

Corrigan, P., & Leonard, P. (1978). *Social work practice under capitalism: A Marxist approach.* London: Macmillan.

Crawley, J. (1989). Marital casework: Option or necessity: A case study in the dilemma of social work. *Australian Social Work, 13*(1), 3-13.

Crinall, K. (1999). Challenging victimisation in practice with young women. In B. Pease & J. Fook (Eds.), *Transforming social work practice: Postmodern critical perspectives* (pp. 70-83). London: Routledge.

De Maria, W. (1992). On the trail of a radical pedagogy for social work education. *British Journal of Social Work, 22*(3), 231–251.

DeMaria, W. (1993). Exploring radical social work teaching in Australia. *Journal of Progressive Human Services, 4*(2), 45-63.

Flowers, R. (1998). How effective are youth workers in activating young peoples' voices? *Youth Studies Australia, 17*(4), 34-40.

Fook, J. (1987). Empowerment as a goal in casework: Structural perspectives in casework: Can they guide practice? *Australian Social Work, 40*(4), 43-44.

Fook, J. (1990) Radical social casework: Linking theory and practice. In J. Petruchenia & R. Thorpe (Eds.), *Social change and social welfare practice* (pp. 20-27). Sydney: Hale & Iremonger.

Fook, J. (1993a). Editorial: Towards an Australian radical social work for today. *Australian Social Work, 46*(1), 1-2.

Fook, J. (1993b). *Radical social casework: A theory of practice.* Sydney: Allen & Unwin.

Fook, J. (1995, November 28). *Beyond structuralism?* Paper presented at Narratives of Change conference, Monash University, Melbourne.

Fook, J. (2000). Critical perspectives on social work practice. In I. O'Connor, P. Smyth, & J. Warburton (Eds.), *Contemporary perspectives on social work and the human services* (pp. 128-138). Melbourne: Longman.

Fook, J. (2002). *Social work: Critical theory and practice.* London: Sage.

Fook, J. (2003). Criical social work: The current issues. *Qualitative Social Work, 2*(2), 123-130.

Fook, J. (Ed.). (1996). *The reflective researcher: Social workers' theories of practice research.* Sydney: Allen & Unwin.

Franklin, J., & Eu, K. (1996). Comparative employment opportunities for social workers. *Australian Social Work, 49*(1), 11-18.

Fook, J., & Pease, B. (1999). Emancipatory social work for a postmodern age. In B. Pease & J. Fook (Eds.), *Transforming social work practice: Postmodern critical perspectives* (pp. 224-229). London: Routledge.

Freire, P. (1972). *Pedagogy of the oppressed.* Harmondsworth: Penguin.

Furlong, M. (1987). A rationale for the use of empowerment as a goal in casework. *Australian Social Work, 40*(3), 25-30.

Galper, J. (1980). *Social work practice: A radical perspective.* New Jersey: Prentice Hall.

Gibson, D. (1995) Empowering the empowerers. In *Mediation throughout the family life cycle* (pp. 21-29). Conference proceedings, Lane Cove, NSW.

Goodman, J. (1998). Ideology and critical ethnography. In J. Smyth & G. Shacklock (Eds.), *Being reflexive in critical educational and social research* (pp. 50-66). London: Falmer Press.

Graetz, B. (1996). Class and inequality. In A. Kellehear (Ed.), *Social self, global culture* (pp. 153-168). Melbourne: Oxford University Press.

Graycar, A., & Jamrozik, A. (1993). *How Australians live: Social policy in theory and practice.* Melbourne: Macmillan.

Hallahan, L. (1997) Exploring partisanship: Towards an emancipatory paradigm of independent social advocacy. In M.L. Caltabiano, L. Hil, & R. Frangos (Eds.), *Achieving inclusion: Exploring issues in disability* (pp. 35-51). Townsville: James Cook University.

Harley, B. (1999). The myth of empowerment: Work organisation, hierarchy and employee autonomy in contemporary Australian workplaces. *Work, Employment and Society, 13*(1), 41-46.

Healy, B. (1993). Elements in the development of an Australian radical social work. *Australian Social Work, 46*(1), 3-8.

Healy, B., Rimmer, J., & Ife, J. (1986). Cultural imperialism and social work education in Australia. In R. Berrenn, D. Grace, & T. Vinson (Eds.), *Advances in social work education* (pp. 92-101). Kensington: UNSW.

Healy, K. (1995). *Rethinking power in activist social work.* Paper presented at the Australian Association of Social Workers Conference (AASW), Launceston, Tasmania, 3 July 1995.

Healy, K. (1999). Power in activist social work. In B. Pease & J. Fook (Eds.), *Transforming social work practice: Postmodern critical perspectives* (pp. 115-134). London: Routledge.

Herbert, C.L. (1998) The ideology of empowerment: Governing community development. *Northern Radius, 5*(3), 30-31.

Hodges, J. (1997). Women and mental health: Policy, service delivery and practice issues. *Women Against Violence: An Australian Feminist Journal, 2*, 22-30.

Hurst, M. (1995). Counselling women from a feminist perspective. In W. Weeks & J. Wilson (Eds.), *Issues facing Australian families* (2nd ed.). Melbourne: Longman.

Ife, J. (1997). *Rethinking social work.* Melbourne: Longman.

Ife, J. (2000). Community-based options for social work: Sites for creative practice. In I. O'Connor, P. Smyth, & J. Warburton (Eds.), *Contemporary perspectives on social work and the human services* (pp. 139-149). Melbourne: Longman.

Jackson, M., & Dilger, R. (1995). An empowering approach to women's domestic violence groups. *Australian Social Work, 48*(1), 51-59.

Jones, M.A. (1996). *The Australian welfare state.* Sydney: Allen & Unwin.

Jupp, J. (1996). From white Australia to multiculturalism: Immigration and the Australian welfare state. In J. Wilson, J. Thomson, & A. McMahon (Eds.), *The Australian welfare state: Key documents and themes* (pp. 174-188). Melbourne: Macmillan Education Australia.

Karapanagiotidis, K., & Kilkeary, S. (1997). *A human rights model for mental health.* Paper presented at Social Work Influencing Outcomes: 25th Australian Association of Social Workers National Conference Proceedings, 1991, 21-24 September, Canberra.

Laragy, C. (1997). Social and welfare workers in the year 2000. In J. Fook, F. Lindsey, & M. Ryan (Eds.), *Advances in Social Work and Welfare Education, 2*(1), 104-113.

Leonard, P. (1997). *Postmodern welfare.* New York: Sage.

Liddell, M. (1997). *Privatisation, contracting and non-government organisations: Child welfare abandons logic and freedom.* Paper presented at Social Work Influencing Outcomes Conference, 25th Annual National Conference Proceedings, 1991, 21-24 September, Canberra.

Liffman, M. (1978) *Power for the poor.* Sydney: George Allen & Unwin.

McDonald, C. (2000). The third sector in the human services: Rethinking its role. In I. O'Connor, P. Smyth, & J. Warburton (Eds.), *Contemporary perspectives on social work and the human services* (pp. 84-99). Melbourne: Longman.

Marchant, H., & Wearing, B. (Eds.). (1986). *Gender reclaimed: Women in social work.* Sydney: Hale & Iremonger.

Matthews, J.J. (1984). *Good and mad women.* Sydney: Allen & Unwin.

Millstein , K.H. (1993). Building knowledge from the study of cases. In J. Lard (Ed.), *Revisioning social work education: A social constructionist approach* (pp. 255-279). New York: Hapworth Press.

McLellan, B. (1995). *Beyond psychoppression: A feminist alternative therapy.* Melbourne: Spinifex Press.

Mullaly, B. (1998). *Structural social work.* Toronto: Oxford University Press.

Mundine, K. (1993). Indigenous people's perspective on justice and empowerment. In S. Rees, G. Rodley, & F. Stillwell (Eds.), *Beyond the market: Alternatives to economic rationalism* (pp. 136-145). Sydney: Pluto Press.

Murray, H., Ryan, M., Grace, M., Hawkins, E., Hess, L., Mendes, P., & Chatley, B. (2000). Supply and demand: A study of labour market trends and employment of new social work graduates in Victoria. *Australia Social Work, 53*(1), 35-41.

Nichols, J. (1973). The silent majority. *Australian Social Work, 26*(4), 35-43.

O'Connor, I., Smyth, P., & Warburton, J. (2000). The challenges of change. In I. O'Connor, P. Smyth, & J. Warburton (Eds.), *Contemporary perspectives on social work and the human services* (pp. 1-10). Melbourne: Longman.

O'Connor, I., Wilson, J., & Setterlund, D. (1995). *Social work and welfare practice.* Melbourne: Longman.

Parker, S., Fook, J., & Pease, B. (1999). Empowerment: The modern social work concept par excellence. In B. Pease & J. Fook (Eds.), *Transforming social work practice: Postmodern critical perspectives* (pp. 150-159). London: Routledge.

Parton, N. (1994). Problematics of government, (post) modernity and social work. *British Journal of Social Work, 24*, 9-32.

Pease, B. (1990). Towards collaborative research on socialist theory and practice in social work. In J. Petruchenia & R. Thorpe (Eds.), *Social change and social welfare practice* (pp. 86-100). Sydney: Hale & Iremonger.

Pease, B., & Fook, J. (Eds.). (1999). *Transforming social work practice: Postmodern critical perspectives.* London: Routledge.

Peers, I. (1990). Participative case planning. In J. Petruchenia & R. Thorpe (Eds.), *Social change and social welfare practice* (pp. 135-145). Sydney: Hale & Iremonger.

Pemberton, A., & Locke, R. (1971). Towards a radical critique of social work and welfare ideology. *Australian Journal of Social Issues, 6*(2), 29-35.

Petruchenia, J., & Thorpe, R. (Eds.). (1990). *Social change and social welfare practice.* Sydney: Hale & Iremonger.

Quiggin, J. (2000). Human services and employment in the postindustrial labour market. In I. O'Connor, P. Smyth, & J. Warburton (Eds.), *Contemporary perspectives on social work and the human services* (pp. 30-44). Melbourne: Longman.

Regan, S., & Lee, G. (1992). The interplay among social group work, community work and social action. *Social Work with Groups, 15*(1), 35-50.

Reiger, K. (1996). Understanding the welfare state. In A. Kellehear (Ed.), *Social self, global culture* (pp. 169-178). Melbourne: Oxford University Press.

Rees, S. (1991). *Achieving power.* Sydney: Allen & Unwin.

Rees, S. (1995). Biographies of youth: Implications for empowerment. *Australian Social Work, 48*(2), 11-18.

Robertson, M. (1990). A feminist approach to madness. In J. Petruchenia & R. Thorpe (Eds.), *Social change and social welfare practice* (pp.180-195). Sydney: Hale & Iremonger.

Rosenman, L. (2000). Turning threats into challenges: A positive perspective on the future. In I. O'Connor, P. Smyth, & J. Warburton (Eds.), *Contemporary perspectives on social work and the human services* (pp. 190-197). Melbourne: Longman.

Rossiter, A.B. (1996). A perspective on critical social work. *Journal of Progressive Human Services, 7*(2), 23-41

Rummery, F. (1996). Mad women or mad society: Towards a feminist practice with women survivors of child sexual assault. In R. Thorpe & J. Irwin (Eds.), *Women and violence: Working for change.* Sydney: Hale & Iremonger.

Ryan, M., Sheehan, M., & Hawkins, L. (1997). Postgraduate social work education in Australia. In J. Fook, F. Lindsay, & M. Ryan (Eds.), *Advances in Social Work and Welfare Education, 2*(1), 109-117.

Saunders, P. (2000). Global pressure, national responses: The Australian welfare state in context. In I. O'Conner, P. Smyth, & J. Warburton (Eds.), *Contemporary perspectives on social work and the human services* (pp. 12-29). Melbourne: Longman.

Skenridge, P., & Lennie, I. (1978). Social work: The wolf in sheep's clothing. *Arena, 51,* 47-92.

Summers, A. (1975). *Damned whores and God's police.* Melbourne: Penguin.

Tesoriero, F. (1999). Will social work contribute to social development into the new millennium? *Australian Social Work, 52*(2), 11-17.

Throssell, H. (Ed.). (1975). *Social work: Radical essays.* Brisbane: University of Queensland Press.

Tomlinson, J. (1977). *Is band-aid social work enough?* Darwin: Wobbly Press.

Weeks, W. (1980). Towards non-sexist social work education. *Contemporary Social Work Education, 3*(2), 144-157.

Weeks, W. (1996). Women citizens' struggle for citizenship. In J. Wilson, J. Thomson, & A. McMahon (Eds.), *The Australian welfare state: Key documents and themes* (pp. 70-85). Melbourne: Macmillan Education Australia.

Wood, C. (1997). To know or not to know: A critique of postmodernism in social work practice. *Australian Social Work, 50*(3), 21-27.

6

Critical Anti-Racism Praxis: The Concept of Whiteness Implicated

June Ying Yee

The anti-racism perspective began in the 1970s as a critical response to existing understandings about how to deal with difference and diversity in Britain. Anti-racism can be deemed critical because of its theoretical roots in the orthodox Marxist tradition (Cox, 1948) and neo-Marxist tradition (Miles, 1989). In these earlier theoretical works, Marxism is negatively viewed as "composed of a unified set of dogmas" (Rex & Mason, 1986, p.85). These metanarratives provided an overly economic deterministic viewpoint; that is, the domination and exploitation of racial minority groups were seen to serve the profit motives of a dominant group in capitalist societies. Yet, in the field of social work practice, many social workers noted that forms of domination enacted upon racial minority clientele did not necessarily serve the conscious motives of an elite group. Rather, explanations were sought to account for the unintended exclusionary practices found within agency structures and practices. Consequently, more sophisticated variants of Marxism have critically accounted for the instances of non-class sites of domination. In particular Louis Althusser's (1971) work shows the overdetermination of social processes in both class and non-class sites of domination. Such an interpretation allows for the creation of a subject capable of resistance and, consequently, extends the discussion beyond a simple class analyses interpretation. Likewise, Antonio Gramsci (1971) examines the ways in which the dominant group in power produces and reproduces its relations of power through ideology in the form of hegemony, an important mechanism of class reproduction.

To better understand the dominant group, a theoretical understanding of the concept of whiteness is required. As commented by Dei (2000, p.31), often in social service agencies "antiracist workers may recognize and discuss systemic racism and yet fail to see themselves as implicated in the structures that perpetuate and reproduce racism." Whiteness as "institutionalised privilege" that perpetuates a "system of dominance" can only be unravelled once the concept of whiteness is critically deconstructed. Racism occurs through the process of false consciousness and is "rooted in commonsensical thought and the material and non-material human condition" (ibid., p.16). The material condition referring to the "socially created structures" (ibid., p.45) that maintains racism and the non-material human condition referring to the knowledge production created about ethno-racial minority people enables their subjugation to the power and privilege of a system of whiteness.

In everyday life, anti-racism began as a social movement that aimed to expose the deep-rooted ideologies that historically (and currently) determined people's attitudinal and institutional responses to those who do not conform to the dominant and/or majority group. Unfortunately, academic writers and social work practitioners who work in the area of anti-racism have been confronted with many barriers and difficulties in trying to carry out this fundamental principle. In the interest of trying to implement the theoretical underpinnings of an anti-racism approach, many academic writers and social work practitioners unintentionally collude with the dominant power structures by perpetuating the general "white" denial of racism.

The dominant and/or majority group refers to the people who hold the most power to shape the collective norms and values of a given society. In Canada, the ideology of the dominant and/or majority group can be seen to manifest concretely in people's social location, which cuts across axioms of race and gender and, in this context, the historical and current power of "White, Anglo-Saxon, Protestant males" (Henry et al., 2000, p.407). Ultimately, those from the dominant and/or majority group are able to tap into strategies of whiteness as a way to maintain their legitimacy and power without anyone questioning them. Therefore, a key component of anti-racism work is to understand how strategies of whiteness work. Whiteness is a key ingredient in holding together the current racist structural formations evident in social service organizations. Anti-racism work cannot be deemed critical if academic writers and social work practitioners fail to provide a theoretical and historical understanding of the social and cultural processes by which people's identities become subject to a system of domination and subordination.

The main purpose of this chapter, then, is to provide a clearer articulation of what is meant by critical anti-racism praxis. This requires a thorough theoretical understanding of the concepts of whiteness and racism. An interrogation of the unspoken central barriers to the effective implementation of a critical anti-racism praxis is discussed, and the work of academic writers and social work practitioners who claim to be engaging in critical anti-racism praxis work is questioned. People cannot speak about racism until they name whiteness for the purpose of dismantling its hidden basis of power relations. To begin, this chapter introduces the concept of whiteness followed by a discussion of the definition and meaning of an anti-racism approach. The anti-racism approach relies on a historical understanding of how people of colour have become racialized, especially in relation to the dominant and/or majority group.

Ostensibly, this paper examines two areas that show the ways in which racism and whiteness work together to create systems of domination and subordination. First, a history of how race is a social construct that works in tandem with the power of whiteness to create a particular set of social relations is discussed. And second, a critique of the commonly accepted ways of addressing culturally diverse populations is explored for the purpose of highlighting how racism does, indeed, operate as a primary structure of oppression. This system of domination, also known as whiteness, maintains power by everyone's inability to seriously challenge, notice or even question how the status quo works, and only by making everyone aware of its invisibility can these processes of domination be dismantled. Even if one recognizes the power differentials that rest in this system of domination, problems of marginalization, domination and oppression make people collude or abet in the maintenance of the status quo. After all, those in the dominant and/or majority group positions know how to maintain a synergy with subordinate groups as their own preservation rests on a remarkable capacity to repackage themselves according to particular historical and social circumstances. The final outcome is that many academic writers and social work practitioners face barriers and obstacles in capturing the racist formations in institutional structures and practices.

What Is Whiteness?

Whiteness can be defined as a complex social process that perpetuates and maintains the dominant and/or majority group's power within social service organizations and is the primary mechanism that prevents anti-racist workers from changing today's societal and institutional arrangements. According to Gabriel (1998, p.13), whiteness operates through three mechanisms: (1) exnomination, (2) naturalization, and (3) universalization. Exnomination refers to how the language we use in everyday life is taken for granted as representing a particular understanding about white people. For example, the ethnicity of white people is hardly named, while all ethnic minority people are racialized as the "other." Naturalization points to how white people are normatively positioned as the referential norm without ever having to define themselves. And finally, universalization is how white people are able to frame an understanding of the world from their socio-political and historical vantage point without being questioned.

Historically, in North America, anti-racism work began with a focus on "awareness training" and "consciousness-raising" strategies for those who were white in order that the problem of racism could be discussed (Katz & Ivey, 1977; Katz, 1978; Hartigan, 2000). This is not a surprise given that these approaches, which were deemed as a part of anti-racism work, emerged from a racist historical past that keeps intact structurally based racist formations. For example, many do not acknowledge the problematic tensions and contradictions in proclaiming the implementation of cultural competency, multiculturalism and ethnic sensitivity, to name a few, as a useful part of anti-racism work. In fact, from a historical perspective, these approaches were not developed by ethno-racial minority groups themselves but primarily by white practitioners who struggled with gaining cultural awareness, sensitivity and understanding in work with culturally diverse clientele (Yee & Dumbrill, 2003). These approaches, which have dominated and informed the social work knowledge base for some time, run contrary to an anti-racism perspective and, moreover, are heavily steeped in strategies of whiteness.

Anti-Racism in Social Work Practice

Fundamentally, anti-racism practice emphasizes the importance of focusing on the structural aspects of inequality, rather than seeing the problem as simply the cultural prejudice and ignorance of social work practitioners. Often social work educators have argued that the dominant and/or majority group's lack of cultural contact with and cultural knowledge about racial minority groups promotes the problem of racism.

The knowledge base, which informs the concept of anti-racism, stems from a particular theoretical understanding about the concept of race, and raises important implications on how social work practitioners are expected to carry out critical anti-racism praxis work. First, the proactive dismantling of current institutional practices requires these exclusionary acts to be identified, named and problematized if the inclusion of a multiplicity of perspectives can be even considered. Second, a critical understanding on how people's identity becomes socially located within systems becomes significant. And third, racism works by making everyone believe that people can be biologically and culturally defined. If people focus attention on the culture of racial minority groups, then those in positions of power in the dominant and/or majority group can successfully distract social work practitioners from tackling the systemic aspect of prejudicial outcomes. For example, equipping service providers with cultural knowledge about various ethnic groups does little to address the ways in which people perpetuate and reinforce the power base of the dominant and/or majority group. More often the resource, support and service needs of minority groups fails to be prioritized as a doable action within social service agencies because of various minority's group's lack of power in decision-making processes. Instead, much emphasis is placed on educating the ignorant knowledge base of social work practitioners in order to familiarize them with cultural difference.

Today, practitioners and educators in the social work field have adopted a variant of anti-racism practice commonly known as anti-oppressive practice. Anti-oppressive practice "embodies a person-centred philosophy; an egalitarian value system; [and] a methodology focussing on both process and outcome" (Dominelli, 1996, p.3). Little difference exists between the two approaches other than the way the anti-racism approach makes explicit the importance of a theoretical understanding of race as a primary structure of oppression that is rooted in colonialism, capitalism and patriarchy. Often, now, the rhetoric of anti-oppressive practice presents a politically correct code word that has become a method of practice that assumes equality, equity and social justice. In Canadian social work practice, the use of the terms "oppression," "systemic barriers" and "sites of advantage and disadvantage" make many assume that anti-oppressive work is occurring with very little critique (Sullivan, Steinhouse, & Gelfand, 2000; Alaggia & Marziali, 2003; Lacroix, 2003; Tsang & George,

1998). In these approaches, these authors fail to articulate a clearly defined theoretical framework from which such analyses emerge, and more problematically, these approaches have become co-opted into mainstream practices that reinforce the current status quo of focusing on the "other" as opposed to truly challenging the power of the dominant and/or majority group.

One could question whether these practices are truly anti-oppressive given the need to theoretically discuss and flesh out the foundational assumptions upon which each form of intervention is based. Versions of anti-oppressive practice present as progressive and critical work but in no way discuss the means by which minority groups can be empowered to dismantle the primary structures of oppression such as colonialism, patriarchy, heterosexism and ableism. This can be evidenced by many social service agencies' unwillingness to change the current philosophy, which drives the values of the organization and, in the final outcome, justifies their current exclusionary practices.

Henceforth, providing theoretical linkages between the concept of the dominant culture to the study of whiteness analytically moves the discussion from a simplistic generalization of privileged white men to a contemporary understanding of racism that takes into account the ways in which identity, culture and difference work to further perpetuate systemic forms of racism in social service agency practices. Too often, in the Canadian literature, much emphasis rests on minority cultures as opposed to the complex ways that racism works to shape the power base of the dominant culture through a theoretical and conceptual process called "whiteness." In fact, Ruth Frankenberg (1993), bell hooks (1990), Toni Morrison (1992) and Mab Segrest (1994a, 1994b) "were among the first to argue that an important element of the anti-racist agenda is the need to map the terrain of whiteness" (Moon & Flores, 2000, p.99). Yet, many academic writers and social work practitioners tend to speak only generically of white privilege without making visible the processes and strategies by which whiteness operates within social service agencies. One cannot speak about whiteness until one has a firm understanding of how race is a social construction in modern Western culture. Without this background historical knowledge, exclusionary practices cannot be identified and so-called neutral practices will continue to further the power of the dominant and/or majority group.

An Historical Understanding of Racism as a Primary Structure of Oppression

In everyday social work practice, workers aim to provide services that are culturally appropriate and relevant to various ethno-racial minority communities. In doing so, the culture and ethnicity of various communities often become synonymously equated with the concept of race. Race is a socially constructed category often used to "classify humankind according to common ancestry and is reliant on differentiation by such physical characteristics as colour of skin, hair texture, stature, and facial characteristics" (Henry et al., 2000, p.409). Such a definition does not capture the complexity and changing meaning of race that has problematically labelled ethno-racial minority communities in negative ways. Similarly, many people hold the view that culture and ethnicity are objective attributes of people and, in turn, create generalizations about whole communities based simply on culture and ethnicity. Yet, people do not recognize that culture is a dynamic entity constantly in flux and in process according to time, environment and interaction with others. When people are examining the culture of a particular person, they are noting that the person presents a worldview that is different from their own social location, including age, ability, sexual orientation and gender identity. Finding ways to accept different worldviews in relation to one's own self-identity is different from gaining knowledge about cultural characteristics that, regrettably, freezes the fluidity of different worldviews. Social workers need to gain an awareness of their own cultures in order to see the power they hold in making some worldviews valid while making others invalid within agency practices.

Oddly, social work practitioners may readily see the problems involved in racializing particular ethnic communities and, at the same time, have no difficulty in focusing on the culture of ethno-racial minority people. Yet, we know that, in everyday life and in social work practice, race still carries meaning within "political and popular discourse" (Mason, 2000, p.8), and often times creates generalizations and stereotypes about groups of people based on "common sense" (Gramsci, 1971) ideas. When people are held accountable for their generalizations by pointing out to them the instances when their group classifications or categorizations do not work, they will try to diminish or minimize awareness of the connection between race and behaviour by stating that they see no difference at all. Likewise, in cultural competency work, social workers see no difficulty in attributing culture to customs and behaviours (Herberg, 1993). This acceptance of fixing culture to people's identity fails to recognize the ideological power of how the "the culture of whiteness" is Eurocentricly valued as the *only* culture. For instance, why is it that academic writers and social work practitioners choose to use the expression "cultural difference" when speaking about racial minority communities? Perhaps the use of the term "difference" is a relational concept to the referential norm of sameness or rather whiteness. It is, thus, important to recognize that culture, race and ethnicity do indeed structure our political, social and economic relationships in liberal democratic societies.

Understanding the culture of various ethno-racial minority communities is inextricably linked to notions of biology and race; that is, the emphasis on various cultures and ethnicities by social workers reflects the current social relations of power that exist in Western society. For example, the term "ethnicity" can be defined as how people would self-identify themselves in terms of their cultural heritage, practices and values as part of a common group. In Canada the term "ethnic" by itself can mean "the less dominant or less powerful cultural identit[y]" (Thomas, 1987, p.5). The failure to notice white people as having an ethnicity signifies the power differentials experienced between dominant and subordinate groups and, moreover, suggests one of the ways in which whiteness operates to maintain these particular set of social relations. Whiteness has power by remaining unnamed and unmarked in contrast to the racial "other," who is classified, ordered and defined into cultural and ethnic categories.

As mentioned earlier, what we know as social work practice today emerged from a racist historical past. Race, as a modern concept, developed between the end of the eighteenth and middle of the nineteenth centuries, which was a time of global expansion of European societies. In this time of conquest and glory for European society, racial minority communities struggled against these imperial and colonial powers (Mason, 2000). According to Henry et al. (2000, p.406), colonialism refers to "a process by which a foreign power dominates and exploits an indigenous group by appropriating its land and extracting the wealth from it while using the group as cheap labour." Significantly, Europeans expanded their "economic, military, political, cultural hegemony in much of Asia, Africa and the Americas" (ibid.). Furthermore, Mason (2000) notes that the expansion and growth of European influence coincided with the develop- ment and rise of science. Not surprisingly, then, the modern definition of race emerged from the purview of science's tendency to classify and order the social world; that is, the development of a hierarchical typology that would account for and explain the reasons why the biological human differences existed. In the broader social context, modern day examples of these typologies include social Darwinism and the use of race by Adolf Hitler to justify the Holocaust in World War II. Current understandings about race, therefore, cannot be separated from a historical past that has been shaped and plagued by racist thought, ideology and practices.

Similarly, the field of sociology has taken up the concept of race as an area of study and inquiry and has greatly influenced government and policy-makers in knowing how to respond to the harmonious living together of racially different groups of people. One could argue that sociology has been predominated with strategies of whiteness, that is, carried the hidden prejudicial values and biases of society in general. The operation of whiteness did not require intention and relied upon unintentional systemic forms of discrimination in order to have influence and power. An understanding of the ethnic "other" from a white person's standpoint meant that policies and practices developed met the needs of the white people as opposed to the marginalized groups themselves.

In North America, Robert Park, an American sociologist and anthropologist, studied the concept of race in the 1920s as a field of social scientific inquiry and greatly influenced the sociological discourse on race in North America. His analysis created the sociology of race relations, which determined the develop- ment of the assimilation and pluralism approaches that are still in effect to this day. The assimilation approach encourages people from different ethnic back- grounds to conform to the dominant and/or majority group's norms and values, while the pluralism approach works to help people to maintain their ethnic identity, which is seen, for example, in the policy of multiculturalism. The anti-racism perspective, however, critically notes how the race relations approach did not take into consideration the problem of power differentials between dominant and subordinate groups and ignored the problem of racial oppression.

It was not until the 1960s, and due to the influence of social movements such as the civil rights marches in the United States, that a shift in conceptual understandings about the source of racial tension occurred and resulted in the need for sociologists to examine the social, economic and political inequalities that existed between various groups of people. Most notably, the 1967 book *Black Power: The Politics of Liberation in America* by Stokely Carmichael and Charles V. Hamilton provides revelatory insight on the distinction between individual racism and systemic racism. The authors examine how institutions and policies can be influenced by common sense understandings about race. Common sense understandings about race reflected not only the prejudicial values of the time, but also showed how the power of whiteness has historically shaped understandings about the ethnic "other."

Recognizing how the definition and meaning of race has changed over time demonstrates the problematic nature of discussing the concept of race. Therefore, race scholars are apt to use the term with both qualification and caution. Robert Miles (1989), quite correctly, has effectively critiqued the use of the concept of race as an analytical category. Miles centrally argues that race has been created for its ideological effect of masking the economic relations of migrant labourers in the capitalist mode of production. Specifically, he points out that race does not exist as a social or biological category and to grant legitimacy to the concept only helps further mystify people's social relations. Instead, Miles suggests that race exists as an ideological effect of social relationships that have become racialized. Consequently, people's cognizance of the real set of social relations never comes to the fore because processes of racialization are full of myth and illusion and, therefore, are hidden from conscious awareness. Yet, to discount the concept of race as an analytical category altogether can result in the paradoxical effect of what is known as race evasion; that is, to deny the racism exists. For example, in Canadian public discourse, those who oppose recognizing issues of race as a societal problem argue that a focus on race perpetuates and maintains racism. A recent illustration can be seen in the Reform Party's multiculturalism critic Deepak Obhrai's view that Census data collection on race is "divisive and potentially exploitative of visible minorities" (Mitchell, 1998).

Unfortunately, the concept of racism remains a relatively contentious area of inquiry. According to Mason (2000, p.9) the study of racism is either "restricted to the realm of ideas and ideologies" (Banton, 1970; Miles, 1989), which in effect means that there can be no such thing as racist practice in social structures or institutions or, for others, racism means "attitudes, beliefs and ideologies and social actions and structures" (Anthias, 1990, 1992; Carmichael & Hamilton, 1967). Consequently, some writers (Miles, 1989; Mason, 2000) in keeping with the definition of race as ideas or ideologies have arguably contested the empirical study of the concept of racism in our structures and institutions. If one begins with the premise that racism stems from ideas, then one assumes the circular argument that racism causes racism.

The difficulty in knowing what constitutes racism, therefore, requires specifying the conditions and theoretical grounds of what may constitute racism in general and, in turn, determining the remedy. Social work practice interventions such as cultural competency and ethnic sensitivity have been viewed as part of anti-oppression work and anti-racism work. Yet, as discussed earlier, methods of practice must also be informed at a theoretical level in order to understand their purposes and outcomes. Aside from the practical applications shown in the cultural competency and ethnic sensitivity models, several assumptions made in these approaches must be examined in relation to the theoretical assumptions of anti-racism work.

It is commonly known that cultural competency and ethnic sensitivity models work well on the "how to" deal with the individual level of prejudice and discrimination shown by social worker practitioners towards ethno-racial minority people (Herberg, 1993; Lum, 1999; Lynch & Hanson, 1998). The purpose of these approaches is to focus on tackling the workers' ignorance and lack of cultural knowledge about the ethnic "other." In doing so, however, the emphasis is placed on "method and efficiency" (Kincheloe and McLaren, 2000, p.282) as opposed to truly achieving substantive, accessible and equitable services for ethno-racial minority clientele since they require structural changes in the organization. These approaches cannot do so because, as noted by Alkimat (Birrell, 1989, p.216), "prejudice and discrimination are static and descriptive concepts that obscure the ideological power of racism and only provide the lowest level of theory." Subsequently, one could argue that producing cultural knowledge about various ethno-racial minority groups reduces people's behaviour, customs and traditions, and attitudes to static and descriptive information, similar to the many cultural artifacts viewed in a museum of civilization.

One of the strategies in dismantling whiteness requires the racialization of white people; that is, recognizing how people from the dominant culture hold an ethnic identity as well. Otherwise, those who come from a social location of whiteness remain invisible and unmarked. Likewise, neutral practices represent a particular ideology just as much as when people label racism as ideological. Therefore, documenting and tackling the way racism operates, beyond overt prejudice and discrimination, requires an explicit examination of the cultural and social processes by which everyday innocent actions and measures covertly do produce unintentional forms of exclusion and discrimination towards ethno-racial minority people. According to Brown (1985, p.678) and similar to Essed (1991), racism is "given materiality-through-practice in articulation with and by interpellation through the dominant mode of understanding, i.e., the meritocratic/individualistic ideological base of the exchange relationship." The dominant mode of understanding presents as fair and neutral, but most people fail to recognize the ideology from which these practices operate. Cultural explanations may occur among service providers to account for why ethno-racial minority clientele are unable to fully benefit from the services of mainstream agencies. For example, clients seeking employment may need to consult with their extended family about the appropriateness of choosing a certain field within which to work. The worker in the agency may receive cultural sensitivity training in recognizing the cultural differences, but at the same time fail to structurally accommodate these differences because the agency practices reflect the culture of whiteness. Few would dare to racialize the culture of whiteness as most see these practices as fair, neutral and non-ideological. Thus, although overt racism may not take place, the unintentional forms of systemic racism persists.

Therefore, to understand racism as a primary structure of oppression, the meaning and significance of race must extend beyond merely a descriptive variable. As noted by Alkimat (Birrell, 1989, p.216),

> [W]hile concepts of prejudice and discrimination are helpful on an analytical level of theory because they are so easily operationalized and quantified, racism is the more appropriate theoretical description of the problem precisely because it captures the qualitative character of the oppression.

Due to the power of the dominant and/or majority group, the strategies of whiteness must be examined at an ideological level in order to examine the contradictions between the surface appearances of fairness and equality and the below-surface reality of how discriminatory actions occur in everyday practices. Underlying much of current social work practice are racist ideologies or rather strategies of whiteness that work to legitimate the hidden power of the dominant and/or majority group, which helps maintain the status quo. Therefore, moving beyond superficial cosmetic changes requires a documentation of the mechanism and processes by which practices of racism are produced and reproduced and also noting the rationalizations provided by those in power to not make the required changes.

Although more than one axiom of a site of oppression occurs at a time, there nonetheless exists a process that enables social service providers to rely upon a structure of oppression to enforce the subordination of various groups of people, including gay and lesbian, transgendered and transsexuals, the disabled and the poor. Such processes exist because service providers may not be so readily consciously aware of the effects of their actions and, when confronted, often evade or resist the naming of their own practices. This is how whiteness operates. Therefore, the work of critical anti-racism praxis is to "expose the contradictions of world appearances accepted by the dominant culture as natural and inviolable" (Kincheloe and McLaren, 2000, p.292). The difficulty, however, is that dominant and subordinate groups often collude with each other in maintaining and reproducing these primary structures of oppression; that is, systems of race, class and gender oppression. Consequently, racializing the practices of white people for the purpose of revealing how strategies of whiteness operate is an important first step in dismantling the primary structure of oppression known as racism.

Problems in Current Diversity Strategies

More recent works on anti-racism and anti-oppressive practice typically make reference to the problem of white privilege and dominance, without naming whiteness, in preventing racial minority clientele from receiving culturally appropriate service delivery within social service agencies (Williams, 2001; Barnoff, 2001; Bishop, 1994). In the Canadian context, most understand white privilege and dominance to mean those who come from the dominant and/or majority group. However, one of the difficulties in focusing on white privilege and dominance is that this interpretation presents "ideology as a monolithic unidirectional entity that was imposed on individuals by a secret cohort of ruling-class czars" (Kincheloe & McLaren, 2000, p.284). This point of view fails, at both theoretical and conceptual levels, to show how such a group can effectively maintain privilege and power. Perhaps examining how the dominant and/or majority group uses strategies of whiteness to create systems of dominance can better illustrate the productive and reproductive functions of power and control. Frankenberg (1993, p.1) defines three central components that constitute whiteness: (1) "whiteness is a location of structural advantage of race privilege; (2) it is a 'standpoint,' a place from which white people look at ourselves, at others, and at society; and (3) 'whiteness' refers to a set of cultural practices that are usually unmarked and unnamed." A good example to illustrate strategies of whiteness in operation is to trace general trends in the cultural diversity literature in the last few decades.

Much of the literature in cultural diversity (Este, 1999) grew in response to the changing demographics of the North American population, especially in the area of racial and cultural diversity. As a result, human service professionals have had to develop models that specifically focused on the cultural and racial needs of diverse populations as the more traditional models of counselling did not work well with those who did not come from the dominant culture, and more importantly, social workers did not feel comfortable in working with cultures different from their own. Often social workers came from the dominant and/or majority group and had little experience and knowledge in working with difference. In the larger socio-political context, and up to the 1980s, much of the social work literature about ethno-racial minority communities carried many of the prejudicial values of the times. In fact, Tsang & George (1998, p.74) point out that, from the 1960s to the early 1980s, ethno-racial minority communities were largely viewed from the superior position of the dominant and/or majority group as reflected in some literature and reviewed by Casas (1985):

> The inferiority or the pathological model (Padilla, 1981), the deviant model (Rubington & Weinberg, 1971), the disorganizational model (Moynihan, 1965), the culturally deficient model (Padilla, 1981) and the genetically deficient model (Hernstein, 1971).

The psychologization and pathologization of culturally diverse communities reflected the prejudicial biases of the time, which was inherently steeped and imbued with racist understandings about difference. Clearly, the dominant and/or majority group's ability to shape, define and determine the knowledge base about minority cultures documents not only their power to speak on behalf of those who are marginalized in society, but also how society itself normalizes the inferior position of minority cultures. These social processes that take place, without people being consciously aware, are known as whiteness.

During the 1970s and 1980s, some shifts in the cultural diversity literature began as the visibility of ethno-racial minority communities took more of a foothold within North American society. For example, in the 1970s the colour-blind approach, which focuses on the denial of difference, looked to ways of having the culture of ethno-racial minority people recognized as much as the dominant culture by advocating for the practice of multiculturalism. Multiculturalism encouraged racial minority groups to maintain their culture and, in effect, assumes that all cultures are equal. However, this approach effectively denies the occurrence of racism and stands above issues of inequality.

Whiteness operates by making sure that the dominant culture never defines itself while defining all the so-called "different" cultures of society or rather ethnic minority communities as owning a culture. The failure to recognize cultures other than whiteness creates inequality because within the structures and process of social institutions there lies a multiplicity of needs in terms of access to resources, power and services. But also, too, the earlier use of the term "difference" can be deemed problematic because ethnic minority groups are unfairly set in comparison to the dominant culture. So in our use in language of the word "difference," we are reinforcing at an unconscious level the unequal position of racial minority cultural groups.

The discourse of multiculturalism in the 1980s, which recognizes the plurality of cultures, created the demand for practitioners to seek knowledge about the cultural characteristics of clients. An example of such literature is the book by Monica McGoldrick entitled *Ethnicity and Family Therapy*, which provides a dictionary-type understanding about various ethnic cultures such as Jewish, Chinese and Italian people. Many social work practitioners wanted to acquire cultural information about ethno-racial minority groups in order to feel comfortable in working with difference. This attitude prevailed within a broader socio-political context where ethno-racial minority people were stereotypically deemed as the "other," that is, as foreign and exotic to the dominant cultural norm. Moreover, many of these practices and norms reflected the norms and values of the dominant and/or majority group and, therefore, failed to respond to the "different" cultural and linguistic needs of various ethno-racial minority communities. Social work practitioners did not need to know the culture they came from, but focused more on knowing the culture of their clients. Often, when asked about working with cultural difference, social workers would comment that they would like a brochure or book that would inform them about "different" cultural practices.

Sociological understandings about race continue to this day to affect the social work practice literature and perpetuate a static understanding of culture where much sensitivity and empathy about the cultural adjustment of racial minorities is emphasized while discussion of racism and systemic barriers remains hidden. By the late 1990s, the social work literature on ethnic-sensitive social work practice figured prominently in the mainstream discourse in working with culturally diverse populations (Lynch & Hanson, 1998; McAdoo, 1993). For instance, Devore & Schlesinger (1999, p.3) discuss the ethnic experience as "a source of cohesion, identity and strength; at the same time; it is a source of strain, discord and strife. Some of the strain is related to the struggle to adapt to the possibilities as well as to the stressful expectations of the new society." The ethnic experience assumes to focus on newcomers to the country. Certainly, one cannot discount the cultural adjustment issues of newcomers to the country. However, the responsibility of the host country to provide resources, services and supports in that adjustment process rests less on the part of newcomers and more on the ability of agencies to accommodate to these so-called "differential" needs. This kind of approach also negates the point that native-born racial minorities still experience systemic and structural barriers in receiving full access and opportunities in social service agencies.

Finally, the stereotyping of cultures is commonly found in social work practice work. For example, Fong & Furoto (2001, p.5) point out that the worker must culturally understand that the "Chinese traditionally value achievement and education." Therefore, if the worker, hopefully, understands these values of achievement, then he or she can better plan the service. This kind of cultural understanding puts people from a Chinese ethnicity into a pre-defined, frozen cultural identity. That is, if a person who is Chinese does not fit this cultural stereotype, does that make the person less Chinese in relation to the referential norm of whiteness? In other words, have these writers, who typically believe in culture as "different" from that of the cultural norm, socially constructed what is considered typical and normal for people of Chinese descent? Although Tsang & George (1998, p.75) argue that these models of cross-cultural practice "show less prejudice and increased awareness of the meaning and significance of cultural and ethnic differences," the titles of the models show the referential norm of whiteness playing in the background as a comparison to what is considered normal. Other similar models known in the social work field include "the culturally different model, the multicultural model, and the culturally pluralistic or culturally diverse model" (ibid.).

Conclusion

More recently, it should be noted that critical anti-racism work has come under attack from scholars who are sympathetic to the politics of the New Conservative Right (Dei, 1999). In fact, the "intellectual dismissal of race-centric politics" (Dei, 1999, p.396) has manifested through fears of McCarthyism and accusations of "political correctness" where people, especially white people, interpreted the practice of anti-racism as forced confessions to acts of racism. This has caused critics to "question the validity, usefulness and relevance of race-centric knowledge and practice" (ibid.). Such criticisms reinforce a kind of historical amnesia to the history and context of racial domination, which, in turn, helps to reinforce strategies of whiteness. This is not surprising given the power of whiteness is to find ways to re-centre its Eurocentric knowledge base as the *only* knowledge. Prior to the development and implementation of the anti-racism perspective, Humphries (1997, p.293) makes the observation that Gilroy (2002) warned about the "end of anti-racism" by stating the

> (i) uncertainty and confusion around the meaning of racism; (ii) the conception of "race" as a fringe question; (iii) the fragmentation of antiracism into culture and identity; (iv) the isolation of "race" from other political antagonisms, particular class and gender; and (v) the dominance of an instrumentalist curriculum in professional education.

Throughout this chapter, I have discussed the ways in which racism has been conceptually and analytically understood and some of the barriers to its study. But, more significantly, recognizing how various social work practice approaches do focus very much on culture and identity, as opposed to how people are circumscribed into a set of social relations of domination and subordination, brings to light the question of whether models such as cultural competency can be considered to be a part of anti-racism work. By focusing on the method of practice, that is, the "how to," and without a strong theoretical and conceptual understanding of racism that is placed in the context of one's own social location, there is a tendency to view working with cultural "difference" as nothing but mere task- and competency-based work that safely renders intact the primary structures of oppression. Cultural competency work can be seen as part of an instrumentalist curriculum and, therefore, these practices contribute to what Gilroy (2002) calls the "end of anti-racism."

Hence, one of the ways to resolve this dilemma is to be mindful of the need to show how any theoretical understandings of racism can be meaningfully applied to practice. This is why Dei (1996, p.253) argues that, to carry out effective anti-racism work, the person must be both an excellent "theorist and practitioner for social change." Otherwise, without a theoretical understanding of race and racism, anti-racism does become prey to a battle over language and representation rather than "analyzing racialized relations within broader sociological theory which takes into account of the interplay of political, economic and ideological and historical forces" (Macey & Moxen, 1996, p.301). In addition, the value and importance of locating particular individual experiences to the wider social problem of oppression enables one to move beyond the ways in which knowledge is created about the ethnic "other," which results in "difference" and inequality to the actual lived, material conditions that people experience.

Certainly, examining how the concept of race is a socio-political construct, or rather more than a ideological construction that has structural expressions within social service agencies, means that anti-racism activists should focus on the processural nature of knowledge. Dei (1996) and Calliste (1996) have argued that racism creates "race." Therefore, racism must be recognized as a process because structures and ideologies do not exist outside the everyday practices through which they are created and confirmed. Critical anti-racism work cannot be effectively carried out if there is no praxis involved. Harvey (1990, p.22) defines praxis as "practical reflective activity" and is "what changes the world." Moreover, praxis can only be carried out when there is a

> critique of the knowledge we have. Knowledge changes not simply as a result of reflection but as a result of activity too. Knowledge changes as a result of praxis... For critical social research this means that an analysis of oppressive social structures is in itself a political act. (Harvey, 1990, p.23)

Henceforth, critical anti-racism praxis can only change the social work knowledge base if catalytic validity is accomplished in transformative social change work. This involves questioning and critiquing how people come to know what they know, why people no longer question what is taken for granted as valid knowledge and when the outcomes of social work practice work will cause everyone to want to transform the structures of oppression.

References

Alaggia, R. & Marziali, E. (2003). Social work practice with Canadians of Italian background: Applying cultural concepts in bicultural and intergenerational issues in clinical practice. In Alean Al-Krenwai and John R. Graham (Eds.), *Multicultural social work in Canada: Working with diverse ethno-racial communities* (pp. 150-173). Don Mills: Oxford University Press.

Alkalimat, A.I. (1972). The ideology of Black social science. In J. Ladner (Ed.), *The death of white sociology* (pp. 173-189). New York: Random House.

Althusser, L. (1971). *Essays on ideology.* London: Verso.

Anthias, F. (1990). Race and class revisited—conceptualizing race and racisms. *Sociological Review, 38*(1), 19-42.

Anthias, F. (1992). Connecting "race" and ethnic phenomena. *Sociology, 26*(3), 421-438.

Banton, M. (1970). The concept of racism. In Sami Zubaida (Ed.), *Race and racialism* (pp.17-34). London: Tavistock.

Barnoff, L. (2001). Moving beyond words: Integrating anti-oppression practice into feminist service organizations. *Canadian Social Work Review Journal, 18*(1), 67-86.

Birrell, S. (1989). Racial relations theories and sport: suggestions for a more critical analysis. *Sociology of Sport Journal, 6*(3), 212-227.

Bishop, A. (1994). *Becoming an ally: Breaking the cycle of oppression.* Halifax: Fernwood Publishing.

Brown, K.M. (1985). Turning a blind eye: Racial oppression and the consequences of white "non-racism." *Sociological Review, 33*(4), 670-690.

Calliste, A. (1996). Antiracism organizing and resistance in nursing: African Canadian women. *The Canadian Review of Sociology and Anthropology, 33*(3), 361-390.

Carmichael, S., & Hamilton, C.V. (1967). *Black power : The politics of liberation in America.* New York: Random House.

Casas, M.J. (1985). A reflection on the status of racial/ethnic minority research. *The Counseling Psychologist, 13*(4), 581-598.

Cox, O.C. (1948). *Caste, class and race*. New York: Doubleday.

Dei, G.S.J. (1996). Critical perspectives in antiracism. *Canadian Review of Sociology and Anthropology, 33*(3), 247-267.

Dei, G.S.J. (1999). Knowledge and politics of social change: The implication of anti-racism. *British Journal of Sociology of Education, 20*(3), 394-409.

Dei, G.S. J. (2000). Towards an anti-racism discursive framework. In *Power, Knowledge and anti-racism Education* (pp.23-40). Halifax: Fernwood Publishing.

Dei, G.S.J., & Calliste, A. (Eds.). (2000). Mapping the terrain: Power, knowledge and anti-racism education. In *Power, knowledge and anti-racism education* (pp. 11-22). Halifax: Fernwood Publishing.

Devore, W., & Schlesinger, E.G. (1999). *Ethnic-sensitive social work practice* (5ᵗʰ ed.). Toronto: Allyn and Bacon.

Dominelli, L. (1996). De-professionalizing social work: Anti-oppressive practice, competencies and postmodernism. *British Journal of Social Work, 26*(2), 153-175.

Essed, P. (1991). *Understanding everyday racism: An interdisciplinary theory*. London: Sage Publications, Inc.

Este, D. (1999). *Professional social service delivery in a multicultural world*. Toronto: Canadian Scholars Press.

Fong, R., & and Furoto, S.B.C.L. (Eds.). (2001). *Culturally competent practice: Skills, intervention and evaluations*. Toronto: Allyn and Bacon.

Frankenberg, R. (1993). *White women, race matters: The social construction of whiteness*. London: Routledge.

Gabriel, J. (1998). *Whitewash: Racialized politics and the media*. London: Routledge.

Gilroy, P. (2002). The end of antiracism. In P. Essed & D.T. Goldberg (Eds.), *Race critical theories* (pp. 249-264). Oxford: Blackwell Publishers, Ltd.

Goodman, P.S. (1997). Conference seeks to clear up what it means to be white; Berkeley talks draw high turnout. *The Washington Post* (p. A16).

Gramsci, A. (1971). *Prison notebooks*. New York: International Publishers.

Hartigan, J. (2000). Object lessons in whiteness: Antiracism and the study of white folks. *Identities: Global Studies in Culture and Power, 7*(3), 373-406.

Harvey, L. (1990). *Critical social research*. London: Unwin Hyman.

Henry, F., Tator, C., Mattis, W., & Rees, T. (2000). *The colour of democracy: Racism in Canadian society* (2nd ed.). Toronto: Harcourt Brace Canada.

Herberg, D.C. (1993). *Frameworks for cultural and racial diversity*. Toronto: Canadian Scholars Press.

Hernstein, R. (1971). I.Q. *Atlantic Monthly, 228*(3), 43-64.

hooks, b. (1990). *Yearning: Race, gender, and cultural politics*. Boston: South End.

Humphries, B. (1997). The dismantling of anti-discrimination in British social work: A view from social work education. *International Social Work (40)* 289-301.

Katz, J. (1978). *White awareness: Handbook for anti-racism training*. USA: University of Oklahoma Press.

Katz, J., & Ivey, A. (1977). Whiteness awareness: The frontier of racism awareness training. *The Personnel and Guidance Journal, 55*(8), 485-489.

Kincheloe, J.L., & McLaren, P.L. (2000). Rethinking critical theory and qualitative research. In N. Denzin & Y.S. Lincoln (Eds.), *Handbook of qualitative research methods* (pp. 257-313). Thousand Oaks: Sage Publications.

Lacroix, M. (2003). Culturally appropriate knowledge and skills required for effective multicultural practice with individuals, families and small groups. In A. Al-Krenwai & J.R. Graham

(Eds.), *Multicultural social work in Canada: Working with diverse ethno-racial communities* (pp. 23-46). Don Mills: Oxford University Press.

Lum, D. (1999). *Culturally competent practice: A framework for growth & action.* Pacific Grove, CA: Brooks/Cole.

Lynch, E., & Hanson, M. (1998). *Developing cross-cultural competence: A Guide for working with young children and their families* (2nd ed.). Baltimore, MD: Brooks.

Macey, M., & Moxon, E. (1996). An examination of anti-racist and anti-oppressive theory and practice in social work education. *British Journal of Social Work, 26*(3), 297-314.

Mason, D. (2000). *Race and ethnicity in modern Britain* (2nd ed.). Oxford: Oxford University Press.

McAdoo, H. (Ed.). (1993). *Family ethnicity: Strength in diversity.* Newbury Park, CA: Sage Publications.

McGoldrick, M. (1982). *Ethnicity and family therapy.* New York: Guilford Press.

Miles, R. (1989). *Racism.* London: Routledge.

Mitchell, Alanna (1998). Face of big cities changing: visible minorities are nearly one-third of Toronto, *The Globe and Mail,* February 18, p.Al.

Moon, D. and Flores, L.A. (2000). Antiracism and the abolition of whiteness: Rhetorical strategies of domination among "race traitors." *Communication Studies, 51*(2) (summer), 97-115.

Morrison, T. (1992). *Playing in the dark: Whiteness and the literary imagination.* New York: Vintage Books.

Moynihan, D.P. (1965). *The Negro family: The case for national action.* Washington, D.C.: U.S. Department of Labor, Office of Policy, Planning and Research.

Padilla, A.M. (1981). Competent communities: A critical analysis of theories and public policy. In O.A. Barbarin, P.R. Good, O.M. Pharr, & J.A. Siskind (Eds.), *Institutional racism and community competence* (pp. 20-29). Rockville, MD: U.S. Department of Health and Human Services.

Rex, J., & Mason, D. (1986). *Theories of race and ethnic relations.* Cambridge: Cambridge University Press.

Rubington, E., & Weinberg, M.S. (1971). *The study of social problems.* New York: Oxford University Press.

Segrest, M. (1994a). *Memoir of a race traitor.* Boston: South End.

Segrest, M. (1994b). When We Don't Get Race, It Kills Us. *Race Traitor: Treason to Whiteness is Loyalty to Humanity, 3,* 23-32.

Sullivan, N.E., Steinhouse, K., & Gelfand, B. (2000). *Challenges for social work students: Skills, knowledge and values for personal and social change.* Toronto: Canadian Scholars Press.

Thomas, B. (1987). *Multiculturalism at work: A guide to organizational change.* Toronto: YWCA.

Tsang, A.K.T., & George, U. (1998). Towards an integrated framework for cross-cultural social work practice. *Canadian Social Work Review, 15*(1), 73-93.

Williams, C. (2001). Confronting the racism in research on race and mental health services. *Canadian Social Work Review, 18*(2), 231-248.

Yee, J.Y., & Dumbrill, G.C. (2003). Whiteout: Looking for race in Canadian social work practice. In A. Al-Krenawi & J.R. Graham (Eds.), *Multicultural social work in Canada: Working with diverse ethno-racial communities* (pp. 98-121). Don Mills: Oxford University Press.

7

Radical Drama with Children: Working with Children Using Critical Social Work Methods

Trevor Spratt

Why, we might ask ourselves, is the development of new methods for social work necessary? To answer this question it is necessary to understand how social work has developed particular forms of intervention based on identifiable ideological premises. Consequently, this chapter begins with a critique of recent developments in social work practice in the United Kingdom before describing the development of a social work methodology informed by critical theory and encompassing techniques derived from radical drama. While the focus is on the U.K., the literature indicates comparable patterns of difficulties in the relationship between the state and the family in other countries, including the United States (Besharov, 1990) and Australia (Thorpe, 1997). Given this commonality of experience, it is likely that the methods described here could be adapted for use in a variety of practice settings.

Recent History of the Child Welfare System in the United Kingdom

The starting points for this project appear more substantial in retrospect than they did to us at the time. My colleague, Stan Houston, and I had together spent some years working as social workers and social work managers in Northern Ireland and had witnessed a number of significant changes to the organization and practice of social work with families and children. The organization of social work had become increasingly bureaucratized (Howe, 1992), and the practice of social work had become increasingly professionalized. Such developments led us to experience a measure of concern and dissatisfaction. We were supportive of the attempt to rationalize the organization of practice and to have social workers become more accountable for their practice. We were concerned, however, that these processes were having unintended and unhelpful consequences. Social work agencies, ever more concerned to limit their exposure to child protection risks, were evolving increasingly prescriptive and restrictive rules and protocols governing the actions of social workers. Social workers themselves were evolving professional identities around child protection work, effectively distancing them from the lived experience of families and communities.

The sense of unease we felt in relation to such developments was mirrored by concerns expressed by researchers and policy-makers within the U.K. Indeed, by the mid-1990s, a concern that a concentration on child protection work had distorted the balance of the entire child welfare system had become the central reference point in any discussion with regard to family and child care social work. This discussion, which became known as the "refocusing debate" (Jack, 1995), centred on the problem of making real the intentions of legislators in practice. The introduction of the 1989 *Children Act* had provided a legislative framework within which a new balance had been struck between the require-ment for the state to intervene in family life in relation to child protection risks and its duty to provide supportive services (termed "family support") to families to meet the developmental needs of their children. The expectation within the professional community that this new legislative balance would help shift practice away from a narrow concentration on child protection risks towards a wider consideration of family difficulties, resulting in the provision of family support, was not realized. Research, commissioned by the government (Depart-ment of Health, 1995), revealed that social work agencies were tending to route many families through the child protection system, even though the nature of their circumstances did not justify this approach. While a number of these families would have benefited from the provision of family support services, they were made wary of accepting offers of services as a result of their often damaging experience of the child protection system (Cleaver & Freeman, 1995). As a result of this research, it became government policy to encourage a refocusing of practice away from a concentration on child protection risks and towards a wider understanding of child and family needs (Parton, Thorpe, & Wattam, 1997).

Critique and Ideology

The refocusing debate was to be a catalyst for our own consideration as to how social work students might best be prepared in university courses to address the issues raised by the debate in practice. With fundamental assumptions as to what constituted good social work practice under question, we felt liberated to imagine alternative methodologies and to share these with the students.

The first step in this process was to develop a critique of current social work practice in the United Kingdom. We began by identifying the ideological influ-ences that had led social work to become preoccupied with either socio-medical concerns to identify and treat the victims of child abuse or socio-legal concerns to identify and control those likely to perpetrate child abuse (Parton, 1991). We considered such influences to have created a basic contradiction for social work agencies and social workers. How could they identify with families and provide them with effective services if they were preoccupied with managing risks via the creation of bureaucratic structures and the development of "professional as expert" identities? How might they develop understandings of practice to chal-lenge the domination of the concept of risk and introduce strategies of intervention to address the restrictions imposed by the professional-client relationship? Would it be possible for social workers to develop more inclusive understandings of their work, based on the concept of family needs, while retaining responsibility for the management of child protection risks? To begin to address these questions we argued that it was necessary to develop a critical social work ideology. Such an ideology might provide an ethical and intellectual foundation upon which new methodologies for practice might be built. We suggested that this ideology would have four key features.

1. A structural approach to the understanding of individual problems, with the large majority of family difficulties (with the exception of child sexual abuse) being understood as the outworking of poverty and poor resourcing leading to stress and breakdown in coping mechanisms (as opposed to understanding family difficulties as products of individual or familial pathology);

2. The role of relationship considered as crucial in responding effectively to the needs of families (as opposed to bureaucratic and procedural responses to family problems);

3. The interrelationship between communication, reason and action would be informed by the critical theory of Jurgen Habermas (1970, 1984). As a counter to the colonizing power of "instrumental reason," which seeks to govern human relationships through reduction of communication to the codified forms of bureaucratic efficiency, Habermas proposes the use of "communicative reason," based on the idea that meanings in human relationships are the product of shared understandings achieved through open and honest two-way communication (Blaug, 1995); and

4. There would be new rules of engagement between professionals and families. These would involve a democratization of the rules of engagement. Habermas' concept of the "ideal speech situation" is useful in establishing an ideal type governing practice. The key elements necessary for fair and equitable interchanges are the opportunity for all to speak, for all to be listened to and for all to be allowed to question. If these conditions are fulfilled, then open and fair communication between parties is possible.

From Ideology to Method

The next challenge was to find ways to build upon our embryonic critical social work ideology by developing new practice methodologies. We were concerned with using the ideal of communicative reason alongside the moral checklist provided by the ideal speech situation to inform the development of such methodologies. However, given the concerns of social workers to manage child protection risks, would it be possible for them to practice in such open and democratized ways? While such changes in practice might be officially sanctioned with reference to the refocusing debate, the continuing influence of socio-medical and socio-legal ideologies inhibited such changes in practice.

Perhaps the key issue here was how we might move beyond individualistic conceptions of practice, and the risks associated with these, towards collective strategies for action.

Augusto Boal: Borrowing Methodologies from Radical Drama

Meeting this challenge involved a casting of the intellectual net beyond familiar waters and trawling for ideas that might prove useful in adding method to theory. We eventually turned to the work of the radical Brazilian dramatist Augusto Boal (1979, 1992, 1995). The basic premise upon which Boal's work is built is that social change can be brought about through a process of "conscientization" (Freire, 1972),that is, the development of the subject's understanding of oppression through learning. For Boal this learning is achieved through empowering the hitherto powerless spectator, enabling them to become an actor rehearsing for real changes in their own lives. Boal conceives the social actor as one who performs different scripts, dictated by the different roles played in everyday life. The scripts, however, may only be regarded as guides to performance and are not prescriptive texts. The actor retains the ability to interpret the script creatively and bring innovation to their performance. This creativity is beneficial to both the individual and their community, as innovation creates possibilities for the solution of common problems. However, releasing the potential for such creativity is restricted because we tend to delegate the responsibility of representing our own interests to others. Boal's antidote to such pacifity is to teach people communication skills, release their latent creativity and allow them to find their voice and tell their story. This is achieved via the utilization of dramatic methodologies through which people may rehearse problems in their own lives and creatively find practical solutions to these.

Those most likely to lack a voice are, of course, most frequently found in poor and marginalized communities. It was within such communities that Boal began his work. In his *Theatre of the Oppressed*, Boal (1979) teaches impoverished rural farmers how to learn and how to listen. This is done by allocating fictional roles to participants that allow them to debate sometimes prohibited, always controversial, issues without the attendant risks if they were to tackle such problems outside the safety of an assumed role. Political theatre has always had this function, allowing debate of forbidden or controversial subjects through creation of farce, comedy and tragedy within fictional worlds that closely parallel the real one. Breaking, however, with the traditions of political theatre, Boal suggests a breaching of the barriers created when scripts are produced by professional writers and interpreted by professional actors. He proposes that such processes should not be owned by professionals but by the communities who are experiencing oppression. For example, Boal (1979) developed ways of creating group solidarity among the rural farmers. This involved the theatre workshop facilitator helping the farmers to identify the source of their oppression (the large landowners). The farmers were then encouraged to share their feelings and to build mutual acceptance and trust with each other. This was achieved through a series of "image theatre" techniques. These are designed to capture the non-verbal expression of ideas through slow motion or "freeze frame" images. These images are often ambiguous in nature, portraying the participants' nuanced and conflicting responses to the issues of their own lives. The farmers were then asked to sculpt (using their bodies to produce a tableau depicting interrelationships) their actual relationships with the landowners. The resulting set of images was then interpreted by the group as a whole. Where forms of oppression exist, the images usually reflect inherent contradictions, conflicts and uncertainties in relationships. The next step involved asking the farmers to sculpt ideal images, expressing the types of relationships they would wish to have with the landowners. These portrayed situations where the farmers exercised greater control over their economic and social destiny. Finally, the farmers were asked to sculpt a transformative image. This intermediate image suggests how their situation may be changed from the image of the present to the image of the ideal. This is termed the "proposition for action." In relation to the farmers this might involve, for example, the forming of a workers' collective. For Boal the goal of this theatre is to aid oppressed groups by helping them to identify sources of oppression, imagine emancipatory ideals and creatively construct strategies for action to achieve these ideals.

Using Image Theatre Methodology with Social Workers

Boal's methods were designed for use with groups suffering from economic and social oppression, and had not been hitherto used with groups outside of this traditional conceptualization of the oppressed. In our view, however, the actors in the child welfare system in Northern Ireland were members of oppressed groups. This was certainly true for children subject to child welfare interventions; sometimes abused, often with developmental needs unmet and almost always sad, apathetic or angry in response to the situations they found themselves in. It was also true for many of their parents, with their own experiences of poor upbringing, economic deprivation and social and emotional conflict. It might also be argued, however, that child welfare professionals experience their own measure of oppression. In occupying the narrow zone in which, as the official representatives of the state, they meet those most marginalized from society, social workers are forced to address the duality of their responsibilities. They face the contradiction of having to govern the family (Parton, 1991) while being aware of being part of the structures of society that contribute to the difficulties faced by families. One notable feature of this position is the isolation of such social workers, who often fail to identify with each other. Yet, as with Boal's rural farmers, social workers may work in isolation from one another but have interests in common, best served by collective action.

It was with these thoughts in mind that we considered the possibility that image theatre might be of help in testing out our hypothesis that social workers share many of the characteristics of an oppressed group. My university colleague, Stan Houston, and I sought to test out this hypothesis with two groups of students. The first group comprised twenty students from a post-qualifying child care program held at The Queen's University in Belfast. This group were well versed in the operationalization of the child welfare system. Because of this experience we characterized the views of this group as the "voices" of practice. The second group comprised twenty-nine mature students on a Diploma in Social Work course at the University of Ulster. While this group had substantial pre-qualification experience, many of them in the field of child care, they lacked any direct experience of operating the child welfare system. What knowledge they had was founded in teaching programs that provided an overview of the child welfare system. Given this lack of first-hand experience, we characterized the responses of this group as "echoes" of practice.

The image theatre sessions undertaken with these two groups were therefore of an experimental nature. Participants were informed that the purpose behind the sessions was to re-examine the child welfare system in the light of the refocusing debate, highlighting the need to find alternative ways of working with children and families. There followed an introduction to the work of Augusto Boal and the core principles underpinning his approach. These included the accessibility of the medium for expressing ideas, the full and democratic participation of all, and the requirement to take ownership of creative ideas and translate these into actions in everyday life. Having gained the assent of the groups to begin the work, they were introduced to the facilitator, Tom Magill, a professional actor with considerable experience in the utilization of Boalian methodologies with a variety of oppressed groups.

Tom's way of working is to divide these methodologies into three distinct phases: trust building, imaging and sculpting. The trust-building exercises are designed to enable participants to gain confidence in expressing their ideas in non-verbal ways. They help unify the group as participants experience the mutual risk taking involved in expressing previously suppressed sentiments in unfamiliar ways. As Boal puts it, recalling an earlier quote from Guevara, "solidarity means running the same risks" (Boal, 1992). Participants were encouraged to use their bodies to portray simple emotions such as love and hate, and having made such images, read meaning into the images made by others in the group. As embarrassment faded, so confidence and enthusiasm grew.

The next phase involved imaging the key actors in the child welfare system: social workers, teachers, doctors, managers, the police and lawyers, as well as the children and parents themselves. The images of social workers produced by the groups' illustrated some differences in perception. The "voices" group most frequently expressed negative images of social workers, seeing them(selves) as "stressed" and "frustrated" by the work and constrained by the bureaucratic and ineffective nature of practice. In contrast, the "echoes" group were more optimistic in their choice of images. They viewed their future selves as "empathetic," "supportive" and "caring," acknowledging, however, that the effects of work with children and families could lead to " confusion," "despair" and " "isolation." The images of other professional stakeholders made by the "echoes" group tended to reflect either their personal experiences or imagined roles while the "voices" group reflected images from their practice experience. So, for example, the "echoes" group largely imaged schoolteachers as "critical" or "controlling," reflecting, perhaps, their own experiences of education. The "voices" group, by contrast, imaged teachers as "cautious" in sharing their views with regard to children and "ambivalent" with regard to their role in child welfare work. There were also contrasts in how each group imaged children and parents caught up in the child welfare system. The "echoes" group imaged parents positively, emphasizing characteristics such as their provision of "love," "care" and "protection." They also empathized with the "stress" such parents felt. The "voices" group were more concerned with the reactions of parents to child welfare interventions. As a consequence they imaged a range of emotions such as "anger," "blame" and "aggression" tempered by an appreciation of vulnerability, often leaving parents "helpless," "fearful" and "despairing." There was greater uniformity between the groups in the images used to portray children. These were of a very negative nature, seeing children as "small," "insecure," "unhappy" and "lonely."

The third phase was to dramatize the relationships between the various stakeholders in the child welfare system. Participants were asked to form subgroups and within these to dramatize the child welfare system as they perceived it to be at present. With each participant adopting the role of a stakeholder in the system, they used their bodies to sculpt the hierarchies and attitudes that characterize interprofessional relationships; detailing relative degrees of inclusion or exclusion, power or powerlessness, and involvement or disinterest. Participants were then asked to view each subgroup's sculpt and choose the one that most accurately reflected the current child welfare system. Following this, participants were asked to image an ideal child welfare system as well as a transitory image, representing how the ideal might be achieved. As with the image of the present system, participants were asked to choose the most desirable ideal image and the most practical transitory image. It is worth describing in some detail the series of images chosen by the "echoes" group. These vividly portray something of the seriousness of intent and creative intellectual and emotional energy invested by the participants.

The image chosen to portray the present system featured a judge (standing on a desk) listening to evidence given by a policeman. A social worker sat cross-legged on the floor, with palms up in an open gesture. Standing above him were various professionals, with hands linked but pulling in opposing directions. The child's mother stood with her back to the proceedings, lines of worry deeply etched upon her face. The child knelt on the floor, her back to the proceedings, but far from her mother and staring at the ground. In articulating this image the group drew attention to the hierarchy of power relationships: the judge at the top with police and guardian *ad litem* taking their instructions from her. Other professionals are concerned for their status, protecting their interests and refusing to co-operate with each other. The mother is excluded and worried.

The child is excluded and depressed. The social worker is vainly attempting to reconcile the interests of the professionals with those of the family.

The ideal image featured a kneeling child encircled by also kneeling parents and professionals, each with their right hand placed upon the child and their left hand upon the shoulder of the person on their left, forming an interlocking circle. The judge stands over the group with her arm outstretched above the child's head. In reading this image the group stated that the child could only be protected if there were co-operative and equal relationships between professionals as well as between professionals and parents. The standing judge represented the overarching importance of the law in protecting the rights of the child. The group felt that, while their ideal image might not be fully realizable in practice, there existed possibilities for movement in that direction.

The transitory image portrayed professionals reaching out to one another before collectively approaching the judge. This, the group explained, signified a will to subsume individual professional interests within a desire to promote the child's best interests. Strategic alliances between professionals could be made in recognition that the child's best interests superseded individual interests. Approaching the judge signified collective lobbying to ensure that the judiciary upheld the law, built upon the principle of the child's interests being paramount. In evaluating their work, participants emphasized that the methods had enabled them to understand how collective action at the "grassroots" level could act as a counterweight to the fractured, hierarchical and isolated nature of current social work practice with children and families.

There is some evidence from this work to support the hypothesis that social workers bear many of the features of an oppressed group. They are marginalized within the matrix of professional power relationships and disheartened by the outcomes of their individual efforts to solve the contradiction inherent in forming communicative partnerships with parents while remaining constrained by agency bureaucracy. Current ways of working are characterized by interprofessional rivalries and hierarchical managerial structures, which result in bureaucratic and defensive practice. The utopian vision of the future provides a moral benchmark against which current realities may be judged, as well as an aspirational goal, while the transitory image revives long-dormant notions of strategic alliances utilized to challenge traditional power bases. Building upon these results, we sought to address a second question. Could Boalian methodologies be used in direct and immediate ways to address oppressions suffered by children and families?

Using Forum Theatre Methodology with Schoolchildren

To address this second question we required a research site. This presented itself in the form of an invite from a community theatre group to train a group of actors in the use of Boalian methodologies. The group had been set up with the purpose of using theatre as a means of enabling socially and economically marginalized communities to participate in wider society through a realization of their creative potential. The initiative was funded by a combination of education, health and local government agencies in the Republic of Ireland. The actors in the theatre group had been formally trained in traditional theatrical methods prior to being introduced to the work of Boal. They had found these traditional methods to be of limited use in their work with members of the wider community, where they had sought to raise awareness of collective interests to help tackle endemic problems of rural isolation and economic and social marginalization.

The methodology used with this group was "forum theatre." Forum theatre was developed by Boal with the same oppressed and marginalized groups with whom he had developed image theatre. The aim of forum theatre is to seek solutions to problems through the provision of a forum in which open debate may take place. It begins with a group of people identifying a common problem or area of oppression. Because they know more about this aspect of their lives than does anyone else, they can easily imagine the context and the characters (both the oppressed and the oppressors). They know how the scene begins, how it develops and how it ends. They understand that some will acquiesce with oppression and others resist it; they can identify potential allies as well as enemies. Because they have this knowledge, they are better qualified than anyone else to represent the story of their own lives. This essentially is the basis of forum theatre — people playing themselves, as protagonists, in a theatre of their own reality.

Boal (1995) identifies three main characters who are always present: a "protagonist," whose role is to epitomize and represent the oppression experienced by the group; an "antagonist," who represents the oppressor; and a "joker," who acts as a link between actors and spectators by providing a running commentary on the unfolding drama and inviting directions from the spectators as to how the drama should unfold. In forum theatre, there is no formal separation between actors and spectators. To symbolize this, the auditorium is bathed in light as well as the stage; no one is left "in the dark." This emphasis on demystification also extends to the drama itself. There is no unfolding plot and therefore no suspense. The joker introduces the main characters to the spectators, describes the context of the dramatized oppression and tells them what is going to happen before the scene begins. The spectators are also informed that the scene is incomplete and that they will have to propose solutions to the problems faced by the protagonist. The scene is then performed. This will portray how oppression happens. The joker then asks the spectators what the protagonist might do differently to solve the problem of oppression. Incorporating this advice, the scene is then performed a second time. On this occasion, spectators may direct the actors to stop. A spectator may then replace the protagonist in the scene and act out their own intervention to address the oppression. The rest of the spectators, as well as the actors, then evaluate the intervention. Was it realistic? Did it have the potential to be effective? Could it be a rehearsal for action in real life? Because of the involvement of the spectators, forum theatre enables the sharing of strategies that have the potential to move the scene from one of oppression to liberation. This is a collective process in seeking realistic solutions to actual problems, empowering the formally passive to take control of their own lives. In echoes of Habermas' ideal speech situation, everyone is allowed to speak, everyone has the right to question and everyone has the right to be listened to.

The objectives in working with the theatre group were threefold: first, to train them in the use of Boalian methods; second, to produce a forum theatre piece based upon a common experience of oppression; and third, to introduce this piece of forum theatre to spectators who might identify with this form of oppression. The common experiences of the theatre group were feelings of social exclusion brought about by unemployment and poverty. This commonality of experience, however, was regarded as a backdrop to their oppression rather than the source of it. They identified their primary source of oppression as the experience of being bullied. Although their individual experiences differed in context and content, the group were able to identify the universal features of the archetypal aggressive and insatiable bully in their collective experience. They were also able to identify common emotional reactions to being bullied: pain, shame and isolation.

The piece of forum theatre the group produced portrayed a school bully as the antagonist and a schoolchild as the protagonist. The other characters included members of the class as silent spectators and a pupil with the potential to empathize with the protagonist. The scene opened with the protagonist seeking to join his peer group, but being prevented from doing so by the antagonist utilizing techniques of exclusivity (the protagonist is alone in not possessing designer sportswear) and shaming (the protagonist is called "smelly." Later in the scene this oppression becomes internalized (Fanon, 1986) to the extent that the protagonist attempts to wash his body free of imagined smells. The protagonist seeks help from his parents, but is offered contradictory advice: his mother tells him to "turn the other cheek" while his father instructs him to "fight back." The oppression develops with the antagonist directing the class to steal the protagonist's schoolbag. The teacher blames the entire class for the incident who in turn victimize the protagonist because of this. Finally, the antagonist leads the class in beating the protagonist until a small act of grace occurs: the empathetic child returns the stolen schoolbag to the protagonist.

In forum theatre the next step is to invite the spectators to intervene in the drama, to propose solutions and to test these out on the stage. In this case, the spectators were rural Irish schoolchildren. When contacted regarding the possibility of taking forum theatre into schools, staff had indicated that the issue of bullying was likely to find resonance with the children as many of them had had experience of this form of oppression. It was, however, an open question as to whether the representation of bullying produced by the theatre group would resonate with the experiences of the schoolchildren. While the format of forum theatre might shock traditional theatre audiences, schoolchildren, unversed in the ways of theatre, responded without difficulty. They proposed a range of solutions to the protagonist's problems. These included the use of violence against the antagonist, telling the teacher, talking again to the parents, forming an alliance with the empathetic classmate and undermining the antagonist through the use of humour. These potential solutions were then acted out by their proposers, with actors and spectators responding spontaneously to these performances, evaluating the efficacy of each. Boal conceives such processes to be rehearsals for changes to be enacted in real life. In follow-up interviews, actors and schools reported a common regard for forum theatre, both as a method for raising consciousness with regard to difficult issues and in its potential to release creative solutions to these issues.

Conclusion

We started out by asking whether or not new methodologies for social work practice were really necessary. We would suggest that they are, for three reasons. The first of these is concerned with the necessity for social work to develop a coherent critique of the ideological influences that have helped shape it as a profession. It is only by doing so that we may come to appreciate how far our consciousness has been shaped by individualistic conceptions of practice, which in turn have created difficulties in how we relate to other professionals as well as to families and children. In the U.K. context, our inability to achieve shifts in practice that would herald a less forensic and more holistic understanding of family needs is but one manifestation of this problem. However, while the development of a critical social work ideology is of some importance, it is necessary for such ideas to become harnessed to methods if we are to witness real changes in practice. This brings us to the second reason for change. There is a need for social workers to understand the problems faced by their clients as (in the main) products of structural forces. Consequently, interventions should be aimed at empowering such clients by offering them opportunity to appreciate the shared nature of their oppression. The paradox here is that social workers may not be able to take forward such strategies until they examine the nature of their own oppressions. This is linked to the third reason for new methodologies. There is a need for collective solutions that do not locate problems within individuals, but link common experiences of oppression with the sources of such oppression and offer potential solutions to these. Such solutions may be found in the development of new practice methodologies.

The process of developing a critical social work ideology offers a basis for the development of practice methodologies that are compatible with its intellectual and ethical foundations. This work, however, poses something of a challenge to the development of social work as a profession, wherein the individual worker, entangled by bureaucratic constraints, prescribes individual solutions to the problems of individuals. Critical social work ideology is based on the premise that traditional social work practice represents an historic "wrong turn" by the profession. Instead of appreciating the commonality of our client's experiences, we became enamoured with the possibilities of professional kudos and bought the lie of capitalism that the cause of the individual's problems are not to be located elsewhere. Where the profession has sought to develop collective methodologies, these have often focused on group support models where the emphasis has been on learning adaptive and coping skills to difficulties, rather than forming the basis for collective challenge to the source of such difficulties.

Can social workers emulate these ideas and methods in their own practice context? Given agency structures and embedded ways of working, it would not be easy. There is, however, no mystery to the method. Boal's techniques are accessible and transparent. Indeed, social workers with basic group work experience should have no difficulty mastering the methodologies. However, as with our own work, the starting point for most social workers involved with children and families may be a need to share their own oppressions and, through this, build collective visions of what may be possible alongside collegiate strategies for their realization. This is really the work of consciousness raising. And, if in this postmodern age, this term sounds a little old fashioned, no apology is made.

Author's Note: While this chapter has one author, the work upon which it draws has three. Over the past four years I have worked collaboratively with Stan Houston and Tom Magill. We published the results of our work in three linked articles in the journal Child and Family Social Work *(Spratt and Houston, 1999; Spratt et al., 2000; Houston et al., 2001), and this chapter is based upon those publications.*

References

Besharov, D. (1990). *Recognising child abuse: A guide for the concerned.* New York: The Free Press.

Blaug, R. (1995). Distortion of the face to face: Communicative reason and social work practice. *British Journal of Social Work, 25,* 423-439.

Boal, A. (1979). *Theatre of the oppressed.* London: Pluto Publishers.

Boal, A. (1992). *Games for actors and non-actors.* London: Routledge.

Boal, A. (1995). *The rainbow of desire.* London: Routledge.

Cleaver, H., & Freeman, P. (1995). *Parental perspectives in cases of suspected child abuse.* London: HMSO.

Department of Health. (1995). *Child protection: Messages from research.* London: HMSO.

Fanon, F. (1986). *Black skin, white masks.* London: Pluto Press.

Freire, P. (1972). *Pedagogy of the oppressed.* Penguin: Harmondsworth.

Habermas, J. (1970). *Toward the rational society.* Boston: Beacon Press.

Habermas, J. (1984). *The theory of communicative action.* Boston: Beacon Press.

Houston, S., Magill, T., McCollum, M., & Spratt, T. (2001). Developing creative solutions to the problems of children and families: Communicative reason and the use of forum theatre. *Child and Family Social Work, 6*(4), 285-294.

Howe, D. (1992). Child abuse and the bureaucratisation of social work. *Sociological Review, 40*(3), 491-508.

Jack, G. (1997). Discourses of child protection and child welfare. *British Journal of Social Work, 27,* 659-678.

Parton, N. (1991). *Governing the family: Child care, child protection and the state.* Basingstoke: Macmillan.

Parton, N., Thorpe, D., & Wattam, C. (1997). *Child protection: Risk and the moral order.* Basingstoke: Macmillan.

Thorpe, D. (1997). Policing minority child-rearing practices in Australia: The consistency of "child abuse." In N. Parton (Ed.), *Child protection and family support: Tensions, contradictions and possibilities* (pp.59-77). London: Routledge.

Spratt, T., & Houston, S. (1999). Developing critical social work in theory and in practice. *Child and Family Social Work, 4*(4), 315-324.

Spratt, T., Houston, S., & Magill, T. (2000). Imaging the future: Theatre and change within the child protection system. *Child and Family Social Work, 5*(2), 117-127.

PART 3
Theories and Critical Perspectives on Social Work

8

A Reflexive Materialist Alternative

Gerald de Montigny

What is critical social work? To answer the question should we turn to texts, or should we look at those who call themselves critical social workers? If we eschew the enterprise of taxonomically determining the ideas, concepts, arguments and positions that belong to an as yet to be determined corpus of critical social work to instead to turn our gaze back onto the embodied and present lives of those who profess to be critical social workers, we are led to ask: What are the desires, the passions and longings that have led such people, in generation after generation, to develop a "critical" analysis and a critical practice? From out of what locations, what forms of life, what emotional matrices are the impulses to be critical derived? What are the implications of critical social work for practice?

Such questions about the embodied presence of critical social workers, or for that matter any social worker, draws attention to the social organization of social workers' practices and accordingly suggest what I have chosen to call a reflexive materialist analysis. A reflexive analysis provides a troubled and troubling ground for social workers' use of language, understandings and knowledge. Yet it is in the acknowledgement of the troubles of a social ground, which not only is, but becomes and is transformed by dint of action and will, that the arrogance of positivism and the rhetoric of power founded in objectivity is displaced by a profound epistemological humility. It is in such an accomplished terrain of self and a social world that analysis celebrates rather than seeks to displace the shadows of an inescapable recursiveness, though not of "signs" à la Derrida (Palmer, 1990, p.3) but of will, agency and a practice that both encounters and shapes a material world. By holding to practices as socially organized, social workers can develop a working analysis of client situations as rooted in what Wittgenstein has called a "form of life" (1958, p.8e), or what Marx called a "mode of production and social formation" (Marx, 1970; Bologh, 1979, p.47).

Social workers perhaps more than other helping professionals are led to recognize that the mundane activities of our lives, and the connection between these particular activities and those of others, are not idiosyncratic, random, incoherent, formless or normless. Rather, in parallel with ethnomethodology (Garfinkel, 2002), such mundane activities express not only the every day and every night construction of self, but equally importantly the construction of an ongoing, coherent and largely unremarkable — that is, taken for granted — social landscape and social world. Such a broadened appreciation of the fundamentally social character of mundane activities is hinted at in the Marxist notion of "practice" (Lenin, 1976; Mao, 1967). Practice designates a nexus articulating active presence, embodied particular being, intercorporeality, coordinated performance, from which knowledge of the world emerges. Practice allows for an appreciation that specific and local activities articulate ongoing, interwoven, past and presently realized courses of action. Further, as Lenin (1976, p.216) noted, "man's practice, repeating itself a thousand million times, becomes consolidated in man's consciousness...[P]recisely...on account of this thousand–million fold repetitions, these figures have the stability of a prejudice."

Practice indicates the integral connection between a fluid and perpetually contingent constitution of "self" and a socially organized world, brought into being moment-by-moment and day-by-day through coordinated activities. Bourdieu (1990, p.81) noted, "because it is entirely immersed in the current of time, practice is inseparable from temporality, not only because it is played out in time, but also because it plays strategically with time and especially with tempo." Indeed, it is this unfolding, temporally rooted nature of in vivo practice that comes to be expressed as our everyday lives that we produce and reproduce, not only ourselves as members of a social world, but the sociability or sociology of the world itself (Campbell & Gregor, 2002).

Reflexive Analysis

While I may see myself reflected in a mirror, or in the faces and talk of others, at the moment of reflection, what I encounter is an object among other objects. The mirror reflects back my body as an image, though in real time and space it is an image that changes and moves, grimaces, smiles back on itself and performs before the mirror. Precisely because this image stares back at me, moves as I move, I am caught in its uncomfortable and seemingly intractable material properties. My body, the light and the mirror reflect into my eyes and are recognized by my brain as I am at that moment, but not exactly as I was at previous moments. This tension between then and now, and a practice before the mirror of playing with the image, point to the limits of reflection, suggesting not just presence but active creation of forms of being. A simple moment of reflection fails to penetrate beyond the visible object. When in a moment of reflection I may note the transformations of the image before the mirror, the trouble of interrogating that which troubles my eye is avoided. Yet in the reflection of self are the phantoms and shadows of a background that threatens to shift my gaze from the mirror to the room, the house, the windows and the world outside.

Though I might play with my image before the mirror, I am only temporarily transfixed by the reflection. I may turn and walk away from the mirror to pursue other activities, or may struggle to penetrate the troubles of the shadows against the image. Though in a moment of reflection I might be transfixed as Narcissus, unlike the mythical character I am not locked in a gaze unto death. In my life, in a lived world, I break from the play of reflection and move elsewhere, beyond and outside the grasp of the mirror. I live. I live among others.

Following from reflection, there is for those of us who live beyond this moment the historically emergent and "unsettling" (Pollner, 1991) possibility of reflexivity. A reflexive analysis pushes past the object present in reflection and turns the gaze of the observer back before the mirror, and after the mirror, to penetrate beyond appearance to interrogate not only the performance of self before the mirror but self and one's knowledge as actively accomplished in ongoing and embedded forms of life. When Pollner notes, "Intrinsic to radical reflexivity is an 'unsettling,' i.e., an insecurity regarding the basic assumptions, discourse and practices used in describing reality" (1991:370), it is important to see that what is unsettled are the mirrors of taken for granted and common sense understandings.

The reflexive turn points to the historical and social background, which allows for my reflection in the mirror. In a reflexive analysis I interrogate, not only my presence, but the trajectory of my arrival before the mirror as a subject rooted in time and space, who is not only able to reflect but to think about the possibility of that reflection. A reflexive turn ensures that this reflection is not narcissistic, not individualized and certainly not such that I am emptied of embodied location so that I become an abstract philosophical "subject." A reflexive analysis is filled with wonder as it opens enquiry out from the frag- mented moment into the plenitude of an ongoing stream of historical and socio- logical reality. A reflexive analysis opens up a space for questioning how it is that the shapes and shadows of what "I am" discovers itself, and lives in partici- pation in the practices and the labours of others.

A reflexive practice forces me to recognize that the very possibility of a "me" as a subject arises, comes to be, gains form and emerges as such in and through social relationships, practices (and yes language) with others, who along with me produce being in the world. Pollner (1991, p.370) explains: "Radical reflex- ivity — the recursively (Platt 1989) comprehensive appreciation of the 'accom- plished' character of *all* social activity — enjoins the analyst to displace the discourse and practices that ground and constitute his/her endeavors in order to explore the very work of grounding and constituting." Indeed, the notion of accomplishment points to practical production, day-to-day practices and mundane activities as contemporaneous co-production of being in social rela- tions as a shared ground (Bologh, 1979).

Clearly a reflexive analysis is "radical" analysis as it does explicate the roots of phenomena, that is, their roots as nurtured, fed and cultivated in a social world. Alvin Gouldner writing in the 1970s called for a "reflexive sociology" by which he meant a transformative sociology. Gouldner aimed to shift the socio- logical practice from creation of "information," which he defined as knowing in order to control (p. 491), to "awareness," which was an "opening of self inward" (p. 492). Whereas the focus on information "thingified" man, awareness is char- acterized by attention to relations between persons (p. 494). In a passage that is apt for sociologists and social workers alike, Gouldner urges that the sociologist must confront himself or herself as "molded by all that he [*sic*] is and wants, by his [*sic*] courage no less than his [*sic*] talent, by his [*sic*] passion no less than objectivity" (p. 493).[1] A reflexive social work, like a reflexive sociology, is of necessity moral, courageous, dedicated to truth as lived and encountered, transformative of self and society, and able to grapple with power and hegemony.

In using the concept "reflexivity," it is important to avoid a transformation into what Kress and Hodge (1979) call a "nominal." A nominal is produced when the mundane activities, situations, and ground of a phenomenon are erased, such that in this case, "reflexivity" becomes a thing in itself.[2] When addressing "reflexivity" it is necessary to gaze through the phenomena to the specific practices that have reflexivity as their effect. The apparent durability of reflexivity as a mundane feature of everyday life (Mehan & Wood, 1975), though indicating a direction for enquiry, is simultaneously and always a puzzle, hence, that which remains to be explored and explicated as we ask "how is it done?" As Wittgenstein observed, "Every sign by itself seems dead. What gives it life?–In use it is alive" (1958, p.128). Similarly, Harold Garfinkel, the father of ethnomethodology, speaks of reflexivity to bring to attention analytic practices for addressing "in vivo" practices. Thus making sense emerges in, through and as practice, which performs, references and relies on — in a mundane indexical fashion — the practical production of the "social" (2002, pp. 203-204).

The Social Ground for Social Work

The concept of materialism designates that there is a "real" world, a world not freely chosen by ourselves, a world that is intractable and obdurate in its press upon on our bodies and our lives. Yet, in the forms in which the materiality of the world appear to us, as seen, heard, tasted, smelled and touched, we are not passive. Rather, not only is the world reflected in and through the forms of our lives, but we change the forms of the world as we act on the world. That which we count as experience articulates the complex evolutionary and fundamentally social processes through which we as a species have come to be with our bodies, our senses, and the possibilities and range of our sensorium. The materiality of the world is expressed not only in the form of our bodies, but in the forms of life that obtain in any given historical epoch. Materialism of necessity points us to examine the historical evolution of not only society but social work as a nexus of practices, identifications and knowledge.

Social work was a child of urban industrial capitalism and continues, appearances notwithstanding, to be a child of a capitalism, albeit a capitalism that now

---

[1] Though it should be noted that Bourdieu distances his notion of reflexivity from that of Gouldner and Garfinkel by insisting on a political foundation in which the challenge is "showing that this world is the site of an ongoing struggle to tell the truth of this world" (Wacquant, 1989, p.35).

[2] Kress and Hodge (1979) provide an homey example in which a "wife" might ask her husband, "Has the garbage been taken out yet?" while meaning "Have you taken out the garbage?" In this example, the person who takes out the garbage has been eliminated from the sentence, and while such transformations are possible in language, they are not possible in the real world. Hence, the garbage will sit and rot until someone takes it out.

operates out of "the metropolises of the world market — London, New York, Tokyo, Hong Kong, São Paulo, Paris, Frankfurt, and so on —" (Beck, 2000, p.29) with considerable wealth and power, and able to restructure local lives according to the imperatives of globalized capital. Capitalism has survived the hiccups of the Bolshevik revolution; the Great Depression; the rise of fascism across Europe; the leadership of Chairman Mao; the revolution of Castro; the brief flickering of a youthful left movement in the West during the sixties; the anti-colonialist struggles in Zimbabwe, Vietnam, Cambodia and a host of other third-world countries; the overthrow of apartheid in South Africa and so on. Left theorists, particularly those who hypothesized that capitalism would collapse due to its own contradictions, have watched as the Western centres of capitalism have moved at an unprecedented rate towards integration of production on a world scale, to aggressive development of trade agreements to foster the expansion of "global" capital and the rapid reorganization of commodity production into countries with cheap sources of labour. Capitalism has proven to be incredibly resilient.

Social workers who often hunger for justice, equality and an end to human deprivation and misery have not been immune to a renewed neo-liberal and triumphalist capitalism (Naiman, 1995). Certainly social workers today, as in the past, are witnesses to a surplus of human pain, suffering and despair. In the nineteenth century our profession grew out of middle-class anxiety and fear caused by a growing urban under class (what Marx 1969a, 1969b] called the lumpenproletariat) and the dangers posed to social order by a fractious industrial working class. For the ruling elites and an emerging professional middle class, these social fractions posed a danger to "society" and accordingly needed to be disciplined (Donzelot, 1979), educated (Prentice, 1977) and controlled (Pfohl, 1985). Through the efforts of the friendly visitors, or the settlement workers, usually good Christian folk inspired by some variant of the gospel message to uplift, affirm and support "the poor," our profession was born (Christie & Gauvreau, 1996; Little, 1998; Valverde, 1991; Struthers, 1994; Splane, 1965). It is important to recognize that the suffering social workers address today, although aggravated by the political climate of neo-liberalism, cutbacks, downsizing and deregulation, was and continues to be a product of life in a capitalist society.

As social workers encounter the wreckage to social security wrought by globalization and its handmaid neo-liberal ideology (Teeple, 2000), it is important to avoid romanticizing the past. Sadly, the effects of boom and bust cycles on social security has been a familiar problem that has been addressed by generations of social service workers. Porter Lee, a pre-eminent social worker of the 1930s and 1940s, delivered an address in 1933 in the midst of the Great Depression, which he entitled "Social workers: Pioneers again." He observed:

> For four years the creeping paralysis which has afflicted our civilization and its institutions has disclosed to us the wilderness aspect of the world in which we work. We are suddenly aware of helplessness in the face of forces which we have hitherto

manipulated with confidence. We have come to distrust many of our methods and we
have begun to realize the inadequacy of some of the foundations upon which we have
built. What had come to seem a reasonably well-charted territory has again assumed
the aspect of a wilderness in which new trails must be blazed. Trail blazing is not a
task for the settled denizen of a sophisticated social order. It is a task for the pioneer.
It calls for faith, competence, and the adventurous spirit. (1937, p.179)

The assault on social services and the values of our profession with the rise
of the neo-liberal New Right has created a demand for social workers similar to that identified by Lee.

As social workers, we must resist the malaise of despair occasioned by the
rise of global capitalism and the New Right. We must help clients and ourselves
to organize in solidarity and community. As Kuyek argued, "We have to learn to
trust and work together in groups...Our organizations should reflect the kind of
world we want to create: co-operative, honest, caring and exciting places"
(1990, p.6). Organization for resistance can only emerge from a firm, consistent
and insistent focus on the centrality of human relationships even if, as Dominelli
points out, "the concern with relationship building is...becoming redundant"
(1996, p.159). The centrality of relationships affirms core values in social work.
Helen Harris Perlman, writing over thirty years ago in a decidedly modernist
tone, explained:

No matter what the theoretical model by which one human being attempts to be of
help to another, the most potent and dynamic power for influence lies in relationship.
The human drive and need for social connectedness and social recognition (to at least
one "other") are lifelong movers and shapers of the personality. These are what any
"meaningful" or "potent" relationship contains: caring and respect, love (in one of its
many faces) and social exchange and affirmation. (1970, p.150)

Perlman's affirmation of the centrality of "relationship" and its forms of
expression rooted in caring, respect and love remains a beacon guiding our
response to globalization and the economic reorganization of our local
worlds.

To be a social worker today, as in the past, demands occupying a social
location of profound alienation and contradiction while opening the possibility
of acting as a witness to the harsh realities of our society, and speaking the truth
about human affairs. Being a social worker often means encountering the
physical poverty, deprivation and loss of freedom of others while attempting to
survive our own existential poverty, deprivation and loss of freedom. While
succumbing to despair creates the dangers of cynicism, hostility and anger
towards oneself and one's clients, social workers, by holding firmly to the loyal-
ties of personal relationships and local places, can find a source for resistance.
Social workers, by holding to the centrality of relationships, can struggle against
becoming simple functionaries who interpret and carry out the provisions of
law, organizational power and authority.

Understanding the powers that lead social workers against the people with
whom they work demands explicating the social organization of social work
practice. At the core of social work are various activities of what Gramsci (1971)

called "intellectual production," that is, assessments, narratives, therapeutic interventions, records and so forth. Being a social worker provides a salary, which allows for the consumption of goods and services produced by others. As consumers, rather than producers of commodities, we can avoid being directly involved in the dirty, hard physical, and often dangerous, labour. Being a social worker brings with it the exercise of authority and command, but perhaps somewhat ironically and irritatingly, it does not bring ownership of the means of production or the command of social wealth. Perhaps at the heart of being a social worker is the frustration of having a semblance of mastery over the lives of our clients — through the exercise of organizational orders — without necessarily having a commensurate mastery over our own lives.

Precisely because so much of social work is exercised in the form of talk, through the orders of texts and in the writing of records, it is little wonder discourses, ideas, theories and knowledge have come to be valorized over mundane practice. It is easy enough for social workers to see that they arrive at work to interview a client. What is less easy to see is that the possibility of the workplace arises in and through the hidden labours of countless others, whether the hydro workers who supply electricity, the linesmen who keep the power grid working, the water and sewer workers who ensure a flow of water for toilets and sinks, or the janitors who empty the wastebaskets, sweep and vacuum the floors, and clean the furniture. The possibility of social work practice articulates, not only the background from which it arises, but the profound alienations of class and orders of production, which become manifest in and through the bizarre turns of what comes to count as social work (sociological, political science and so on) theory.

Although social work practice emerges through socially organized forms of life, social workers are not alone in their alienation. Social workers are fortunate as the core of their practice is oriented towards explicating the social as it impinges on the lives of their clients. This is their professional mission. The attention to the social of necessity has the potential to bring into play a dialogue and a communication across socially organized sites of production. Social workers can enter into the daily worlds of their clients, at least vicariously through talk, and as visitors into the places where they live. They can build genuine relationships and dialogue with those who inhabit forms of life organized by imperatives far different from those that obtain in social service agencies and organizations. As such, social workers are able to build through their relations with others, not only solidarities, but a critical reflection on the organization of their own practice.

Returning to the Social

The strengths of social work are rooted in an abiding attention to the social as the very fabric of each of our lives. This is a strength clearly evident in the work of Mary Richmond's *Social Diagnosis*, published in 1917, and which has survived in social work scholarship over the past century. Social workers need not the tools of deconstruction, but tools for reconstruction of the social. The social is far richer than is suggested by a focus on talk, discourse or the realm of ideas. Social workers' tools must recognize the reflexivity of practice in a material world, a world in which their thought and their practices are grounded irremediably, ever presently and incorrigibly. It is as we live in this world, as we move about day by day, as we engage in the mundane current of living activities coordinated and linked with others, pondered over, written and talked about, that contours of the world come into focus as what we call experience.

The invitation of both new and old social workers to "critical" practice must be appreciative of danger. Critical social work must offer more than a clever critique and certainly more than a contrarian approach to others. Social workers who desire congruence, and who practice with courage and conviction, need a secure "epistemological" foundation. This is an epistemology rooted not in the mere flow of words, discourses or ideas, but in the stuff of material existence, in the social relations of life itself. Social relations are not "other" to any individual. They are not an external duality from which one's self and one's knowing emerges. Social relations are the very matrix in, against and through which we come to be. This was, and continues to be, the brilliance of social work. The continuation and survival of our living being depends on such relations. As the work on women's caring makes so evident, the possibility of our existence speaks to the care of those others who sustained us from infancy through childhood into adulthood (Baines, Evans, & Neysmith, 1998).

Of course, as we saw from Perlman above, at the core of a focus on the social is a celebration of human relationships. Do we value our relationships with people or do we value things? Do we devote our intellectual attention to impersonal discourses, talk and text,[3] or are we devoted to personal and face-to-face interaction with others? Today each social worker is forced to weigh out and make fundamental choices in the workplace. Do they commit themselves to building relationships of trust and care with clients, or do they comply with the machine demands of the organization? Do they spend their time doing home visits, or do they allow themselves to be chained to their desks completing paperwork? Do they muddle alongside clients with a spirit of solidarity in a joint effort to understand and to survive daily life, or do they take refuge in the standpoint of expertise, authority and power? Do they reach out for the human dimension of interaction, or do they satisfy themselves with administering universal-

---

[3] Marx in *Capital* (1996) developed an analysis of commodity fetishization, essentially pointing to the tendency for social relations to be understood as "things" with a life or an agency of their own. Thus in political economy commodities, money, capital are treated as things with agency rather than as expressions of determinate social relations (Rubin, 1972, p.59). Similarly, social workers encounter products of organizational processes, legislation, policy manuals, directives, which appear to have a life of their own. Textual fetishism, similar to that of commodity fetishism, as Marx pointed out in *Capital* (1996, p.83), "has its origin...in the peculiar social character of the labour that produces them."

ized policies — wherein the very structures of dehumanization and erasure are reproduced in client's lives?[4]

The incarnate forms of their practice, as accomplished day by day in face-to-face encounters are marked not just by the words spoken, not just by the stories told, not just by the documents produced, but by the spaces in which social relations are effected, produced and sustained. A focus on social relations leads us to ask how mundane and taken-for-granted phenomena, such as interviews, clients, agencies, policies, and so on come to be produced through what actual people do day-after-day in concert. While "talk" is often necessary for practice it is not in itself sufficient.[5] Social workers do not live by talk alone.

A Reflexive Materialist Method: Focus on Practice

A reflexive materialist approach to knowledge insists that there is a necessary relationship between what is known, the mundane and local practices of knowing, and the articulation of these practices to historical and social forms of organization. Attention to these relationships not only corrects arrogance, but points back to a humility that promises to ground social work and, I might add, science. A reflexive materialist approach to knowledge recognizes that there is social and intellectual progress. A reflexive materialist approach, while recognizing that there is a dark side to science and technology (Beck, 1999, 1992), also appreciates that a substitution of medicine with chants, dances around the fire or magical incantations is not acceptable.

The sustenance of our lives, whether Kraft Dinner or cappuccino, binds us to very real, ever-present, incorrigibly pressing and globalized socially organized practices and relations. No matter how deliciously different narratives might be, there remains this ineluctable stuff of material daily life. Though we might imagine that the trip from the dining table to the toilet[6] should provide sufficient corrective to the overvalorization of postmodernist excess, the aesthetics produced through capitalist fetishization give rise to myriad forms of fantasy and self-delusion. Fetishized chimera, whether discourses or simulacra, can be understood only by assiduously and unrelentingly "grounding" and thereby

---

[4] Beck (1992, p.21) binds risk to "reflective modernization" and observes that "risk may be defined as a "systematic way of dealing with hazards and insecurity induced and introduced by modernization itself." The social forms that generate child abuse and neglect as problems generate the attention to these "problems" in the form of state-controlled government ministries and Children's Aid Societies.

[5] Against an "idealism" that "fetishizes" language, Volosinov (1973, p.21) stated: "The form of signs are conditioned above all by the social organization of the participants involved and also by the immediate conditions of their interaction. When these forms change, so does sign. And it should be one of the tasks of the study of ideologies to trace this social life of the verbal sign. Only so approached can the problem of the relationship between sign and existence find its concrete expression; only then will the process of the causal shaping of the sign by existence stand out as a process of genuine existence-to-sign transit, of genuine dialectical refraction of existence in the sign."

[6] Mary O'Brien (1981, pp. 38-39) argues, "From our own digestive processes, we are conscious of…our own participation in the opposition of externality and internality, and of the unification and transformation of objects." For O'Brien, the possibility of a "dialectic" arises as "living consciousness apprehends the living body primordially as a medium of the opposition of internality and externality, of mediation, of negation and of qualitative transformation" (p. 39).

explicating (Bologh, 1979) our corporeal, presently experienced and materially constituted lives inside historically determined and socially organized relations.

It is in these bodies, as they are located in differentiated social relations, that we live and die. Our place, our identities and our lives are not reducible to discourse, nor to a clever play of differences (Derrida, 1974). Though I may agree with Baudrillard (1975) that there are times for play, those of us who work for a wage, and work maintaining a home, know only too well the inexorable necessity for work. When we face as social workers the pain of hunger in a child, the suffering of disease among the elderly, the violence of some towards others, a response is needed beyond excess, prodigality and play. While such clever postmodernists turn work to disturb order, regimes and regulations of "truth," we who grapple with what Lillian Rubin called "worlds of pain" (1976), are impelled to move beyond words. We are impelled to struggle for change. Change is not just spoken, it is worked. As work, social change is brought about in the sweat of our brow and in the span of our lives.

Marx argued that it is in and through work as organized under capitalism that workers are alienated, not only from that which they produce, but from that which they become. As "labour," workers become yet another commodity to be bought and sold. The central tenet of Marx's critique of political economy centres on labour power (Capital, 1996, 1970); that is, the living expenditure of energy transferred from the active worker to the things at hand and the socially organized processes that result in the purchase and transformation of this life force into things or commodities. Marx's focus on labour power was an entreaty never to lose sight of the incarnate, living individuals who in social coordination produce the world around them.

Despite the primacy of living, local and incarnate action, ours is a society where the very forms of life (Bologh, 1979, p.46) mask, mystify and disguise the fundamental and ongoing processes by which living human beings produce the world. The practical effect is that agency is continually attributed to things, that is, to the state, bureaucracy, the organization, documents or, more recently, discourses, which are presumed to perform, to act or to believe. This way of making sense is what Marx called "idealism," and its ultimate consequence is to transform the things that we produce into fetishes (Rubin, 1972), that is, into objects with agency.

Against such ways of making sense, against erasing real living "subjects," against seeing ourselves as simply interpellated into discourse, I want to insist that living people, in and through their bodies, make themselves as "subjects," not just as they please, but inside densely woven networks of social relations. Against a way of working that would speak about state powers, I want to look at how social workers coordinate their working activities, case by case, document by document, into the coordinated institutional nexus we call an agency, and the ways that agencies are practically coordinated into the nexus we call the state. I call for a way of working that recognizes that is through the mundane, practical, day-by-day coordination of multiple activities in concert that empty buildings are filled, policies are read, interpreted and acted on, and dust-collecting files are resuscitated by readers and actors with the breath of life. What the agency is, is as the people who work there make it collectively.

The materiality of the world is never unmediated, never just there, but always as worked, laboured, sweated, pondered and reflected. The materiality of the world is never just of one individual's making but always and everywhere present through the labour, the effort, the embodied enunciation and putting of pen to paper of co-conspirators against and inside the world. The materiality of the world is emergent, not in any form, but in and through the concrete, detailed forms through which we live and reproduce ourselves day after day.

I want to insist that there is indeed a "reality" rooted in the encounter between our bodies intertwined with a world (Merleau-Ponty, 1968), which provides a substrate, a "trace," an origin and thick substance to utterances and to language itself. Before language, we are present in bodies that suckle, nurse, grope and gaze. Merleau-Ponty observed,

> If we were to make completely explicit the architectonics of the human body, its ontological framework, and how it sees itself and hears itself, we would see that the structure of its mute world is such that all the possibilities of language are already given in it. (1968, p.155)[7]

Of course the possibility of human bodies that move about, interact and also think depends on the work of others, first mothers who bring those bodies into the world, then suckle, feed and nurture infants into children and into adults. It continues to amaze that so much of what adults produce as philosophy acts as though we were never children, as though we did not nurse, eat, defecate, and get cleaned up by others.[8] That we are here to talk, write and think speaks to the labour of our caregivers, our mothers and fathers.

The Socially Organized Materiality of the Body

It is through our bodies, our physical existence and presence, that the world as present arises for us as a pressing series of sensations demanding mediation, engagement and synthesis. Harré, using Merleau-Ponty's phenomenology of perception, observes, "In touching oneself perceiver and perceived are simultaneously given to consciousness" (1991, p.96). Indeed it is in touch, in and through our bodies as we live in real historical time and socially organized spaces, that our presence, our ontology and our consciousness arises. Of course, that which is, is never finally realized but always unfolding, coming into being

---

[7] There has been a growing body of work that explores the "body," whether in the form of the sociology of the body (Turner, 1992), the implications of physical being for "experiences" (Harré, 1991), or the body and the construction of gender (Gallop, 1988).

[8] This insight is rooted in the work of Mary O'Brien (1989, p.41) who reflected, "There is a sense in which male species integration stops dead at the moment of ejaculations. Historically, at some time birth had no meaning for men." Against the alienation and refraction she identifies in universal theory and the universal state, she proposes, "It can be transformed only by a concrete turning toward community and life, integration of people and the natural world, to a practice which integrates the web of species and persistence with the realities of personal and social being" (p. 42).

and becoming something other through the transformations of life itself. Always we sense an ineffable embodied existence beyond language. This ineffability of being fuels a curiosity rooted in intercorporeality, and pushes us to join with others. This beyond the word, this compulsion for community and solidarity, has unfortunately often been dismissed as emotion and therefore as lesser than reason.[9] Yet, it is this ineffability and mystery at the core of corporeal being that ruptures the power of language. It is this other beyond language that presses on us as a well of innovation, inspiration and change. Beyond the word is the body, and as we live inside and through these bodies, we grapple, in material space and in lived time, to accommodate that which is around us to socially organized and expressed needs and desires.

The failure of the word to capture the plenitude of embodiment is marked in moments of speechlessness. We know this sensation well when we turn to a beloved and utter the words, "I love you." In even such an utterance we sense a fissure, and a chasm between the desire and the word. We mourn for the inadequacy of the utterance. We reach across this space with our arms and our bodies to embrace, to breathe in the scent, to feel the warmth, and to rejoice in the touch and the body of the other. We reach past our individual bodies through our skin, through the shades and colours of the morning, beyond the utterance, to fracture the seeming coherence of the word.

Before we dressed up as adults, and before we came to value words over life, all of us were children. As children we rejoiced in the sensation of water crashing over our bodies as we ran into the surf. We felt the pulse of waves moving us back to shore. We tasted the sea salt on our lips and tongue. Though such sensations may be reawakened by language, they can never be captured by language. We are never bound by language. Language is but one form of embodied practice, for a voice that speaks is conjoined with lungs that inhale and exhale, with arms and hands that gesticulate, lips that smile and corners of eyes that wrinkle and turn up with laughter. Language may aid us to recall a wind raising prickly goosebumps over our wet bodies, but it is neither the wind nor the moment of the flesh responding to the embrasure of the world. Language may recall grains of sand, the sun's heat, the smell of suntan oil and the colour of the sea, but it is none of these things in itself. To pretend that language is a sealed box from which we cannot escape is to imagine a prison that is inside out, for language is but a moment, which ruptures, fractures and bleeds in the wounds of the body.

---

[9] Talcott Parsons (1968, p.16) wrote that empirical facts could be thought of "as a 'spot' in the vast encircling darkness, brightly illuminated as by a searchlight…[W]hat lies outside the spot is not really 'seen' until the searchlight moves, and then only what lies within the area into which its beam is newly cast." He used this metaphor to develop the notion of "residual categories," which he identified as the darkness surrounding the illuminated spot (p. 17). In a simple materialist conversion of Parsons' metaphor we reinsert actual people engaged in socially coordinated activities using tools in hand — whether flaming torches or battery-operated flashlights — to peer into the darkness surrounding them as they go about trying to accomplish discrete, particular and grounded activities. It is the forms of socially organized life and the mucking about together that brings into focus certain types of problems, questions and enquiries, and knowledge.

As a father I have seen my three children born, and along with my wife, I have cared for them. None would have survived the weeks after their birth without care. That these children have come to speak, to act in a social world, is itself an expression of the labour and the love performed by their mother and I. As a social worker I appreciate that caring for infants and children does not just happen. Every day when doing child protection I witnessed failures in the care of infants and children. Parents cannot pretend to act as do postmodern philosophers. They cannot fail to attend to the materiality of bodies. They cannot fail to recognize the sharp edges and dangers of a material world. Though play is essential for human health, perhaps even the play of postmodernism, there comes a time when even Samuel Beckett's actors in *Waiting for Godot* (1965) step off stage to eat their suppers, brush their teeth and crawl into bed to sleep. Social workers cannot afford to play at abdicating the onerous responsibility for judgement. We cannot abdicate our place in the world as "relatively autonomous human subjects" (Leonard, 1997, p.167).[10] We cannot act as though one "account" or "narrative" is as good as another (Parry & Doan, 1994). In child protection, social workers must exercise judgement. Social workers must evaluate and assess objective conditions or else children will die. Social workers must insist that certain narratives are more accurate and better guides for survival than others. As anyone who has done house renovations knows, along with deconstruction there must be a reconstruction, or else life becomes unbearable.

Conclusion

Marx understood that in times of transition certain philosophies, certain ways of working, emerge that though dressed up in progressive, revolutionary and transformative language, carry inside a reactionary core.

> Men make their own history, but they do not make it just as they please; they do not make it under circumstances chose by themselves, but under circumstances directly encountered, given and transmitted from the past. The tradition of all the dead generations weighs like a nightmare on the brain of the living. And just when they seem engaged in revolutionizing themselves and things, in creating something that has never yet existed, precisely in such periods of revolutionary crisis they anxiously conjure up the spirits of the past to their service and borrow from them names, battle cries and costumes in order to present the new scene of world history in this time honoured disguise and this borrowed language. (Marx, 1969a, p.15)

As social workers we must insist that there is a "real" or "material" world, and although this is not our "preferred reality" (Freedman & Combs, 1996), it is the "reality" with which we must grapple. We are bound by our professional history

---

[10] Leonard's work stand apart from other social workers who write about postmodernism, for although he is interested in the topic and borrows some features of postmodernist analysis, he dedicates his work, following Doyle and Gough (1991) to a project that aims to construct "emancipatory universals around which solidarity might be formed" (1997, p.27). Indeed, Leonard (1997) provides an erudite analyses of Marxist, socialist and class theory, and accordingly a reticence to abandon the "subject" and an insistence on the cogency of common human needs.

not to abandon the social in social work. Social workers must insist on the pre-eminent place of socially organized practice as that which brings the contours of a world worked on and shared in common into view. How we conceive of the world arises from how we live in the world, not just as individuals, but as members of a society. As we struggle along with our clients to figure out how to live in this world shaped by the reified forces of global capitalism, it is more important than ever to insist on a material anchor in the world, that is, an anchor that sinks beneath the reflection on the water through the water itself, to find the sedimentation, the soil and the ground of an intractably social materiality.

References

Baines, C.T., Evans, P.M., & Neysmith, S.M. (1998). Women's caring: Work expanding, state contracting. In C.T. Baines, P.M. Evans, & S.M. Neysmith (Eds.), *Women's caring: Feminist perspectives on social welfare* (2nd ed., pp. 3-22). Don Mills, ON: Oxford University Press.

Baudrillard, J. (1975). *The mirror of production* (M. Poster, Trans.). St. Louis, MO: Telos.

Beck, U. (1992). *Risk society: Towards a new modernity.* London, UK: Sage.

Beck, U. (1999) *World risk society.* Cambridge, UK: Polity Press.

Beck, U. (2000). *The brave new world of work* (P. Camiller, Trans.). Cambridge, UK: Polity Press.

Beckett, S. (1965). *Waiting for Godot: A tragicomedy in two acts.* London, UK: Faber and Faber.

Bologh, R.W. (1979). *Dialectical phenomenology: Marx's method.* London, UK: Routledge.

Bourdieu, P. (1990). *The logic of practice.* Stanford, CA: Stanford University Press.

Campbell, M., & Gregor, F. (2002). *Mapping social relations: A primer in doing institutional ethnography.* Aurora, ON: Garamond.

Christie, N., & Gauvreau, M. (1996). *A full-orbed Christianity: The protestant churches and social welfare in Canada 1900-1940.* Montreal, PQ: McGill-Queen's.

Derrida, J. (1974). *Of grammatology* (G.C. Spivak, Trans.). Baltimore, MD: Johns Hopkins.

Dominelli, L. (1996). Deprofessionalizing social work: Anti-oppressive practice, competencies and postmodernism. *British Journal of Social Work, 26,* 153-175.

Donzelot, J. (1979). *The policing of families* (R. Hurley, Trans.). New York, NY: Pantheon.

Doyle, L. & Gough, I. (1991). *A theory of human need.* New York, NY: Guildford.

Freedman, J. & Combs, G. (1996). *Narrative therapy: The social construction of preferred reality.* New York, NY: W.W. Norton.

Gallop, J. (1988). *Thinking through the body.* New York, NY: Columbia University Press.

Garfinkel, H. (2002). *Ethnomethodology's program: Working out Durkheim's aphorism* (A.W. Rawls, Ed.). Lanham, MD: Rowman & Littlefield.

Gouldner, A. *The coming crisis of Western sociology.* New York, NY: Basic Books.

Gramsci, A. (1971). *Selections from the prison notebooks* (Q. Hoare & G. Smith, Eds. and Trans.). New York, NY: International Publishers.

Harré, R. (1991). *Physical being: A theory for a corporeal psychology.* Oxford, UK: Blackwell.

Kress, G., & Hodge, R. (1979). *Language as ideology.* London, UK: Routledge and Kegan Paul.

Kuyek, J.N. (1990). *Fighting for hope: Organizing to realize our dreams.* Montreal, PQ: Black Rose Books.

Lee, P. (1937). *Social workers: Pioneers again.* Address delivered at **[complete reference]**

Lenin, V.I. (1976). Conspectus of Hegel's Science of Logic. In *V.I. Lenin collected works* (Vol. 38, Philosophical notebooks). Moscow, USSR: 1976.

Leonard, P. (1997). *Postmodern welfare: Reconstructing an emancipatory project.* Thousand Oaks, CA: Sage.

Little, M.J. (1998). *No car, no radio, no liquor permit: The moral regulation of single mothers in Ontario, 1920-1997.* Toronto, ON: Oxford University Press.

Mao, T. (1967). On Practice: On the relation between knowledge and practice, between knowing and doing. In *Selected works of Mao Tse-tung* (Vol. 1). Peking, China: Foreign Languages Press. (Original work published 1937)

Marx, K. (1969a). *The eighteenth brumaire of Louis Bonaparte.* New York, NY: International Publishers.

Marx, K. (1969b). *Class struggles in France 1848-1850.* New York, NY: International Publishers.

Marx, K. (1996). Capital (Vol. 1). In K. Marx & F. Engels, *Collected Works* (Vol. 35). New York, NY: International Publishers.

Marx, K. (1970). *Wages, price and profit.* Moscow, USSR: Progress.

Mehan, H., & Wood, H. (1975). *The reality of ethnomethology.* Malabar, Florida: Robert E. Krieger.

Merleau-Ponty, M. (1968). *The visible and the invisible* (A. Lingis, Trans.). Evanston: Il.: Northwestern University Press.

Naiman, J. (1995). *Beyond oppression, beyond diversity: Class analysis and gender inequality.* Paper presented at Society for Socialist Studies annual conference, Montreal, PQ.

O'Brien, M. (1989). *Reproducing the world: Essays in feminist theory.* Boulder, CO: Westview Press.

Palmer, B.D. (1990). *Decent into discourse: The reification of language and the writing of social history.* Philadelphia, PA: Temple University Press.

Parry, A. & Doan, R. (1994). *Story re-visions: Narrative therapy in the post-modern world.* New York, NY: Guilford Press.

Parsons, T. (1968). *The structure of social action: A study in social theory with special reference to a group of recent European writers* (Vol. 1). New York, NY: The Free Press.

Parton, N. (2000). Some thoughts on the relationship between theory and practice in and for social work. *British Journal of Social Work, 30*, 449-463.

Perlman, H.H. (1970). Problem solving. In R.W. Roberts & R.H. Nee (Eds.), *Theories of social casework* (pp. 131-179). Chicago, IL: University of Chicago Press.

Pfohl, Stephen J. (1985). *Images of deviance and social control: A sociological history.* New York, NY: McGraw-Hill.

Pollner, M. (1991). Left of ethnomethodology: The rise and decline of radical reflexivity. *American Sociological Review, 56*, 370-380.

Prentice, A. (1977). *The school promoters: Education and social class in mid-nineteenth century upper Canada.* Toronto, ON: McClelland and Stewart.

Richmond, M. (1917). *Social diagnosis.* New York, NY: Russell Sage.

Rubin, I.I. (1972). *Essays on Marx's theory of value* (M. Samard_ija & F. Perlman, Trans.). Detroit, MI: Black and Red.

Rubin, L.B. (1976). *Worlds of pain: Life in the working-class family.* New York, NY: Basic Books.

Smith, D.E. (1999). *Writing the social: Critique theory and investigations.* Toronto, ON: University of Toronto Press.

Splane, R. (1965). *Social welfare in Ontario, 1791-1893: A study of public welfare administration.* Toronto, ON: University of Toronto Press.

Struthers, J. (1994). *Limits of affluence: Welfare in Ontario, 1920-1970.* Toronto, ON; University of Toronto Press.

Teeple, G. (2000). *Globalization and the decline of social reform: Intro to the twenty-first century.* Aurora: ON: Garamond Press.

Turner, B.S. (1992). *Regulating bodies: Essays in medical sociology.* London, UK: Routledge.

Valverde, M. (1991). *The age of light, soap, and water: Moral reform in English Canada, 1885-1925.* Toronto, ON: McClelland and Stewart.

Volosinov, V. N. (1973). *Marxism and the philosophy of language* (L. Matejka & I.R. Titunik, Trans.). New York, NY: Seminar Press.

Wacquant, L.J.D. (1989). Toward a reflexive sociology: A workshop with Pierre Bourdieu, *Sociological Theory, 7*(1), 26-63.

Wittgenstein, L. (1958). *Philosophical investigations* (3rd ed., G.E.M. Anscombe, Trans.). New York, NY: Macmillan.

9

Unfinished Fictions: Becoming and Unbecoming Feminist Community Organizers

Sarah Todd

Traditionally, it has been difficult to remain committed to the work of white feminist community organizers while simultaneously considering the various ways these women reproduce oppressive relations. In the past, structural social work practice has often situated the work of radical white women who work as community organizers as "good" social work (see Carniol, 2000; Mullaly, 1997). Alternately, Foucauldian critiques leave it floundering as part of an overriding practice of controlling the poor and/or powerless (Cruikshank, 1999). Neither option has seemed particularly helpful at attending to the complexity of white female social workers' community activism. While sitting in the middle of this tension, I began to read various rewritings of critical social work (see Rossiter, 2001; Harris, 2001; Healey, 2001) and began to ask what an integrated post-structural-critical approach to social work, as described by Jan Fook (2002), could offer us when trying to make sense of feminist organizing. This chapter is an initial attempt to use this theoretical integration to understand how white feminist organizers' ways of knowing, our practices and our self-recognitions are caught within specific histories and social relations, some of which we transform, and others we reproduce. I outline the various social, cultural and historical meanings of community that shape white women's organizing practices and describe three narratives that social work offers feminist organizers to make sense of their work. These include the narratives of professionalism, radicalism and, less often, skepticism. I suggest that an integration of post-structural analysis with critical social work makes it possible to attend to the complicated social relations that shape and are shaped through community practice. In this way, I draw on the work of Healey (2001), Rossiter (2001) and Fook (2002) to interrogate the discursive terrain of community organizing, and through this begin to reflect on the concrete effects of our work. Further, this analysis highlights the possibilities for a community practice that, in attending to the multiple and subtle ways it operates as a disciplinary practice, can simultaneously take advantage of anti-oppressive opportunities. This chapter outlines a particular framework, developed from post-structuralism and critical social work, through which we can envision possibilities for liberation within complex social relations, rather than solely working towards the myth that emancipation is the core of community practice.

For me, such critical reflection facilitates my engagement with Steve Pile's (1997, p.17) query as to whether "the production of 'inner spaces' marks out the real break point of political struggle." In Pile's understanding, resistance is no longer solely recognizable in terms of large social protests, but has become both a public and private phenomenon. By challenging the public-private divide that so cleanly defines what is political in our practice as social workers, it seems that we begin to ask whether resistance may be as much an internal practice as an external one — neither privileged, but rather co-existing and supporting each other. Thus the discursive fields we draw upon to think of ourselves as feminist community organizers shapes, narrows and distorts our work. By understanding the intimate sphere of our public practices maybe we can understand the "break point of political struggle." This combined approach draws upon critical social work's attention to the social context and its continued connection with individual experience to provide a comprehensive theoretical understanding of our practice (see Fook, 2002).

This chapter unfolds as two distinct sections. The first explores the various tropes of community upon which feminist community organizing relies. I consider how the idea of community has evolved in Western society to offer contradictory possibilities for securing and resisting established social orders. In unpacking the ways in which our knowledge of community organizing is produced, we can challenge taken-for-granted power differences that evolve from the truths we envision through social work. These tropes symbolize the ideals we draw upon and reinscribe in our work to organize communities. In the second section I explore three narrative structures that offer meaning to feminist organizing. The narrative strategies that I propose here are analytical categories and interpretive strategies. They include radical, professional and skeptical stories about feminist community organizing. There is never a single narrative at work in conversations about feminist organizing; rather, I suggest that they rely on a mixture of familiar stories, or backdrops. The three narratives that I propose are "worked up" in a dialectical fashion, teased out of various transcripts of conversations I have had with feminist community organizers (Todd, 2002) and various writing about feminist organizing specifically, and community organizing generally. This combined deconstruction of community and an unpacking of the narratives employed by feminist community organizing makes visible the taken-for-granted ways in which our practice is historically and discursively situated to maintain certain social hierarchies.

Community as a Trope

Feminist organizing is made possible within a trope of "community." This trope is full of histories and theories; it works as ideology, interpreting the "real." "Community" clearly has a common sense usage that provides a sense of identity, belonging and purpose for people whose lives are otherwise characterized by isolation and alienation (Muller, Walker, & Ng, 1990, p.15). What makes it so appealing is both its fluidity and its overdetermined metaphorical meaning. The prolific circulation of "community" ensures that there need not be an agreed-upon signification to activate our collective imaginations (Singer, 1991). My analysis of "community" is designed to provide an understanding of the broad social histories, ideologies and investments that fashion white feminist organizing as a set of practices and as identities. In turn, these "imagined communities" form the backdrop against which we come to know ourselves as a particular type of social worker.

The call to an ideal community is a "non-negotiable consequence of our being in relation and in difference" (Singer, 1991, p.129). It is the apparatus into which our presence becomes possible. We could not ontologically exist without the pre-existence (in terms of memory rather than time) of community. For the most part, its function has "largely been that of managing, consolidating, or overriding the dissembling effects of a *non*regulated interplay of differences" (Singer, 1991, p.124). "Community" becomes the ideological and physical space in which we firm up our identities. Thus, when organizing communities we are creating a self-identity as well as coming to know those with whom we work.

This creation of identity is one effect of democratic societies requiring the technologies of community to manufacture the self-regulating, active subjects (see Cruikshank, 1999). While community is often appealing because it can challenge hegemonic notions of sameness and difference, its use simultaneously recreates dominant notions of citizenry and participation. Without communities or a

> vibrant public sphere, democratic citizenship is impossible; there are no contexts to generate the kinds of selfhood, friendship, power, and relations to the wider world that democracy demands. The point is dual: participation in the public sphere helps cultivate a sense of community, so that people care more, and think more, about the wider world; and second, participation becomes a source of meaning-making power. (Eliasoph, 1998, p.11)

This view of "a citizen" is not only self-regulating, but also a "*moral* subject accountable to him-or herself in ethical terms" (Heron, 1999, p.84). As such, a citizen is recognizable as a "good person." This morality is also central to community practice. Community workers are often attempting to create communities that regulate themselves through particular types of participation that we, and subsequently they, see as signifying good health.

Community does not only function to organize "other" bodies, but also operates through our individual desires for belonging in imagined, self-evident, pre-existing spaces of general commonalties (see Anderson, 1997). As a compelling performance, community participation offers a specific way of knowing oneself in relation to others. Not only do we, as community organizers, know ourselves in terms of sameness and difference, but we also attach certain moral meanings to this signification of difference. We want to recognize our community participation and subsequently ourselves as "good," while also desiring that the community participation of others be reshaped towards the ideal of "good" we imagine ourselves emulating.

Community ideology, on the other hand, also offers the possibility for resisting pre-established distributions, to claim the visibility of differences that were previously subsumed within the hegemony of social ordering. It provides both familiarity and a "not-quite-public sphere" where groups of people can question established orders. Susan Stall and Ralph Stoecker, reviewing the resistive possibilities of community, assert that

> behind every successful social movement is a community or a network of communities. When these communities are effectively organized, they can provide social movements with important benefits...[They] provide a free space where members can practice "prefigurative politics," attempting to create on a small scale the type of world they are struggling for. (1998, pp. 729-730).

Thus, "community's" containment effects can be read as both practices of resistance and governance, two sides of the same functions of modern power (see Cruikshank, 1999). These co-existing yet oppositional possibilities interfere with (and also depend on) each other, often making governance and/or resistance unstable. It is this paradox, the possibility of social discipline and denial, that community organizers are often trying to resolve through the way we talk about community practice. Our selves are recognized through radical and/or professional or skeptical versions of white feminist community organizing stories that provide competing possibilities of identity and practices. In trying to make visible the ways in which we use concepts such as community and the narrative structures of our work, we let the contradictions of our practice become visible, which opens up the opportunity for a reflective practice.

In the organizing process a community can be described, named, counted, assessed and changed. In organizing literature, communities are known as groups of people who organize themselves into various "types": geographic, functional or a group that comes together around an interest (Lee, 2001, p.17). But this is only an initial observation. It is also clear that a community can be evaluated in terms of their "capacity," "competency" and even degrees of "goodness" (see Fellin, 1987; Kretzmann & McKnight, 1993). It is with these assessments that the site of community becomes the mechanism through which moral citizenry is the idealized goal. Although such terms of evaluation are developed outside of disadvantaged communities, in academic and professional contexts, they offer a particularly universal seduction.[1] For a competent, good community that is full of capacity is also a respectable community. Respectability becomes the moral marker of middle-class superiority (Razack & Fellows, 1998, p.346), offering a tempting payoff for rehabilitating oneself as an active citizen. Such rehabilitation is often envisioned and enacted by community workers who encourage citizenry through the roles of volunteer, advocate and community leader.

---

[1] Though seductive these evaluations are often resisted. Seductions style bodily desires. They offer the visions into which we make ourselves. While ever present, subjects possess the agency to resist or comply with progressing seductions. People excluded from the middle-class respect ability resist the markers of respect ability through innumerable practices that are recognized as disrespectable. Such resistance also holds a particular appeal, for the role of enemy can offer its own seduction.

Configurations of Whiteness in Community Practice

Feminist organizing, when imagined through histories of social work, is largely remembered within the white middle-class project of social reform that formed alliances with the struggles of racialized communities (see Ware, 1992, p.108). Part of knowing feminist organizing as a "good" project came through white women's alliances with abolitionist and civil rights struggles. While these alliances are often remembered as white women's acts of saving "other" women, they also provide the possibility of a feminist organizing subject (Heron, 1999, pp. 76-78). In other words, they helped constitute spaces of public subjectivity for white women (Rogers, 1998, p.103), and as a result, feminist organizing constituted notions of a gendered citizenship performed by white women "helping others."[2]

Though Sojourner Truth, Harriet Tubman, Ida B.Wells and Rigoberta Menchu (among others) all present possibilities for remembering feminist organizing as a multi-racial project, mainstream organizing narratives tend to see these bodies as contesting the meanings of feminist organizing. Most often these women's stories are remembered as the struggles of "others," while the beginnings of a "professional" feminist community organizing, and connectedly social work, rely on white bodies to signify an organizer in relation to poor women of colour as members of the communities who were to be organized (Adamson, Briskin, & McPhail, 1988; Mitchinson, 1987; Wills, 1992; Valverde, 1991). The practices of what we might now define as "feminist organizing" by women of colour remain largely inaccessible within entrenched narrative possibilities (see Hill Collins, 1990, pp. 139-161; Guitierrez & Lewis, 1995). So a woman of colour who engages with practices of feminist organizing is seen as disrupting an established norm (in terms of radical activism), and not performing within knowable versions of the "professional" community organizing story. Feminist organizing practices are part of the narrative through which white women can be thought of, and think of themselves as, white (Heron, 1999). It shores up the certainty that one is white by positioning bodies within racially appropriate practices (Rogers, 1998).

Tropes of community and histories of whiteness haunt contemporary community organizing by white women. In the next section, I explore how the contradictions of a colonialist-radical history are managed in today's community organizing discourse. Through such an exploration, I hope to find ways that white feminist community organizers may be able to attend to the ambiguities

---

[2] There are some complexities to this story. First, claims to citizen ship have often been made through alliances. It is possible that such movements, in and of themselves, demand "helping" others. So, for instance, Fred erick Douglas's fight for citizenship among black people also involved allying with the predominantly white women's struggle for suffrage. Also important to note is that femi nist struggles for gendered citizenship have required that women help themselves. Finally, notions of the interconnectedness of systems of oppression have shaped the ways in which white women become active in the public sphere. Many feminist struggles have rested on notions of needing to transform oppression generally, not just for certain groups of women and have perceived their work as requiring a broader struggle than one based solely upon women's liberation (see Adamson et al. 1988).

and uncertainties of our work (see Rossiter, 2001). To do so includes attending to the narratives that suggest that working with communities is radical, in fact, revolutionary. At the same time, we need to attend to how our vision of radical community practice intersects with other narratives that mobilize community as an object of professional intervention, a means by which white feminist organizers can secure themselves as members of the middle class. And finally, we also need to respond to the whispers that our work is, in fact, not creating the revolution we so often speak about, but instead secures existing relations of inequality. All three of these narratives are made possible through tropes of community that offer the fluidity to imagine our work as holding innumerable possibilities for social change and middle-class security.

Narrativity and Community

I am going to draw out narratives of "professionalism," "radicalism" and "skepticism" and in order to understand the shape of the terrain upon which white feminist community organizers recognize and understand others and ourselves. My choices of these three storylines is problematic, since they are so embedded among a series of ever-shifting narratives that to highlight them separately is to stabilize feminist organizing in a way that fails to reflect the fluidity of our identity claims. However, for the purpose of beginning this exploration, I am highlighting these stories as unfinished "fictions" of white feminist community organizing. The contradictory and unending nature of these fictions provides both the language to speak as a knowable subject and the hiding spaces, vulnerabilities and, most importantly, the uncertainties that locate the performance of feminist organizing as an act of becoming (rather than being) an organizer. This makes visible the claims feminist organizers make towards certain idyllic representations that are mourned and/or affirmed through radical, professional and skeptical narratives. What follows, then, is an exploration of the concrete and symbolic practices that are negotiated when white women claim the location of feminist organizer through performances of self as radical, professional and/or oppressor. These narratives continually evolve and shift, twist against one another and expand. Such a deconstruction makes visible some of the more subtle ways in which structural relations are deeply connected to the ways in which we limit and produce ourselves in everyday life.

The "professionalism" version

When I look through stories of white feminist organizers, professional narratives are often most clearly visible in moments where they signify a desire for middle-class security through social work. These narratives focus on middle-class histories of interventions into the social, but supporting them are the whispers of radicalism. To recognize white feminist organizing on these terms requires forgetting the possibility of community organizing as enabling relations of dominance. The breadth and fluidity of professionalism make such patterns of recollection possible.

Narratives of professionalism trace late nineteenth- and early twentieth-century interventions into poor communities onto present practices and identities. They draw on century-old memories of upper middle-class, religious white women intervening in the homes of people who were considered poor, and often "foreign" (see Mitchinson, 1987). Professional narratives weave through feminist organizing stories, locating these nineteenth-century men and women as the precursors of contemporary social workers, a category that would eventually expand to include some feminist community organizers.

Professional narratives capture the emergence of the "social worker" between 1910 and 1930, when various paid workers in social welfare services mobilized to distinguish themselves from charity workers and those involved in organized philanthropy (Walkowitz, 1999, p.27). Through articulating a category of "social work," these workers made claims to a scientific and/or technical authority and middle-class respectability. Professional narratives signify this authority and status, but remain difficult to situate firmly within specific class locations (Burrage, 1990). Radical narratives intersect with professionalism, mobilizing the concept as both an authoritative claim to middle-class status and as an object of authority and status that organizers critique.

There are at least three narratives regarding how community organizing came to be considered as a part of a profession called "social work." The first plot relies on a pre-existing profession of social work that splits in two directions. Some workers are remembered as intervening at the level of communities while others continued to intervene in individualized spaces (Woodroofe, 1971, pp. 56-61). A second narrative suggests that social work came to know itself in terms of its diversity and fragmentation, with workers in various locations (i.e., settlement houses, hospitals and so forth) (see Walkowitz, 1999, p.35). A third story remembers community organizing in terms of a rather loosely organized group of individuals interested in rejuvenating democracy, but without any shared training or specific practices, who found themselves caught within social work's "administrative structure" (Lubove, 1968, p.180). In each of these versions community organizing is accounted for in terms of its connection to a social work structure, and it is when links between social work and community organizing evolve that professional narratives are most visible.[3]

Even within professional narratives of feminist organizing, however, claims for a professional identity are uncertain. Social work itself must faithfully repeat demands to be recognized as a legitimate profession, continually mourning why it is often not recognizable as such. Claims to professional (read: middle-class) locations are equivocal when social work is measured against the empirical certainties of medicine, law and engineering, professions that are more easily

---

[3] There is a significant amount of community organizing that has not emerged from social work. In fact, the Alinsky style of organizing (1971), for example, emerged as a critique of social work, but would later be co-opted by some who practice and/or teach community organizing from within social work. There are also many globally diverse approaches to community organizing such as the African examples explored by Barbara Heron (1999) or the work of Paulo Freire (1972).

imagined in terms of scientific authority and middle-class security. So to secure recognition as a profession, social work systematically attempts to re-signify itself in terms of measurable, teachable technologies that are located in a code of ethics.[4] To mediate any uncertainty, professional narratives of community organizing offer an imagined talk of teachable expertise — skills, strategies, tools and tactics (see Burghardt, 1982; Lee, 1999; Shaw, 1996). For the most part, the narrative of professionalism is disembodied, referring to specific practices and skills that when performed by certain bodies in certain contexts signify a "professional" organizer (Cox & Garvin, 1970; Kretzmann & McKnight, 1993).

At times, feminist community organizers draw upon such narratives in attempting to make themselves visible within generalist (masculine) constructions of community organizing (see Adamson, Briskin, & McPhail, 1988; Acklesberg, 1988; Dominelli, 1995; Weeks, 1990). Early practices of community organizing were largely created by first-wave feminists (Wills, 1992; Guitierrez & Lewis, 1995), but after World War II, community organizing was largely perceived as a masculine practice of social work and became increasingly known in terms of masculine memories. As a result, many contributions of feminist organizers were forgotten (Wills, 1992; Dominelli, 1995) and are, at times, being reclaimed through professional narratives.

At the same time, professional narratives also enable a forgetting of feminist organizing. In a discipline that is liminally recognized as a profession, the more quantifiable practices of social work, those that can be articulated in terms of "scientific" theories (for example, therapy drawing on psychoanalytic theories) tend to dominate. Meanwhile, less scientifically based practices such as organizing are sidelined within the academic curriculum (Lee et al., 1996). As a result, community organizing stories often lament a lack of recognition as a secure professional practice. This practice of struggling against erasure forefronts narratives of professionalism, particularly normative masculine thinking about "the professional," so we may reposition ourselves as legitimate practitioners.

As we contemporary white feminist organizers reclaim our own history, the variety and complexity of community organizing — particularly, as I have noted, the practices of women of colour and working-class women that may not fit within "professional" ideas of organizing — is often forgotten or offered up in terms of marginal contributions (Gutierrez & Lewis, 1995). In an effort to be recognized we attend to those practices that are easily made visible within existing frames of knowledge, namely white middle-class conceptions of community organizing. This is not to suggest that feminist organizing literature does not tell stories of organizing with women of colour, but what becomes most visible in terms of professional feminist organizing are practices by women who declare themselves as feminists and work explicitly towards the liberation of

---

[4] Attempts to shore up the scientific efficiency of social work have been part of the making of social work itself. Mary Richmond and her infamous efforts to systematize case work is an early example of such attempts (Margolin, 1997).

women. This can make it more difficult to recognize the contributions of women whose work and lives are not necessarily signified in terms of white middle-class feminism.

The imagined autonomy of community organizing suggests that the organizer herself is a self-regulated, moral citizen who does not require supervision. At the same time, job insecurity, low salaries and occasional (or not so occasional) acts of social protest against the resurgence of laissez-faire capitalism suggest that these claims are shaky. So, while professional community organizing is most easily situated as the property of the middle class, it often signifies some of the uncertain edges of notions of class. In the end, professional narratives promise the possibility to secure claims to the middle class while attempting to remain innocent of the relations of dominance upon which the idea of professionalism rests. It is a promise that is never obtained, always unfinished and haunted by other narrative possibilities that make for unstable terrain. In fact, it is the haunting of radical narratives, often left unspoken in professional discussions, that provides the conceptual promise of an "innocent professional."

The "radicalism" and/or heroic version

Radical narratives are most often, though not always, mobilized by people within progressive movements to account for the actions of many working-class people and people of colour whose practices are marginalized within notions of professionalism (for example, see Matthiesson, 1973; Grant, 1990). At the same time, they offer middle-class white women a route to understanding their motives as organizers as "good." Without relinquishing the possibilities of radical stories of oppressed groups achieving progressive social change, I want to unpack the ways in which heroic narratives work to stabilize certain stories of white feminist community organizing.

A heroic narrative of feminist organizing is a second path white women use to account for our practices of naming ourselves and "saving others." At times it is firmly based in women's reclamations of our contributions to achieve social change. Cheryl Hyde observes that

> contributions of women activists have been virtually ignored by the field of social work. Consequently, social work has a diminished knowledge base and has alienated large numbers of talented women. Ironically, both the past and the future of community organizing is tied intimately with the action of women. Foremothers include Jane Addams, Dorothea Dix and Lillian Wald. (1986, p.545)

Given the exclusion of many women's contributions from collective memories of the past, these are important celebrations of a women's history — or at least a white women's history. At other moments, feminist organizing has been, and remains, a practice of "saving other" women, and these acts are similarly made sense of in heroic terms. Radical narratives invoke a sense of agency and allow the possibility of recognizing what are often undervalued, difficult to work towards, idealized notions of social justice. They are narratives that can engender hope at times when it is often difficult to envision the possibility of social change (see Bishop, 1994).

Stories of radicalism are broadly woven throughout practitioners' images of community organizing. Here, community organizers are recognized through their heroic resistance to oppression and their links with social change movements, and include the likes of Mohandas K. Ghandi, Malcolm X, Saul Alinsky, Caesar Chavez, Rigolberta Menchu, Sylvia Pankhurst and Dorothy Day. Again, some of these heroes are remembered for their work to change conditions for themselves and people whose struggles they share, while others are remembered for their support of struggles for social change in communities of "others."

Although, or maybe since, most community organizers remain in relative obscurity, it is the stories of heroes and heroines that promise the ideals of social change, community and organizing towards which our practices are oriented. These are memories that affirm ideals and often resist dominant social discourses. The trickiness of the heroine terrain is that it lets us avoid certain truths about the ways in which our work is complicit in relations of dominance — stories that rely on our agency make it difficult to address the uncertainties and dangers of organizing practices.

The possibility of speaking about community organizing as a radical practice requires a story that is somewhat distant from representations of the professional. This reconstruction is imagined by disconnecting community organizing from modernity and reconstructing it as a transhistorical story (see Lee, 1999). It is also supported by re-envisioning modern histories to accentuate the intimacy of organizers with disadvantaged communities and their distance from other exclusionary professional groups. To achieve this, writers such as Fred Cox and Charles Garvin tell stories of early organizing in the following terms:

> charity organization leaders were persons closer to the upper classes of society, and epitomized *nobless oblige*. They favored either reforming the poor or modifying the most adverse of their social circumstances. Although exceptions on both sides can be cited, the settlement house workers were a different breed. Typically well educated and drawn from the middle-classes, they were frequently critics of the social order who identified with and shared the lives of the poor in some measure. (1970, p.42)

Such remembrances obscure many of the similarities between community organizers and clinical social workers while enhancing organizers' proximity with disadvantaged communities. This requires faith in the possibility that people who are not poor can "share" in the lives of people who are poor and, moreover, give useful advice to them. It is a belief in the promise of friendly relations between classes.

Within radical and/or heroic narratives we therefore come to know ourselves as allies with the dispossessed. This styling of self makes it difficult to consider oneself as a feminist community organizer without positing oneself as innocent in oppressive relations, or even more than innocent, as actively resisting hierarchical practices of social ordering. The heroic narrative is linked to the necessity of a moral citizenry; it is the possibility to be "good." For example, Lena Dominelli describes the Greenham Common women's Peace Movement strategies as exemplifying one of women's most exciting attempts at organizing ourselves in massive numbers according to the principles of feminist community action in modern times. Capturing the imagination of the public worldwide, it terrified the Anglo-American military machine. (1995, p.137)

Although providing an account of feminist organizing, the dramatic language of heroism leaves little room to envision feminist community organizing as *in excess* of acts of social-political resistance. The veracity of this fiction is supported by the difficult nature of the work — it becomes impossible (or so we believe) to put in the long hours and the often-unappreciated work if one does not firmly believe that such work promises social justice. By avoiding the problem of our complicity in maintaining systems of race and class, we keep alive a sense of inspiration and hope based in the apparent righteousness of our tasks.

At times identity formations are externally motivated. Our assertions of radical agency are partly in response to the intensity of broad social responses that understand feminists as dangerous or ineffective. Heroic narratives offer the possibility to rehabilitate feminist activism historically. Throughout their history feminists have been posited as members of the "dangerous classes" (see McClintock, 1995, p.5), and this representation of feminist organizing continues to resonate across society.[5] In opposition to such social perceptions, feminists re-present themselves as heroines in the struggle for social change, offering the possibility of recognizing themselves as moral citizens within societies that question the morality of feminism. In other words, in an effort to value past contributions of women who have historically been considered socially deviant, feminists rewrite them as heroes.

The "skepticism" version

The skeptical version of white middle-class feminist organizing is particularly seductive for me, as an academic, because of its exclusion, because it is so uncomfortable to confront and so difficult to maneuver around in everyday life. It is perhaps also seductive because, if a white middle-class feminist organizer believes it and speaks it, the skeptical narrative promises another type of innocence.

From one perspective, the problematic feminist organizer, imagined through skeptical narratives, is described in terms of the threat that feminists pose to established relations of racism, classism and sexism. From another perspective, most often situated in academia, white feminist organizers are understood as enabling practices that support oppressive relations. In this latter version, the feminist organizer sometimes takes dramatic form in a Foucauldian universe of discipline and punishment, populated by docile bodies. White feminist

---

[5] Susan Faludi (1991) outlines the various ways in which this stereo type still exists in her book *Backlash: The Und clared War Against American Women* (see especially pages 290-296). More recently, Jerry Falwell, during an appearance on the reli gious television show *700 Club* placed "a lot of the blame [for the terrorist attacks of September 11th]… on pagans, abortionists, feminists, gays and lesbians" (Falwell, 2001).

organizing is revisioned as complicit in broader practices of social reform that are perceived as reproducing oppressive relations in their engagement with "strategies for governing the very subjects whose problems they seek to redress — the powerless, the apathetic, or those at risk" (Cruikshank, 1999, p.2). In these stories altruism and sacrifice are read as gendered, raced, classed narratives obscuring our complicity in practices of containment (Heron, 1999; and more generally, Rogers, 1998; Razack & Fellows, 1998). While seemingly threatening to and condemnatory of white feminist community organizing, such critical narratives also present knowable subjects with definitive practices. Though this narrative proves the most difficult for organizers (and for me) to engage with until our livelihoods no longer rely on organizing, it is only one of many readings of the landscape of feminist organizing. At the same time, skeptical narratives may be part of the stylization of a mournful subject, a lament over the lost heroism in community organizing. They are, for many of us, a practice of separating the lost ideal of an innocent feminist activism outside of ourselves. By remembering feminist organizing solely in terms of its complicities, we are able to disconnect ourselves from the ideal of social change that we had been promised, and that is now lost. In so doing, we attempt to access another kind of innocence, so the distanced academic can speak back to community work to achieve some sort of redemption in her new space.

Skeptical narratives describe the origins of interventions in the social arising from the turn-of-the-century development of cities, full of people of different races, classes and nationalities. This period has been described as one in which

> people were profoundly suspicious of one another, and the monied classes were fearful of uprisings and mass violence, as if the entire community might at any moment erupt into a carnival of murder and crime...Because the sudden accumulation of people mainly occurred from among the foreign born and the impoverished, because these people lived in separate districts and were mostly unheard and unknown their very existence created economic, political and medical panic. Thus, the Haymarket Square riot of 1886 is significant, not so much because someone threw a bomb at a labor union meeting, killing and wounding many police and bystanders, but rather because a whole class of people — the poor, especially the immigrant poor — was held responsible. (Margolin, 1997, p.14)

Here the colonizing anxiety was not about "darkest Africa" but instead focused on the fears of losing control of the city to "internal enemies" (Stoler, 1996, p.96). Although contemporary community organizing is quite different from the organizing work that was practiced at the turn of the century, white feminist community organizers are some of the very few middle-class members who have daily contact with those living in poverty within the city. The colonializing imagery used to make sense of domestic colonial practices such as settlement houses (see Valverde, 1991, p.140) still haunt modern feminist organizing. For most members of modern society, the poor only exist as manifest in the media, and contemporary fears of these populations are evidenced in laws that prohibit panhandling, punitive social assistance programs, and the ever-present NIMBY-ism (not-in-my-backyard) of urban communities.

Feminist community organizers have a fragile, often contradictory, participation in these negotiations. Within skeptical narratives, their work is remembered as the "practical arts of liberal government" (Cruikshank, 1999, p.43) whereby we assuage the anger and resistance of the working-class and poor. This skeptical narrative pales in comparison to the neo-liberal skepticism that imagine feminist organizers as largely ineffectual, but also traitors to middle-class interests.

The skeptical narrative relies on an unrelenting and at times overly enthusiastic engagement with Foucauldian analysis. Although sympathetic to the idealism of community organizing, writers such as Barbara Cruikshank (1999) and Barbara Heron (1999) offer few possibilities for surveying a landscape of white women's community organizing as anything but a doomed project that inevitably facilitates the effective operation of oppressive modern power relations. As Heron notes,

> Although our commitment to development work is primarily about social justice, the *de facto* acceptance of the existence of the development worker option in participants' narratives affirms that our desire for development is deeply organized by the racialized, moral and self affirming (for bourgeois subjects) colonial legacies of planetary consciousness, and entitlement and obligation to intervene elsewhere in the world. All of these normalized through the pervasive operation of discourse, and intersect in Canada's national story of "good guys of the world." From the time of decision to go overseas, the bourgeois narrative of self as moral is invoked, calling nationalistically to "good women" across the prohibitions of Othered spaces. (1999, p.225)

In no small measure, the story of social work villainy arises as a counter-narrative to the postmodern bogeyman of heroic, whiggish histories, which makes it equally difficult to see through it and into possibilities that feminist organizing is constituted by an interweaving of unfinished narratives. While providing an important counterbalance to radical stories, the trickiness of the skeptical version is its reliance on a certain forgetfulness. Here the dramatic changes that have moved us somewhat closer towards ideals of social justice are obscured by a general skepticism of the possibility of friendly relations between classes.

The Legacies of these Stories

While I present them as mutually exclusive, the narratives of the professional, the radical agent of social change and the complicit oppressor are productive precisely because they diverge and cross over one another, the possible and impossible. They also gain currency because they are employed through various community tropes that are so embedded in our democracy. Using a discursive analysis, we can begin to explore the strategies used by feminist organizers to negotiate the desire for and contradictions inherent in the ideals of the radical change agent a, the professional and a performance heavily implicated in strategies of social governance. As a result, we may be able to develop a more critically reflective practice that challenges us to seek out innovative ways of unbecoming white feminist organizers. The goal of such reworkings cannot be to secure innocence in oppressive relations, but rather to engage with the present in all of its ambivalences; to see ourselves as ambivalent subjects, invested in achieving social justice, but also in maintaining a familiar social order in which we secure a significant amount of privilege. The result of this will always be an unfinished web of stories that hold onto traces of past narratives, often weaving together in contradictory ways that allow us to both avoid and explore new terrains towards future possibilities. By drawing on post-structural critical social work, I have explored the way we talk about our work, but also the context in which that talk occurs. By engaging in the project of creating a more critical, reflective community practice, I hope we will begin to imagine new local forms of liberation.

References

Acklesberg, M. (1988). Communities, resistance, and women's activism. In A. Bookman & S. Morgen, Eds., *Women and the Politics of Empowerment: Perspectives from the Community and the Workplace*. Philadelphia: Temple University Press, 1988.

Adamson, N., Briskin, L., & McPhail, M. (1988). *Feminists organizing for change*. Toronto: Oxford University Press.

Alinsky, S. (1971). *Rules for radicals: A pragmatic primer for realistic radicals*. New York: Vintage Books.

Anderson, B. (1997). *Imagined communities: Reflections on the origins and spread of nationalism* (Rev. ed.). New York: Verso Books.

Bishop, A. (1994). *Becoming an ally: Breaking the cycle of oppression*. Halifax: Fernwood Publishing.

Burghardt, S. (1982). *The other side of organizing*. Rochester: Schenkman Books, Inc.

Burrage, M. (1990). Introduction: The professions in sociology and history. In M. Burrage & R. Torstendahl (Eds.), *Professions in theory and history: Rethinking the study of the professions*. London: Sage.

Carniol, B. (2000). *Case critical: Challenging social services in Canada* (4 th ed.). Toronto: Between the Lines.

Cox, F., & Garvin, C. (1970). The relation of social forces to the emergence of community organization practice: 1856-1968. In F. Cox, J. Erlich, J. Rothman, & J. Tropman (Eds.), *Strategies of community organization: A book of readings*. Illinois: F.E. Peacock Publishers, Inc.

Cruikshank, B. (1999). *The will to empower: Democratic citizens and other subjects*. Ithaca: Cornell University Press.

Dominelli, L. (1995). Women in the community: Feminist principles and organizing in community work. *Community Development Journal, 30*(2), 133-143.

Dominelli, L. (1996). Deprofessionalizing social work: Anti-oppressive practice, competencies, and postmodernism. *British Journal of Social Work, 26*, 153-175.

Eliasoph, N. (1998). *Avoiding politics: How Americans produce apathy in everyday life*. Cambridge: Cambridge University Press.

Faludi, S. (1991). *Backlash: The Undeclared war against American women*. Anchor Books: New York.

Falwell, J. (2001, September 13). *700 club* (Television broadcast).

Fellin, P. (1987). *The community and the social worker*. USA: F.E. Peacock Publishers Inc.

Fook, J. (2002). *Social work: Critical theory and practice*. London: Sage.

Freire, P. (1972). *Pedagogy of the oppressed*. Penguin: Harmondsworth.

Grant, J. (1990). Civil rights women: A source for doing womanist theology. In V. Crawford, J.A. Rouse, & B. Woods (Eds.), *Women in the civil rights movement: Trailblazers and torchbearers 1941-1965* (pp.39-50). Bloomington & Indianapolis: Indiana University Press.

Gutierrez, L., & Lewis, E. (1995). A feminist perspective on organizing with women of color. In F. Rivera & J. Erlich (Eds.), *Community organizing: In a diverse society* (pp.95-112). Massachusetts: Allyn and Bacon.

Hall, S. (1996). Introduction: Who needs "identity'? In S. Hall and P. de Gay (Eds.), *Who needs "identity'?* London: Sage.

Harris, P. (2001). Towards a critical post-structuralism. *Social Work Education, 20*(3), 335-50. June 1, 2001.

Healy, K. (2001). Reinventing critical social work: Challenges from practice, context and postmodernism. *Critical Social Work, 2*(1). Retrieved from http://www.criticalsocialwork.com, September 9, 2002.

Heron, B. (1999). *Desire for development: The education of white women as development workers.* Unpublished doctoral thesis, Ontario Institute for Studies in Education, University of Toronto, Toronto, Ontario, Canada.

Hill Collins, P. (1990). *Black feminist thought: Knowledge, consciousness, and the politics of empowerment.* New York: Routledge.

Hyde, C. (1986). Experiences of women activists: Implications for community organizing theory and practice. *Journal of Sociology and Social Welfare, 13*, 545-562.

Kretzman, J., & McKnight, J. (1993). *Building communities from the inside out.* Illinois: Centre for Urban Affairs and Policy Research.

Lee, B. (2001). *Pragmatics in community organizing* (3rd ed.). Mississauga: CommonAct Press.

Lee, B., McGrath, S., Moffat, K., & Usha, G. (1992). Community practice education in Canadian schools of social work. *Canadian Social Work Review, 13*(2), 221-236.

Lubove, R. (1968). *The professional altruist: The emergence of social work as a career 1880-1930.* Massachusetts: Harvard University Press.

Margolin, L. (1997). *Under the cover of kindness: The invention of social work.* Charlottesville: University Press of Virginia.

Matthiesson, P. (1973). *Sal si puedes: Cesar Chavez and the new American revolution.* New York: Dell Publishing Co.

McClintock, A. (1995). *Imperial leather: Race, gender and sexuality in the colonial contest.* New York: Routledge.

Mitchinson, W. (1987). Early women's organizations and social reform. In A. Moscovitch & J. Albert (Eds.), *The benevolent state* (pp.77-89). Toronto: Garamond Press.

Mullaly, B. (1993). *Structural social work: Ideology, theory and practice* (2nd ed.). Don Mills, ON: Oxford University Press.

Muller, J., Walker, G., & Ng, R. (1990). Problematizing community organization and the state. In R. Ng, G. Walker, & J. Muller (Eds.), *Community organization and the Canadian state* (pp.13-28). Toronto: Garamond Press.

Pile, S. (1997). Introduction. In S. Pile & M. Keith (Eds.), *Geographies of resistance* (pp.1-32). London: Routledge.

Razak, S. & Fellows, M. (1998). Race to innocence: Confronting hierarchical relations among women. *Journal of Gender, Race and Justice, 2*, 335-352.

Rogers, K. (1998). *"Fairy fictions": White women as helping professionals.* Unpublished doctoral dissertation, Ontario Institute for Studies in Education, University of Toronto, Toronto, Ontario, Canada.

Rossiter, A. (2001). Innocence lost and suspicion found: Do we educate for or against social work? *Critical Social Work, 2*(1). Retrieved from http://www.criticalsocialwork..com on September 9, 2002.

Shaw, R. (1996). *The activist's handbook*. California: California University Press.

Singer, L. (1991). Recalling a community at loose ends. In The Miami Theory Collective (Ed.), *Community at loose ends* (pp.121-130). Minneapolis: University of Minnesota Press.

Stall, S., & Stoecker, R. (1998). Community organizing or organizing community? Gender and the crafts of empowerment. *Gender and Society, 12*(6), 729-756.

Stoler, A.L. (1996). *Race and the education of desire: Foucault's history of sexuality and the colonial order of things*. Durham, NC: Duke University Press.

Todd, S. (2002). *Organizing narratives: An exploration through friendship and mourning in women's stories of becoming feminist community organizers*. Unpublished master's thesis, Ontario Institute for Studies in Education, University of Toronto, Toronto, Ontario, Canada.

Valverde, M. (1991). *In the age of light, soap and water: Moral reform in English Canada 1885-1925*. Toronto: McClelland and Stewart.

Walkowitz, D. (1999). *Working with class: Social workers and the politics of middle-class identity*. Chapel Hill: The University of North Carolina Press.

Ware, V. (1992). *Beyond the pale: White women, racism and history*. London and New York: Verso.

Weeks, W. (1990). *Feminist principles for community work*. Paper presented at the Women in Welfare Education conference, Sydney.

Wills, G. (1992). Values of community practice: Legacy of the radical social gospel. *Canadian Social Work Review, 9*(1), 28-39.

Woodroofe, K. (1971). *From charity to social work: In England and the United States*. Toronto: University of Toronto Press.

10

Analysis of Social Location and Change: Practice Implications

Ben Carniol

C entral to critical social work is a critical consciousness that helps us to question our own practices. In this chapter, I explore ways that various privileges and oppressions not only influence our subjective view of the world, but also manifest themselves within North American societal structures. I will offer an analysis of social location and change in order to explore how social workers can work more effectively towards transforming oppressive realities into greater social justice.

Among Canadian social work educators, critical consciousness is being applied through a discourse about anti-oppressive practice, endorsed by the Canadian Association of Schools of Social Work. Its Accreditation Standards (2003) state that

> the curriculum shall ensure that students achieve transferable analysis and practice skills pertaining to the origins and manifestations of social injustice in Canada, and the multiple and intersecting bases of oppression, domination and exploitation. (Section 6.7 [c])

To encourage a critical consciousness about these multiple and intersecting bases of oppression, the curriculum of the School of Social Work, where I teach at Toronto's Ryerson University, focuses on a number of "isms." These "isms" include colonialism, racism, sexism, capitalism, heterosexism, ageism and ableism. This material is used as a springboard to support faculty, students and service providers to carry out critical forms of social work (Bishop, 2002; Campbell, 2002; Carniol, in press; Mullaly, 2002; Mullaly 1997).

In recent years postmodernism has unsettled a number of fields, ranging from art to history, from literature to politics. Not surprisingly, given their emphasis on diversity and subjective realities, postmodern theorists have also critiqued social work (Chambon, Irving, & Epstein, 1999; Fook, 2002; Healy, 2001; Rossiter, 2001). In response, some educators have suggested that social work should combine elements from postmodern and structural approaches (Fook, 2002, p.16; Ife, 1997, p.141). In this chapter I explore where such combinations may be feasible in relation to a focus on social location and change. I enter this task with some trepidation, given the sharp contradictions that exist between structural and postmodern approaches.

A benefit that Jan Fook (2002) reports from postmodernism is that it has helped to empower her work, particularly in her relationship to theory development. She states: "I am much more aware of using theory consciously in different ways and of developing a process of creating my own theory" (p.14). Fook suggests that, because it values subjective insights, a post approach frees the theorist-practitioner from some of the constraints of established theory. I must confess, I find it appealing to be able to create theory, and will attempt a bit of it, as I proceed with this chapter. I have picked the following seven areas of analysis based on my sense of what would be strategic in filling the gaps about ways that social workers can further develop emancipatory practices:

1. analyzing the main sources of inequalities: "isms";
2. analyzing harmful polarizations within oppressive realities;
3. analyzing the invisible privileges created by oppressive realities;
4. analyzing our own social location;
5. analyzing the social location of others;
6. analyzing sources of emancipation from oppressive realities; and
7. further practice implications from analyzing social location and change.

1. Analyzing the Main Sources of Inequalities: " Isms"

In my teaching and practice, I have found it helpful to begin by pointing to the reality of the multiple oppressive "isms" that impinge on specific situations. My understanding of these "isms" has meant learning about the deep historical roots and contemporary expressions of systemic inequalities based on such areas as gender, colour, sexual orientation, class and colonial relations. Yet here we bump into one of the major positions of postmodernism as expressed by Jan Fook (2002, p.12): "There is no one universal truth or reality, but instead 'reality' is constructed out of a multiplicity of diverse and fragmented stories."

As I reflect on the impact of the commercial privatization of public resources, I must admit that its impact will be felt differently in Montreal, Shanghai or Capetown. Moreover, each person in those three cities will experience the impact of global corporations in their own unique way. But does that diversity of experience negate the other more universal reality (Graham, Swift, & Delaney, 2003, pp. 90-95; Lightman, 2003, pp. 107-109) of top-down, secretive global decision making by the owners of capital? Just as male violence against Canadian women results in different subjective experiences — does that negate the prevailing reality of patriarchy within Canada and beyond its borders? (Carr, 1996, p.394).

In fairness, the post assumption that there is no one universal or prevailing truth does have emancipatory potential. That potential, it seems to me, stems from the lived experience of how dominant groups try to impose, or universalize, their opinions on everyone else. For example, colonial regimes and their missionaries felt that they represented a more "advanced" state of civilization compared to indigenous populations (Chrisjohn & Young, 1997). In Canada these attitudes of superiority constituted a reality that resulted in the assimilationist policies of forcibly removing young children from their

Aboriginal families and communities to be "educated" in distant Catholic, Anglican and United Church residential schools (Fournier & Crey, 1997). Similar examples of powerful decision-makers imposing their values upon others, as if their assumptions were universally true, can be found within the other "isms." This is similar to what has been called "hegemony": the process whereby the ideas of ruling groups become the ruling ideas (Gitlin, 1980).

Postmodernism helps to fragment such ruling ideas and universal "truths" propagated by domineering groups (Chambon, Irving, & Epstein, 1999). Instead of comfortable conformity to a monolithic version of "truth" as espoused by privileged elites, we are encouraged to recognize the diversity of experience and to value difference in such areas as culture, class and sexual orientation. Indeed here, post critiques and structural approaches, each with different frames of analyses, do undermine the privileging of dominant discourses.

While critical social workers welcome challenges to universal truth-claims that have oppressive consequences, does it follow, as post critiques claim (Davies & Barton, 2000, p.262), that universal truths do not exist? Actually, some post theorists seem uncertain. For example, when outlining what postmodernism has to offer, Karen Healy (2001, p.11) states that it "emphasizes that truths are always constructed through language, context and interpretation." Is she not suggesting a new universal truth? But aside from postmodern ambivalence, a fundamental question has been raised: are there no universal truths?

From my observation, based on four decades of work with diverse individuals and communities, it is self-evident that when it comes to certain values, there are indeed universal truths. For example, real democracy is better than tyranny; respect for human beings is better than killing them; protection of our environment is better than poisoning our air, water and soil; caring about others is better than indifference, prejudice, hatred or contempt.

Such universal values, based as they are on reducing harm to people, are consistent with social work values that seek to optimize human well-being. To practice such values, we need to be clear about another level of reality, namely, the reality of oppressive and exploitative societal structures. Recognition of this structural reality argues neither for its permanence nor for its desirability. That brings us back full circle to the "isms." Despite the diversity of personal stories, that diversity must not eclipse the prevailing reality of today's structural oppression and exploitation. Both sets of realities, I suggest, inform critical social work. This was also the message of theorists such as Maurice Moreau (1989; Moreau et al., 1993), a structuralist, and Helen Levine (1982), a feminist, both of whom were social work educators and clinicians, and who had a major influence on how structural approaches evolved in Canada (Carniol, in press).

2. Analyzing Harmful Polarizations within Oppressive Realities

In offering assistance to social service users, I have found it helpful to explain that oppressive "isms " signify groups of people who gain privileges at the expense of others. Structural theories suggest that a major source of conflict in society stems from the tendency of privileged groups to expand their power while the more powerless attempt to redress the power imbalance in their favour (Dahrendorf, 1970). Such a view, however, is rejected by postmodernism. Fook (2002) summarizes the post critique this way:

> One of the most cogent criticism of modernist construction of identity lies in the problem of dichotomous thinking. This is the tendency for language (and our conceptions of the world) to be constructed as binary opposites, creating forced categories of choice, often opposed to each other, in which one member of the pair is usually privileged. (p. 72)

The tendency that Fook refers to is reflected in familiar examples: rich/ poor, men/women and Whites/Blacks.

As Fook goes on to note, dividing people into polarized groupings de-emphasizes and negates people's real diversity of experiences. While Fook makes a valid point, must we accept the post conclusion, namely, that we should refrain from pointing to such dichotomies? In my opinion, such a conclusion is dangerous because it leads us to negating the very real, brutal and harmful differences of power that actually exist among certain groups.

Let's consider the master-slave dichotomy. While my awareness of it is still growing, there has been ample documentation about the cruelty inherent in the institution of slavery when huge numbers of African people were violently uprooted to be exploited in the Americas. Granted, at the time, there were many variations in the subjective experiences of both slaves and their masters. But there was also another reality: the dichotomous positioning of master-slave where masters coercively extracted free labour from their slaves. These binary opposites were so structured by the very institution of slavery. How could emancipation activists have succeeded in their struggle to dismantle this example of slavery if this vicious dichotomy had been downplayed or ignored?

I feel we must squarely face the dichotomy of "winners" and "losers" from oppressive realities. A current example comes from James Sears' (1997) definition of heterosexism:

> A belief in the superiority of heterosexuals or heterosexuality evidenced in the exclusion, by omission or design, of nonheterosexual persons in policies, procedures, events or activities. We include in our definition not only lesbians and gay men but other sexual minorities such as bisexuals and transgendered persons as well. (p. 16)

The illusion of superiority as part of the lived experience of heterosexists, accompanied by exclusion, not only creates harmful polarization, but it also perpetuates illegitimate privileges. A heterosexist privilege today is the power to define who qualifies for marriage, a turbulent topic in Canada. While attitudes are shifting, heterosexists still assert that only their sexual intimacies are "normal." This type of assertion is part of a long history of sexual minorities being labelled as sinners, criminals, mentally ill and deviant (Brotman et al., 2002). Similar harmful divisions are also experienced on the basis of unequal power between mainstream institutions and Aboriginal communities, between men and women, between the ruling class and everyone else, between Whites and other ethno-racial people, between the able-bodied and people with disabilities, and between adults and "senior citizens" (Carniol, *Case Critical,* in press).

Structural analysis suggests that these harmful polarizations spawn a multiplicity of prejudices and stigmas against those who are oppressed by these diverse social divisions. From my experience it is not unusual for those prejudices and stigmas to be believed and accepted, in different degrees, by service users when they experience disempowerment: this is sometimes called internalized oppression (Mullaly, 2002). Such beliefs can further erode a service user's confidence, motivation and self worth. This may lead to depression and sometimes to suicide. From my experience, when service users are able to discuss their lived reality in terms of externally structured dichotomies (for example, a female survivor of male violence, recognizing the illegitimacy of male power over her), I have noticed a shift in perception, and more precisely, a reduction of self-blame and shame, by service users.

3. Analyzing the Invisible Privileges Created by Oppressive Realities

Social workers are becoming more critically conscious about how internalized oppressions can become a large part of the service user's reality. We are less aware, I suggest, about internalized privilege. In her influential article "White Privilege: Unpacking the Invisible Knapsack," Peggy McIntosh (1998, pp. 147-148) addresses what she was taught *not* to see when educated about racism: "As a white person, I realized I had been taught about racism as something which puts others at a disadvantage, but I had been taught not to see one of its corollary aspects, white privilege, which puts me at an advantage."

She lists some of her white privileges: If she needs legal or medical help, her race will not work against her. She is never asked to speak for all the people of her racial group. She goes on to note that "Whites are carefully taught not to recognize white privilege, just as males are taught not to recognize male privilege" (p. 148). This process has been further analyzed by June Yee and Gary Dumbrill (2002) in terms of the whiteness that shapes the lives of both white people and people of colour in North America: "The essence of Whiteness lies in its power to establish and maintain a silent discourse that so equates normality with White culture that this culture becomes taken for granted as the norm" (p.103).

Consequently, there is little or no questioning of the power exercised by European elites in structuring whiteness as society's reference point for judging different ethno-racialized people. A similar structural analysis within each of the other oppressive "isms" would show that the illegitimate privileges of other dominant groups are also hidden by unquestioned norms. When post theories deconstruct oppressive norms in order to resist them by, for example, challenging the unjustified universality of assumptions held by dominating groups, post critiques reinforce structural approaches. This example suggests that structuralists and postmodernists can find common ground from which to de-legitimize some of the sources of multiple oppressions.

4. Analyzing Our Own Social Location

Postmodernism can probably be credited with our growing awareness about the multiple identities that each person carries. In terms of our lived reality, each one of us is more than the colour of our skin. We also have a gender and sexual reference, an age, and belong to a class. We may also have a disability. We may have an Aboriginal or other ethnic and/or cultural background.

As we consider the totality of our identities, we may feel contradictory pulls because parts of these identities provide us with disadvantages while others bring privileges. Using my own multiple identities as an example, I have received a bundle of privileges due to my being a White heterosexual male, without disabilities, and possessing a decent income. These privileges come from the reality of how the society in which I live is structured today. For most of my adult years, I benefited from privileges such as: never having to wonder about the colour of my skin or my sexuality; being able to have a middle-class standard of living; not being questioned as to my competence due to any disability. At the same time, I am also disadvantaged by my age, having just turned sixty-five. Also, I am Jewish. My age as a "senior citizen" has already caused me to experience ageism, such as being required by law to retire from full-time teaching, though this has been somewhat softened by the university offering me part-time employment. On the ethno-cultural dimension, my parents were killed because they were Jewish during the European Holocaust of World War II; I survived by being a hidden child in Belgium, and was later adopted into the family of my mother's sister living in Canada.

My social location, according to today's stratified societal structures in which I live, is a "snapshot" of the cumulate mix of my privileges and my oppressive circumstances. Yet that picture is incomplete because subjective realities also matter. It matters that I am engaged personally and politically in working to dismantle my systemic illegitimate privileges. Yet my subjective reality makes little difference to my social location at any given time. Privileges continue to flow to me. For example, my retirement income is on average higher than women's, even though at home my gender roles are based on egalitarian and power-sharing relationships.

Similarly, on the oppressive side of my social location, it matters that I am comfortable with my religious roots. It matters that caring people helped me to heal from my early childhood traumas. It matters that within the Jewish community, I belong to progressive networks that carry out activism to support the Israeli and Palestinian peace camps, seeking justice for both peoples in the Middle East conflict.

While these subjective realities make little difference to my present social location, they do make a difference to the kind of helper that I am. From this example and other experiences, I believe one can generalize to suggest that, while not altering one's social location at any one point of time, subjective realities are key to the question of personal agency, that is, to whether or not we will act towards transforming oppressive realities into social justice.

5. Analyzing the Social Location of Others

Once social workers have assessed their own social location, next steps include assessing the social location of the people we work with. Not surprisingly, despite some service users having some privileges, many are multi-oppressed, experiencing considerable stress due to many of the "isms." At the same time, substantial differences exist among oppressive conditions and also among subjective responses to these conditions.

At the very opposite end, within North America's societal structures, are the social locations of upper-class, White, male elites, who are multi-privileged on most if not all of the "isms." Again, subjective responses matter. A multi-privileged person may recognize their illegitimate privileges. More likely, they will see these as entitlements, motivating them to amass more privileges at the expense of others.

In between these extremes of social location are many individuals having a substantial mixture of privileges and oppressive conditions. Such mixture seems to reflect the social location of many public sector workers within health, education and social services. My impression is that this mixture is also common among the social location of many people within the middle and working classes.

Regardless of one's social location, subjective reality matters. While it does not modify that person's social location at any one point in time, subjective realities speak volumes about the direction a person is likely to take, such as wanting more privilege, being apathetic or becoming an activist for social justice. Over time, subjective realities can modify or dramatically change aspects of one's social location in terms of changeable identities. Though neither my age nor my Jewish background can be changed, I can choose to hide these as much as possible to "pass" for what I am not. This would alter my social location as perceived by others. A different kind of subjective reality may motivate someone to have surgery for a sex change, which, in turn, will impact the perceptions of others in terms of gender.

Perhaps the most familiar area of change within one's social location comes from upward or downward mobility due to income and wealth changes; this mobility is sometimes the result of subjective aspirations. At the same time, contrary to the sweeping claims of individualism, it is not accurate to conclude that only subjective reality, such as personal motivation, will determine changes in one's social location. Downward mobility can be caused by a global economic recession, resulting in major job and income losses. Upward mobility may be caused by the inheritance of a family fortune. These are bold reminders about the importance of both subjective and external structural realities in developing a critical consciousness about social location.

6. Analyzing Sources of Emancipation from Oppressive Realities

While the powers-that-be work hard at engineering our consent to various system-created inequalities, there is always the possibility that we will see through their false claims. People will give different reasons why this possibility exists. The explanations that attract me are grounded in an intuitive, subjective sense about the meaning of being human. It is a sense that, as human beings, we share a basic interdependence, anchored to an even deeper sense that life is a precious, sacred gift — a gift that is violated by oppressions yet healed by social justice (Heschel, 1996, pp. 314-317; Hanh, 1991). By social justice, I mean an ongoing process of replacing oppressive realities with greater social inclusion; that is, achieving more equity and more authentic participatory democracy at personal and institutional levels, from the local to the global (Canadian Centre for Policy Alternatives, 2003; Centre for Social Justice, 2003; *Tikkun Magazine*, 2003).

Building upon subjective resistance to oppression, another source of change is the coming together of people who experience similar oppressions, and who organize support to end these injustices. Within each of the multiple areas of inequality, distinct social movements already exist, such as those led by: Aboriginal peoples; feminists; African-North Americans and others disadvantaged by whiteness; gay, lesbian, bisexual and transgendered people; labour movement activists; anti-poverty advocates; older adults; people with disabilities; environmentalists; and anti-corporate-globalization activists (Carniol, *Case Critical*, in press).

These diverse social movements are today typically decentralized, and grassroots. They are fluid, tackling different issues, having an ebb and flow of lesser or greater influence depending partly on their leadership and on public opinion. Social movements are typically trivialized or otherwise marginalized by the backlash of dominating groups who fear a loss of privilege. Nevertheless, social movements seem to be holding their own (Barlow & Clarke, 2001), tapping into subjective resistance and increasingly developing coalitions to carry out their historical role of being catalysts for more democracy and more equity (Piven & Cloward, 1979).

7. Further Practice Implications from Analyzing Social Location and Change

Resistance to oppressive realities

Among their immense contributions to our critical consciousness, feminists exposed the processes of silencing which devalued women's lived experiences. This silencing became understood as one of the tools used by patriarchy to induce women to internalize sexist and misogynist stereotypes. Such internalized oppression was challenged by the Women's Movement several decades ago as it nourished consciousness-raising groups that linked the personal with the political (Miles & Finn, 1982; Adamson, Briskin, & McPhail, 1988;

Bricker-Jenkins, 2002). Feminist social workers, such as Helen Levine (1982), affirmed the importance of subjective experiences and critiqued the artificial split between the private and public spheres of women's lives.

Critical social workers applied feminist approaches to help service users to reclaim their voices and their own stories. I see feminist approaches being at least partly supported by a post emphasis on subjective dimensions to support a diversity of stories, narratives and voices that were previously silenced. These processes also challenged the Women's Movement itself to become more inclusive, to move beyond its earlier history of being primarily White, middle class and heterosexual (Barnoff, 2001).

Feminists and postmodernists have also questioned the tendency of labelling difference as "other." The professional practice of impersonal classification, such as in the mental health field, was often built on a foundation of elitist attitudes, which ended up dehumanizing service users. Challenging such top-down professionalism, postmodernism, along with structural approaches informed by feminism, were joined by another influential source: the writings of Paolo Freire (1971). He felt that to resist oppression, we should begin by explicitly naming it and by analyzing it thoroughly from the vantage point of the oppressed.

Partly as a result of these influences on practice, what follows is a small sample of what critical social workers do: listening, listening and listening more to what service users are telling us; advocating to meet basic needs for food, shelter, money and emotional and/or political support; helping to counteract experiences of being isolated, voiceless and trapped; validating strengths; exploring links between stressors and oppressors; re-framing, using a critical consciousness; sharing the power of our understandings; and helping to unmask various "isms."

Social workers in general respect the individuality of service users and their unique strengths and challenges, but critical social workers go further by challenging the individualism that places total responsibility on that person's shoulders. Social workers in general empathize, communicating an understanding of the service user's feelings about their situation, but critical social workers go further by widening the focus beyond conventional systems and ecological social work. We do this by encouraging social empathy — a recognition of the painful realities experienced by other people similarly oppressed (Fook, 1993, pp. 112-114).

The recognition of commonalities within oppressive realities may lead to collective resistance. Despite suspicion and hostility from funders, there are social workers who persevere in organizing community-wide resistance to multiple oppressions (Lee, 1999). In this area of resistance, skills used by social workers include: organizing public forums and social action campaigns, supporting grassroots leadership, working with the mass media to mobilize public opinion, applying political pressure against harmful institutional practices, helping to build viable and democratic community organizations, linking up with other existing grassroots networks and social movements.

Dismantling privileges

Even in resisting oppression we begin to dismantle privileges because our resistance helps to undermine the legitimacy that surrounds the status quo. Beyond resistance, we use our critical consciousness to deepen our awareness by asking: "What are the invisible, illegitimate privileges that I have? How can I become more involved in structural change aimed at dismantling such privileges?"

This brings me to the teachings of Wabano Kwe (Barbara Riley), a respected Ojibway Elder who has regularly visited our university to assist mainstream social work students and faculty to unlearn myths about colonialism. She teaches about the importance of spirituality within Aboriginal perspectives. When Wabaono Kwe refers to spirituality, she is not referring to theological dogma. She is referring to something that I believe many of us experience — a sense of awe at the delicate yet powerful interdependence of the various parts of the universe. Her teachings about Ojibway culture suggest how spirituality can invigorate our human qualities, such as courage and humility.

Applying Aboriginal teachings (Hart, 2002) to critical social work, I realize it takes courage to face how we, as social workers, have colluded with oppressive realities to reinforce privilege at the expense of others. It takes humility to let go of our subjective and defensive denials about our privileges. For example, it was not easy for me to recognize that for years I have benefited much from life in different North American cities, while all along making no links between my benefits and the genocidal policies that killed Aboriginal peoples in order to steal their land.

Critical consciousness about such privileges is not intended to create guilt. Anne Bishop (2002) has pointed out that what is more helpful than feeling guilty is for us to become allies to oppressed populations. We do that by being responsive to the subjective realities of oppressed individuals while also keeping a focus on dismantling illegitimate privileges.

Just as oppressions across the various "isms" intersect in complex ways, so too are privileges interconnected. That is why coalitions among different social movements are necessary for their transformative efforts. I feel that each of us should become active with at least one such coalition, or one social movement. Most movements welcome people with privilege who are willing to listen, not to lead, and to make their time, talents and professional skill available as allies and supporters of that movement. As Lena Dominelli (2002, p.148) points out, it is a mistake to assume that agency administrators will object to our alliances with community groups. Indeed, there are administrators in social agencies who are proactive in supporting social justice. From her study of three social service organizations engaged in mainstream fields of practice in Toronto, Purnima George (2003, p.56) found reason for hope: "These organizations have demonstrated different ways to adopt a holistic approach which increase their opportunity to engage in diverse activities that contribute towards the process of social transformation."

George's study focused on a structural social work approach that is holistic, which she defined as being inclusive of services spanning the levels from micro all the way to macro practice. She found that these social agencies were able to offer services geared to bringing about greater social justice.

Concluding Comments

This chapter offers ways of analyzing social location and change that hopefully will strengthen the practice of critical social work. On balance, compared with post approaches, I found that structural approaches, contextualized to Canada, were more helpful for emancipatory practice. On the other hand, there were areas where these different approaches found common ground in challenging multiple oppressions. Might there be a way to build on this common ground?

It is my hunch that a different kind of common ground may be feasible if we can develop a healthy climate of acceptance for differences, for example, between postmodern and structural approaches. An acceptance of these theoretical differences may free us as social work educators and as service providers to build greater solidarity among ourselves in resisting the multiplicity of illegitimate privileges. One potential focus for such solidarity is the ominous and ever-widening gulf between the rich and the poor, both within and across national boundaries. No wonder that resentments and hatreds are exploding, along with frantic defensive reactions, all of which are being inflamed into violence near and far.

Our challenge, I suggest, is to harness our courage and humility, by engaging ourselves as allies with social service users, helping to develop their grassroots organizations and social movements, listening to their priorities, their struggles, their needs and their requests for assistance. Once we respond to these realities, informed by our critical consciousness, I believe we will be taking a modest step forward in our quest for social justice.

Author's Note: I am appreciative of a number of colleagues who made helpful comments about earlier drafts: Shari Brotman, Purnima George, Steve Hick, Ken Moffatt, Dorothy Moore, Rhona Phillips and June Yee.

References

Adamson, N., Briskin, L., & McPhail, M. (1988). *Feminist organizing for change: The contemporary women's movement in Canada.* Toronto: Oxford University Press.

Barlow, M., & Clarke, T. (2001). *Global showdown: How the new activists are fighting global corporate rule.* Toronto: Stoddart Publishing.

Barnoff, L. (2001). Moving beyond words: Integrating anti-oppression practice into feminist social service organizations. *Canadian Social Work Review, 18*(1), 67-86.

Bishop, A. (2002). *Becoming an ally: Breaking the cycle of oppression — in people* (2nd ed.). Fernwood: Halifax.

Bricker-Jenkins, M. (2002). Feminist issues and practices in social work. In A.R. Roberts & G.J. Greene (Eds.), *Social workers' desk reference* (pp. 131-136). Oxford: Oxford University Press.

Brotman, S., Ryan, B., Jalbert, Y., & Rowe, B. (2002). The impact of coming out on health and health care access: The experiences of gay, lesbian, bisexual and two-spirit people. *Journal of Health and Social Policy*, *15*(1), 1-29.

Campbell, C. (2002). The search for congruency: Developing strategies for anti-oppressive social work pedagogy. *Canadian Social Work Review*, *19*(1), 25-42.

Canadian Association of Schools of Social Work. (2003). Manual of Accreditation Standards. Ottawa: CASSW. Retrieved from <www.cassw-acess.ca>.

Canadian Centre for Policy Alternatives. (2003). Retrieved from <www.policyalternatives.ca>.

Carniol, B. (1992). Structural social work: Maurice Moreau's challenge to social work practice. *Journal of Progressive Human Services*, *3*(1), 1-20.

Carniol, B. (in press). *Case critical: Social justice and social services in Canada* (5th ed.). Toronto: Between the Lines Publishers.

Carniol, B. (in press). Structural social work in Canada. In *Encyclopedia of social welfare history in North America*. Thousand Oaks, California: Sage Publications.

Carr, G. (1996). Patriarchy. In M. Payne, M. Ponnuswami, & J. Payne (Eds.), *A dictionary of cultural and critical theory* (pp. 394-396). Oxford: Blackwell.

Centre for Social Justice. (2003). Retrieved from <www.socialjustice.org>.

Chambon, A.S., Irving, A., & Epstein, L. (Eds.). (1999). *Reading Foucault for social work.* New York: Columbia University.

Chrisjohn, R., & Young, S. (with Maraun, M.). (1997). *The circle game: Shadows and substance in the Indian residential school experience in Canada.* Penticton, British Columbia: Theytus Books.

Dahrendorf. R. (1970). Social structure, group interests and conflict groups. In M. Olsen (Ed.), *Power in societies* (pp. 58-67). New York: Macmillan.

Davies, M., & Barton, R. (Eds.). (2000). *The Blackwell encyclopedia of social work.* Oxford: Blackwell.

Dominelli, L. (2002). *Anti-oppression social work: Theory and practice.* London: Palgrave Macmillian.

Fook, J. (1993). *Radical casework: A theory of practice.* St. Leonard's, Australia: Allen and Unwin.

Fook, J. (2002). *Social work: Critical theory and practice.* London: Sage.

Fournier, D., & Crey, E. (1997). *Stolen from our embrace: The abduction of First Nations children and the restoration of Aboriginal communities.* Vancouver: Douglas & McIntyre.

Freire, P. (1971). *Pedagogy of the oppressed.* New York: Herder & Herder.

George, P. (2003). *Going beyond the superficial: Capturing structural social work practice.* Research report for the Faculty of Community Services. Toronto: Ryerson University.

Gitlin, T. (1980). *The whole world is watching: Mass media in the making and unmasking of the new left.* Berkeley: University of California.

Graham J.R., Swift, D.J., & Delaney, R. (2003). *Canadian social policy: An introduction* (2nd ed.). Toronto: Prentice Hall.

Hanh, T.N. (1991). *Peace is every step: The path of mindfulness in everyday life.* New York: Bantam.

Hart, M.A. (2002). *Seeking Mino-Pimatisiwin: An Aboriginal approach to helping.* Halifax: Fernwood.

Healy, K. (2001). Re-inventing critical social work: Challenges from practice, context and postmodernism. *Critical Social Work*, *2*(1). Retrieved from <www.criticalsocialwork.com>.

Heschel. S. (Ed.). (1996). *Moral grandeur and spiritual audacity: Essays of Abraham Joshua Heschel.* New York: Farrar, Straus & Giroux.

Ife, J. (1997). *Rethinking social work: Towards critical practice.* Sydney, Australia: Addison Wesley Longman.

Lee, B. (1999). *Pragmatics of community organization* (3rd ed.). Toronto: CommonAct Press.

Levine, H. (1982). The personal is political: Feminism and the helping professions. In A.R. Miles & G. Finn (Eds.), *Feminism in Canada: From pressure to politics* (pp. 175-209). Montreal: Black Rose.

Lightman, E. (2003). *Social policy in Canada.* Toronto: Oxford University Press.

McIntosh, P. (1998). White privilege: Unpacking the invisible knapsack. In M. McGoldrick (Ed.), *Re-visioning family therapy: Race, culture and gender in clinical practice* (pp. 147-152). New York: Guildford.

Miles, A.R., & Finn, G. (1982). *Feminism in Canada: From pressure to politics.* Montreal: Black Rose.

Moreau, M. (in collaboration of Leonard, L.). (1989). *Empowerment through a structural approach to social work: A report from practice.* Montreal: Ecole de Service Social, University of Montreal, and Ottawa: School of Social Work, Carleton University.

Moreau, M., Frosst, S., Frayne, G., Hlywa, M., Leonard, L., & Rowell, M. (1993). *Empowerment II: Snapshots of the structural approach in action.* Ottawa: School of Social Work, Carleton University.

Mullaly, B. (1997). *Structural social work: Ideology, theory and practice* (2nd ed.).Toronto: Oxford University Press.

Mullaly, B. (2002). *Challenging oppression: A critical social work approach.* Toronto: Oxford University Press.

Piven, F.F., & Cloward, R.A. (1979). *Poor people's movements: Why they succeed, how they fail.* New York: Vintage.

Rossiter, A. (2001). Innocence lost and suspicion found: Do we educate for or against social work? *Critical Social Work, 2*(1), 1-10.

Sears, J.T. (1997). Thinking critically / intervening effectively about homophobia and heterosexism. In J.T. Sears & W.L. Williams (Eds.), *Overcoming heterosexism and homophobia: Strategies that work.* New York: Columbia University.

Tikkun Magazine. (2003). Retrieved from <www.tikkun.org>.

Yee, J.Y., & Dumbrill, G.C. (2002). Whiteout: Looking for race in Canadian social work practice. In J. Graham & A. Krenawi (Eds.), *Multicultural social work in Canada* (pp. 98-121). Toronto: Oxford University.

11

Post-Critical Social Work Analytics

Graham McBeath and Stephen Webb

The emergence of "critical social work" from the writings of Peter Leonard, Karen Healy and Jan Fook among others has its roots in the radical social work and community work in the 1970s within the U.K. In its socialist/Marxist guise, radical social work of thirty years ago, ironically given a fillip from the community development projects of the British Conservative Government of the time, opened up the question of social workers as agents of state power. More precisely, the question was about the reconciliation of the contradictory identity of the community worker as part agent of the state and as part agent and/or advocate of the working class (the "client" base). A crude but intelligible dialectics of dominant and subordinate forces, of state and/or social worker "against" the people, of professional language versus the vernacular, emerged from this. Theoretically speaking, this was an "essentialist" approach because of its appeal to a basic set of defined identities, and "reductionist," by explaining matters in terms of class.

Within social theory in the late 1970s "critical" theories emerged that rejected essentialist social explanations shaped by modernity's assumptions. They questioned the philosophical need to start from *universal* concepts such as self-consciousness (rationalism) and/or raw observations (empiricist positivism). Though coming late to social work, such perspectives have more recently led to a re-valuation of social work's universalist and Marxist approaches and of the organization of generic social work agencies (McBeath & Webb, 1991). This *anti-essentialism* claims that there are multiple starting points of equal status rather than one single one from which to assess the validity of social work interventions. It embraces what can be identified loosely as the "postmodern" revolution. This resistance to a basic "ontology" (claims about what exists), for example, God, human nature, "reason," out of which all else is derivable, expresses postmodernism's best-known figure — "fragmentation." Assuming multiple starting points founds explanations not on a single factor or a grounding "unity," but on "difference." "Difference" is basic to critical social work theory. What it is and, how it is used in social work theory and practice, forms much of our discussion.

It is our contention that the "postmodern project" within social work, falling under the broad title of "critical social work," does not fulfill the radical analysis it promises. Critical social workers soften up Michel Foucault's "postmodern" theses about the ubiquity of power to complement ethical ideals about human freedom that critical social work takes from a neo-Marxist critical theory tradition. The result — a simulacrum — a bad copy of radical thinking, has not the escape velocity to free critical social work from the gravitational pull of social work's traditional humanism.

The Idea of Critical Social Work

Critical social work tries to provide an answer to the question of how we can frame social work within the terms of a progressive politics. This partly reflects a desire to eradicate social injustice in contemporary Western economies. Consonant with such a project of linking situation to diagnosis and cure is the social science tradition of signposting a utopia at the crossroads of social analysis (Healy, 2001, p.1; Leonard, 2001, p.1).

Critical social work looks for a metaframework that sustains social and cultural pluralism. Here there is a desire for one account of justice that maximizes diverse individual and collective flourishing. The aim is to identify an essential form of justice without reducing the rich variation of human culture. Drawing on Doyal and Gough's "Theory of Human Need," Peter Leonard (1997, p.29) asks, "Can we...identify some universal preconditions for the expression and satisfaction of culturally produced needs?" The quest for a transcendental yet multicultural social and political theory has remained an unrealized project of the left.

Peter Leonard answers his own question, saying:

> If it were possible to build an emancipatory welfare project on a common understanding, reached through inter-cultural dialogue, of the centrality of difference and exploitation in the constitution of subordinacy, then we might find that a common signifier emerged which, for now, we might call the Universal Other (1997, p.30).

This emphasis on difference signals the birth of a postmodernism from the womb of his earlier class reductionist account of Marxism. Now class is seen as one, if a particularly influential, variable among many. This displacement of class as *the* universal signifier of oppression permits a re-theorization of radical social work in terms of alliances between relatively diffuse oppressed groups. Thus there are some neo-Gramscian tendencies within critical social work involving a strategy of counter-hegemony where essential differences fundamentally dividing "power" are resolved by a fight between the dominant constellation of forces and those seeking to displace it. Critical social workers' identification of "difference" as the driving force of their criticisms of established social work primarily underpins their postmodern turn. Their continuing search for a resolution of "difference," perhaps by new forms of practice, turns them towards Gramsci and critical theory.

Critical social work tends to use postmodernism and critical theory as strategies of thought rather than as specific theories. This allows for a variety of readings and engagements. As Jan Fook (2002, p.17) notes, "There are clearly many points of similarity between post-modern thinking and a critical approach." While critical social work carries with it an idea of an intellectual whole, it is clear there are divergent approaches within it. Critical social work theorists share certain key concepts and theoretical ideas. As Karen Healy (2000, p.13) comments, "[D]espite their obvious variations, what these critical approaches to practice share is their foundation in the critical social science paradigm...[T]here is a general endorsement of critical social science understandings about the nature of the social world and human existence." Critical social work generally understands postmodernism as a derivation of post-structuralism and deconstruction. Their take on critical theory is one that derives from neo-Marxism and feminist theory. Postmodernism and critical theory provide critical social work with the theoretical and political resources to deal with contemporary issues, particularly in relation to social justice, emancipation, power, oppression, exploitation and domination. Pease and Fook's foreword to *Transforming Social Work Practice* captures these emphases when they ask:

> How can we maintain what was positive and liberating in the critical tradition in social work, the emancipatory side of the Enlightenment, but still use post-modernism to deconstruct the problematic elements in the metanarratives of feminism, Marxism, and other critical perspectives to the point where reconstruction becomes possible? (1999, p.2)

Critical social work seeks to understand how dominant relations of power operate through and across systems of discourse, to deconstruct and reconstruct these discourses.

We note that critical social work has high hopes of a better, more expansive future. In summing up the characteristics of the postmodern and critical approach to social work, Fook says that "a post-modern and critical approach to social work is primarily concerned with practicing in ways which further a society without domination, exploitation and oppression" (2002, p.18). In harking back to the ideology critique of the Frankfurt school of critical theory, Richard Pozzuto (2000) explains that "the task of Critical Social Work is to lift the veil of the present to see the possibilities of the future." In his influential book *Challenging Oppression: A Critical Social Work Approach* (2002), Robert Mullaly proposes a psychology of emancipation for social work so that oppressed groups might resist the dominant hegemony that encourages them to internalize and blame themselves for their own oppression by accepting as normal and inevitable the present society and its oppressive social institutions.

Foucault is perhaps *the* most favoured "postmodern" thinker with critical social workers. While his politics are regarded as ambiguous, critical social work regards them as profitably situated in relation to critical theory. He provides theoretical ideas that open up new directions for critical social workers. They find in Foucault the prospects for an emancipatory project through a critique of "dominant discourses" and his notion of resistance to power. In Foucauldian vein, Peter Leonard (2001, p.5) points to the authority of dominant discourses along lines of exclusion and/or inclusion: "as Foucault would put it, those who are culturally authorized to speak for others are excluded from the discourse... The future prospects of critical social work might be determined by who is included in its discourse and who excluded." Self-reflection, reflective practice, dialogue, resistance and empowerment are seen as crucial components for social work in releasing the forces of emancipation in contemporary society (Healy, 2000; Fook, 2001, p.7).

In attempting to pull together postmodern and Foucauldian perspectives, critical social work is concerned with questions about the organization of power and knowledge. Chambon, Irving, and Epstein's *Reading Foucault for Social Work* (1999) problematizes social work as an instrument of state governmentality, a disciplinary agent that reproduces dominant discourses on gender, sexuality, ethnicity and old age. Here, social work is characterized as mediating and regulating the life world of clients in an oppressive way. In this vein it is argued that front-line practitioners exercise power over clients by implementing their versions of truth, social control and normalization. It regards the surveillance apparatuses of social work in conjunction with the state as regulating approved forms of family, intimacy, desire and addiction. And yet there is very little talk, or even recognition of "the state" in Foucault's work. Indeed, he insisted that "technologies of power" cannot be localized in a particular type of institution or state apparatus. His refusal to recognize the power of the state as an originating cause derives from his concern with "the micro-physics of power" (1975/1977a, pp. 26-27). Foucault (1984/1988, p.380) noted that "power is not discipline; discipline is a possible procedure of power." In critical social work, the regulatory function of social work is often coupled to a postmodern critique of social work organizations. Thus the recent restructuring of welfare systems has produced a postmodern "logic of management characterized by de-centered rationality, augmented practices and knowledge, and the dispersal of the individual subject" (Chambon, Irving, & Epstein, 1999, p.xvii). In critical social work thinking, the discourse of social work is similarly regarded with suspicion and viewed as potentially oppressive. As Healy (2000, pp. 61-62) notes, "[T]he insights of post-structural theory invites us to recognize that 'social work,' like all other entities, is constituted through discourse...[and] draws attention to the intolerance of differences that lie at the heart of social work practices, including critical practice approaches." While we are gratified that contingency and difference are seen as radically challenging the hegemonic relationship between social work theory, practice and institution, by mixing and matching various "critical" theories the deconstructive force of critical social work and its hope of producing radical conclusions have been blunted.

Three Doubts about the Identity of Critical Social Work's Postmodernism

We have three primary doubts regarding the validity of critical social workers' analyses.

1. Critical social work mixes two incompatible theoretical sources: Foucault and critical theory.

2. (a) Critical social work's "Foucauldian" critique rests on an outmoded account of power organized by a rather fixed, narrow set of binary oppositions.

   (b) Critical social work misses the importance of the central themes of complexity and the "immanent" process of the flows of power in Foucault's work.

3. Critical social work (and Foucault) does not let loose the full methodological force of the "analytics of power" upon the issues at hand. In the case of critical social work, this leaves largely unaccounted the formation of social work decisions within agencies *and* the relationship between the discursive and the non-discursive.

In the following sections, we will substantiate these doubts, in particular stressing the distinctions that critical social workers should have drawn between the aims of neo-Marxism and critical theory on one side and those of postmodernism and of Foucauldian analysis on the other.

1. First doubt

Firstly, critical social workers make extensive use of Foucault's work, finding congenial the surface appearance of a harmony between its methodological procedures and possible "liberatory" political implications. They tend to subordinate Foucault's work to the purposes of neo-Marxist critical theory despite the contradictions between these theorists' claims. Critical theorists seek redemption in the face of corruption by concentrations of power, whereas Foucault reveals our collective fate by the dispersion and inescapable fact of power. Critical theorists offer moral transcendence; Foucault offers an analysis of unending complex flows of power, the implication being that that there is no outside of power. Critical social work tends to use Foucault's work to support non-Foucauldian purposes, while being happy for it to signal a commitment to postmodernism.

The misappropriation of Foucauldian funds has practical implications. Critical social workers using Foucault and critical theory produce a one-sided account of social work practice. Critical social work often quite subtly explores client-social worker relations, but handles all too reductively the relation between worker and the social work agency (for example, Healy, 2001, pp. 6-7). To stop this, we need to take seriously Foucault's *analytics* of *contemporary* power that stresses the complexity and immanence of power. Unfortunately, his ideas on this are scattered. Gilles Deleuze and his co-writer Felix Guattari, personally and intellectually close to Foucault, provide explanatory concepts that help strengthen Foucault's analyses. We therefore sketch and apply to social work a "Deleuzian" Foucault that offers a radical, materialist analytics of power. We hope that, unlike critical social work, it does not show a failure of nerve by lapsing into (or being led by) humanist moral sentiment.

2. Second doubt

Our second line of argument is that critical social work imposes a structuralist (and *not* a post-structuralist) conception of "difference."

Critical social work tends to accept a view, compatible with Marxist and Foucauldian ideas, that in the nineteenth century identities were regulated by social codes setting out their differences to other identities. While for Marx this was a universalist tale about class, for Foucault the structural dynamics of "disciplinary practices" became more fluid across time. This latter point however, is barely recognized by critical social workers, who apply Foucault's analysis of nineteenth-century regulatory systems of power to the fluid world of social work today.

Foucault sketches an alternative, more flexible, picture of power today:

> From the eighteenth to the early twentieth century…the investment of the body by power had to be heavy, ponderous, meticulous, and constant…And then in the 1960s, it began to be realised that such a cumbersome form of power was no longer as indispensable as had been thought and that industrial societies could content themselves with a much looser form of power over the body. (1977/1980c, p.58)

And he indicates the fluidity of power when he notes:

> [T]his exercising [of power] (to the degree to which it is…nothing other than the instant photograph of multiple struggles continuously in transformation)…transforms itself without ceasing. We need not confuse a power situation…with simple power institutions such as the army, the police, the government etc. (1978/1989a, p.188)

Deleuze comments:

> Foucault's often taken as the theorist of disciplinary societies and of their principal technology *confinement*. But he was actually one of the first to say that we're moving away from disciplinary societies toward control societies that no longer operate by confining people but through continuous control and instant communication. (1995, p.174)

Power (and difference) is not about the ideological effects of the closure or domination of one discursive formation over another. The dynamic *in*-sistence of power is a creative productive process that may temporarily fall into a pattern, only to free up and move on. And our times are these times of the fluid and the mobile. (Bauman, 2002; Castells, 1995; Urry, 2000)

Critical social work ought not only to show the routine *mechanisms* of power in a discursive field, but also try to capture a sense of the "micro-physical" (the tiny fluctuations) fluctuating *movements* of the discursive and the non-discursive that is so basic to Foucault.

3. Third doubt

Our third reservation poses a question for Foucault's work as well as that of critical social workers. We suggest that both parties here depend too heavily upon a formal "black box" model of "governmentality" — that the operations of governance in their specificity are not analyzed to the same degree as their effects upon populations. This image of governmental complexity shoe-horned into a single "black box machine" nudges critical social work towards a rather basic version of critical theory and away from a postmodern analysis that emphasizes the indeterminacies in and of society.

Foucauldian studies of "governmentality" identify the terms of socio-political programs that have attempted to shape the "conduct of conduct" — the management and thus disciplining of populations — and then analyze the "capillary action" or "micro-physics" of these programs upon various strata of society at which they are aimed, for example, Bentham's "panopticon."

For Foucault and for critical social workers, it would seem that policy aims and effects upon the population, the modes of consumption, become the only really interesting matters; that is, the "subjectification" process. The complex variable mechanisms of their production — what's in the "black box" — are largely ignored in both critical social workers' and Foucault's *actual* historical analyses *despite* what is promised by his methodological prescriptions. Our concern is to uncover the complex strata and "subjectifications" of the making and makers of policy.

Critical social work has not looked deeply at the genealogies of the conduct of conduct and of power and/or knowledge within the domain of social work agencies. Critical social work grabs at a mechanistic "black-box" account of the institutional ground of operation of social work upon a subjugated population — the client. This is explained in terms of "the social control functions of social work" and the "authoritarian, bureaucratic or privatised practice contexts where the vast majority of social work occurs in western countries" (Healy, 2001, p.5) Such accounts tend towards the deterministic and do not take seriously enough the flowing variable character of the complex institutional formations of practice. Merely suggesting that for critical practice theory to remain vital it "could usefully focus on a thorough analysis of organisational systems through which human services are now delivered" does not get us very far (ibid., p.7). Such weakness provides critical social work with an all-too-easy link to the strategy of critical theory that gives a picture of a standardized practice constituting and repeating patterns of injustice. With this, we have the opportunity to reinstall the idea of justice through the "negative dialectic," as Adorno might have it, of client resistance — that clients do not fit nicely into the social work agencies' categories or its ideologies (see Held, 1980, pp.212-218). Clients' daily reality exceeds these, and thus provides a gap or moment of critique of the managerial frames of social services and, by inference, of the local and central state apparatuses. But this would seem to replace one universalist conception of justice with another by reversing the logic of operation: that the client world now re-frames the regulatory ideologies of "state" practice — in critical social work's case, by dialogue. And this reversal, though possessing the surface form of "deconstruction," is firmly locked into the project of critical theory.

We reject critical social work's "praxis" — of neo-Marxist notions of an "escape from power" that gets mixed up with arguments from Foucault and postmodern theory. In positive terms we argue that, certainly we should draw substantially upon Foucault's ideas to illuminate an analysis of social work, but in a way that recognizes the impact of Deleuze upon his thought. We hope that this will bring out the fatal aspect of a "post-structural" or postmodern social work: namely, that a world understood as the power and play of "difference" is ultimately irreconcilable. Critical social workers cannot redeem their practice; only analyze it.

The Politics of "Difference" and Critical Social Work's Binary Assumptions

Front-line "radical" social work in the 1970s was little touched by neo-Marxist theories and the post-structuralist critique of them. However, such debates shaped the arguments of the vanguard party of nascent "postmodernists" of the late 1970s and early 1980s. Arguably it was not the substance of these thinkers' works that was taken up, but rather the aura of radical intellectual resistance to Anglo-American "positivism" (always a popular target — so loosely defined that you could not miss).

The motivation for much of Western intellectual thought — that a language would be found that would fully express absolute notions of being and identity — was being "deconstructed." Under postmodern theory, hierarchies of values were shown empirically and theoretically to be illusory. Untroubled by differences between postmodernism, post-structuralism, deconstruction and social constructionism, liberal-left social scientists embraced theories that challenged hierarchy. And herein lay the idea of "difference."

The post-structuralist challenge to foundational ontology, to the idea of a single origin, proposed that there was a necessary other — a point of difference — always threatening to displace the dominant force. Here theories of difference separate into two camps, one based on logic, the other, on desire (Colebrook, 2002, pp. 15-31).

Difference, as theorized by Hegel, Lacan and Derrida, proposed that identities are grounded not by some metaphysical substrate or essence, but by their difference from that which they are not (a lack). This emphasizes difference as a logical negation between two items (Derrida, 2002, p.5). By contrast, Foucault and Deleuze and Guattari's notion of difference was seen as an aspect of "desire" — the *positive* production of the continuously varying connections between bodies. The concern here was with actual movement of *differentiation in itself*. Foucault developed this "immanent" notion of desire as the endless folds or play of acts of power, giving it expression as histories about the ever-present possibilities of counter-insurgency from, or alliances with, others that delimit and/or divert the lines or the flows of power. Foucault and Deleuze do not start from assumptions about fixed hierarchies of difference embedded in social structures, but from the idea that difference is dynamic and undecidable precisely because boundaries are endlessly asserted and erased. No identity is stable.

Foucault's historical research shows how the multiple points from which people speak are filtered through various strategies and technologies of power, thereby allowing some groups to be dominant and other subordinate. This makes "difference" a game of relative claims for inclusion by otherwise marginalized groups, for example, older, disabled or gay people.

Social workers' excitement about "difference" has created a double irony. Due to rough handling, difference has become politicized. For instance, it was a name used as a "ground" from which women could speak *qua women,* rather than having feminism function as part of a more universal discourse such as Marxism. The ironies are that (a) "difference" has become theorized as identical with (rather than as a "power" to create) actual material differences *pre-constituted* by an existing politics, for example, by agendas of feminism, anti-racism, multiculturalism, as if these were necessary and basic; and (b) these pre-constituted political identities *determine* a fixed social field of hierarchical oppositions that can be deconstructed.

For critical social workers "deconstruction" simply involves a reversal of the prevailing social hierarchies (for example, woman-man) under the generic category of central-marginal (see Pease and Fook, 1999, p.13; Healy, 2000, p.42). This means they work within a binary conception of the world: dominated/not-dominated — precisely the thing they said they were not going to do!

Peter Leonard assumes binary thinking when he adverts to Foucault's methodological strategy of "dividing practices," that is, recognizing the operation of such differences as mad-sane, healthy-sick, that are used to regulate populations (1997, p.16). Jessup and Rogerson similarly use "divisive practices" as the means by which persons "since the 17th century" have been subjugated and identified (Pease and Fook, 1999, p.164). Talking about oppositions in this way gives the impression that an organized field of subjugation (a quasi-ideology?) results from the (intended?) arrangement of these. But it makes the direct appeal to Foucault's method problematic. For him divisions are not taken-for-granted binaries as Leonard and others seem to think. The "forms of division" are about the transformation and dispersion of elements, which "instead of drawing up tables of differences (as the linguists do)...would describe systems of dispersion." (Foucault, 1972/1991b, p.37). The emphasis in Foucault is upon transformations of sets of statements. "Transformation" is a factor immanent to "discursive formations." It is not a causal power of an external ideological force.

Karen Healy has a more subtle appreciation of the variable character of social work's discursive practices where she acknowledges devolved categories of identity, that is, the possibility of multiple and contingent categories. She sees that the oppositional categories of social work reduce a range of differences to just two positions: "worker" and "service user" and that there should be recognition of "local variation in power relationships" (Healy, 2000, p.65; 2001, p.5). She does not offer an account of these elements in flux. Critical social work is primarily a synchronic, not a diachronic, portrait of power in social work practices.

Critical Social Work and Critical Theory

Neo-Marxist critical theory attempts to expose and thus transcend the ideo-logical values systems that distort "true" social relationships. In appealing to critical theory *and* post-structuralism, critical social work theorists are faced with the problem of squaring transcendentalist conceptions of free individuals with the claim that identities are necessarily fragmented. The logic of "differ-ence" in critical social work (of dominant-subordinate) founders because it wants to escape power via strategies of service user empowerment and consciousness raising of providers, while using ideas from Foucault that depend on the argument that power is inescapable.

Critical social workers imagine a post-ideological world of equality and shared understanding, where self and other meet in an open dialectic without subordination of one group by another. Healey accounts for this in terms of reflexive dialogue, Fook, in terms of "contextual practice" (Fook, 2002, p.143) and Pease, in terms of "collective memory work" (Pease, in Fawcett and Featherstone, 2000, p.147).

Jim Ife (1999) in his contribution to Pease and Fook argues for a subordina-tion of postmodernism under critical theory: "Critical Theory can readily accept...post-modernism, and the form of critical theory advocated here is one which is informed by and incorporates significant elements of a post-modern position" (p. 219). Ife desires a continuing affirmation of social work's tradi-tional commitment to social justice and "therefore to retain some kind of universal vision" (p. 217). Karen Healy (1999) in her piece in the same volume wishes to reduce power through negotiated understandings between workers and users. Both in their distinctive ways wish to ameliorate the ruses of power by finding strategies for reconciling them with preferred moral ideas and goals. Such attempts at neutralizing power to free up a space for just social arrange-ments has an underlying dialectical structure, namely, that the play of antago-nistic discourses (worker-client contradictions) can be resolved (dialogical synthesis). This assumes a relation of exteriority, and thus rides roughshod over the idea of the notion of immanence and positivity of power central to their most favoured theorist, Michel Foucault.

Ultimately Leonard's and Pease and Fook's ideas seem little different from Marxist analyses of ideology as false consciousness and the role of the social worker as critic and revolutionary leader. Inasmuch as critical social work makes dominant discourses a theme, it aligns itself with Foucauldian terms, but in aspiring to emancipating selves, it is working on a plane of transcendence and redemption. Fook notes, "[E]xpert professional social workers are able to create critical knowledge which potentially challenges and resists current forms of domination, and they are able to maintain commitment to a system of social values which allows them to work with, yet transcend the contradictions and uncertainties of daily practice" (Fawcett & Featherstone, 2000, p.118). This idea of the social worker as manager of the binary switch from false to true consciousness provides for a liberal utopian politics wholly out of sympathy with Foucault. Fook trades on a tired, imprecise but supposedly "critical" notion of "false consciousness" — a term that is rooted in binary thinking if ever there was one. Fook (2002, p.17) notes, "[T]he notion of 'false consciousness' is important...a process of false consciousness operates within capitalist societies." Later on Fook tries to edge her way around the dichotomy she has endorsed. Unfortunately the problem of giving agents of true consciousness (critical social workers) the power of correction and thus domination over those who suffer from false consciousness (clients) is acknowledged by her, but not resolved (p. 60).

Critical social workers' use of neo-Marxist inspired "critical theory" aligns with and ultimately colonizes critical social work's Foucauldian aspects. We will argue that what we have called contemporary power — the mark of which has impressed itself upon social work today — should be explored within the terms of a Deleuzo-Foucauldian analysis, rather than critical social workers trying to fit critical theory around a world for which it was not designed.

Deleuze's Foucault

Foucault and Deleuze have both evaluated the theoretical sympathy between them (Foucault, 1977a; Deleuze, 1988, 1994, pt. 3). "I differed from him on only minor things" (Deleuze, 1994, p.150). Despite half-hearted attempts to identify some differences, critics have agreed that what Foucault and Deleuze have in common is more significant. (see the excellent Callinicos, 1981; Gutting, 1989).

Our broad point so far has been that the tendency of critical social work, among others, to situate Foucault and "postmodern" perspectives within an emancipatory account of social work intervention is misleading. This trajectory is as modernist as any: the familiar nineteenth-century story of a passing from analysis to utopia; contradiction to resolution. The rejection of such a dialectical approach and its persistent ethical nagging is a strength in Foucault and Deleuze. We wish to give a Deleuzian tone to Foucault's analytics of power. In pursuit of a post-critical social work *analytics*, we reject the politics of rereading Foucault as offering another route to a leftist form of utopia.

Where Foucault and Deleuze focus upon a non-dialectical approach is in their idea of the relatively unpredictable flows of social and historical change. An "event" of power is not about specific contradictions (for example, state-people, social worker-client). We may get a sense of what Foucault calls "event," or Deleuze the "diagram," if we think of a snapshot of the complex play of lines of power in movement comprising a surface. We can think of power as a varying plane of decentred intensities rather like the surface of a river as it flows, ripples and eddies, where each "now-state" of the river is its power, its life — where the immanence of power can be grasped as "nothing other than itself." (Colebrook, 2002, p.xxiv). Deleuze and Foucault give analytical descriptions of this "inherence" of power within a socio-historical plane. Naming the object of an analytics of power as a "dispositif" — "concrete social apparatuses" — Deleuze defines Foucault's idea thus:

> [W]hat is a dipositif? In the first instance it is a tangle, a multilinear ensemble, which is composed of lines, each having a different nature. And the lines in the apparatus do not outline or surround systems which are each homogenous in their own right, object, subject, language and so on, but follow directions, trace balances which are always off balance, now drawing together and then distancing themselves from one another. Each line is broken and subject to changes in direction, bifurcating and forked and subject to drifting. (Armstrong, 1992, p.159)

Taking this approach produces cracks in our faith in the unitary "juridico discursive" model of power as the function of the sovereign, state or law. It sets out to make sense of power as an unfolding flow of differentiation. As Foucault (1980/1991c, p.76) says of himself, "[N]o-one is more of a continuist than I am." Rose sums it up neatly when he says that we should

> track force relations at the molecular level, as they flow through a multitude of human technologies, in all the practices, arenas, and spaces where...the administration of others intersect with techniques for the administration of ourselves...in a multitude of programmes, strategies, tactics, devices, calculations, negotiations, intrigues, persuasions and seductions...[T]he State now appears simply as one element in multiple circuits of power. (1999, p.5)

Deleuze's Foucault not only places greater emphasis upon the identity of each tiny little difference and thus of the identity of selves in the pulsing field of power (Deleuze, 1988, p.12), but also upon the speed of changes that are a function of forces that constrain or enable flows. For Deleuze this means that we should grasp this field or plane as endlessly de- and re-territorializing — of its "diagram" or topology in flux. A third important Deleuzian theme that connects to fluctuating identities and to Foucault's discursive formation that critical social work overplays is that of striated versus smooth space. It links to our earlier distinction between rigid modern and fluid contemporary power. We will discuss it in more detail further on, but roughly it refers to the degree of organization operating in society. "Smooth" is the least organized and rule bound; "nomadic space," "striated space," the most. Our degrees of freedom are a function of the number of our connections to smooth or striated space. Of course in keeping with the idea of flux of systems, Deleuze allows that one form can contain the tendencies of the other form, thus producing a conjunctive synthesis of molar and striated (larger-scale organized elements) underlain by the molecular and/or nomadic (small fluctuating particles), for example, unilateral varying of procedures by social workers to cope with work load.

The fluctuating field of the social can be seen in terms of each social action making a difference in the *effective* assemblage of power itself. That which has become ineffective, that is, has become redundant, crosses into the "archive," and the present is the network of active forces that persist in their effectiveness as they are added to by successive social actions (Armstrong, 1992, p.165; Foucault, 1972/1991b, pp. 130-131). In this sense the threshold of the archive is the borderline between the passing (becoming inactive) and the becoming (active forces), each nuance of which is *difference*. Contra-Foucault, critical social work has treated social work as an archaeological object; as an archive constituted by "reified" frozen repeating structures of power and rules-systems. Against this neo-Marxist model we need to try to grasp the becoming of social work as the history of its becoming-present (Rose, 1999, pp. 12-13).

We want to go beyond critical social work to engage in a "reversed platonism," as Deleuze puts it; that is, by analyzing the immanence of social formations involving a complex unfolding of connections between variably conquered and disciplining bodies, rather than a Platonic-type narrative about the emergence of true consciousness from the darkness of ignorance and power.

The Immanent Analysis of Social Work Practice: Critical Social Work and Deleuze/Foucault

In Deleuzian vein, Foucault, in an interview in 1980 for *La Nouvel Observateur*, called for thinking and life to be creative and experimental: "I...dream about a kind of criticism that would try not to judge but to bring a work, a book, a sentence, an idea to life...It would multiply not judgments but signs of existence."

Deleuze and Guattari celebrate conceptual creations giving rise to plateaus of analytical description that resonate with each other. Thus the title of their 1980 work, *Mille Plateaux (A Thousand Plateaus)* and the close affinities of meaning between the members of their conceptual lexicon such as immanent-exterior; smooth-striated; molecular-molar; bodies without organs-organic; state-nomad. On spec, one might charge them with having created binary oppositions, but closer inspection shows that these are non-dialectical in character, that is, they are effects of each other or nested. Deleuze and Guattari show how the distribution of multiple forces through time territorializes (sets up) and de- and re-territorializes (reconfigures) an image of society. For instance, tribes intensify their tribalness precisely by coding and recoding their relation to the earth through myths and rituals. In doing so they image and thus invest the earth with causal powers that then appear *ab initio* to explain the tribe to itself. Causes, as Deleuze and Guattari put it, are "miraculated" on the socius — the social body. This helps to rigidify — reify — a social system. Later it is the sovereign image of the despot in early feudal systems that is the cause and primary (re-) coder. Our modern times are primarily structured through processes of endless de-territorialization of codes as one is exchanged for another, for instance, changes in social policies. All these tendencies overlayer or overcode one another. Deleuze and Guattari show how these forms of material arrangements and thought occur through desiring-production — the impulse to connect leading to a social order, as opposed to an uncoded flux and givenness of "life" (Deleuze, 1994, p.222).

Productions of desire, arrangements of things into functional "machines," are underlain by a projected image of the "body without organs" (BwO). Peter Leonard suggests that a BwO is a social text (1997, p.55). This is precisely what it is not. It is not an organized structure; rather, it is an image of an unorganized, disconnected, potential field of activity or "discourse" — the political, the economic, the cultural, the musical and so forth. We project this plane from the actual situation of intensities in which we find ourselves. The BwO has no intensity because intensities are about active connections, disjunctions and conjunctions — syntheses that give order to life and, for our purposes, social work. In this sense the BwO is not an "exteriority," but an image that gives us an illusion of ground or origin. We could stretch this idea to suggest that it may be used to signal the possibility of making a better world, an "idealized" coding of the BwO. To some degree this is what social work and critical social work has imagined: an *unbiased whole sense* or perfect figure of how things should look, as an invitation to refigure actual social work. In this sense, they seek the very thing postmodernism has most attacked — the "true" original world. We should offer an account of how critical social work makes its body without organs? How does it pretend contra-Deleuze and Foucault that there was a unitary world before difference?

Social work involves persons who relate to each other in various hierarchies of command and respect and within institutions that mediate variable relations of control between "professionals" and between professionals and users. Changes in those hierarchies and relations are "becomings" of the fluid constellations of force — of intensities. They converge in a linear series that Deleuze names as the connective synthesis. But they are hierarchically ordered and thus separated (coded). Deleuze calls this "disjunctive synthesis." However the ordering is not merely to be seen as an arbitrary power, but to be explained by a projection of some underlying value or logic such as "justice" or "saving children." These are immanent in that they are given expression and referred back to in each aspect of the work of the organization. Deleuze calls this process a "conjunctive synthesis." Social workers become conjoined together by an imagined set of basic values into an *apparently* self-justifying field of social work. The operation of these three axes or syntheses creates a relatively clear image of the place of social work. The actual proliferation of change and of power is often ignored. Social workers "slow down" their perception of the endless movement and reshaping of their field of activity and fall into routines of practice. In Foucault's terms, this is about normalization, not of populations but, in this case, of social workers. Neither critical social work nor Foucault adequately scrutinize the micro-physics of this process. As we said earlier, this level of analysis is dropped into a black box. Deleuze gives us ideas of how to analyze such processes.

What we have in Deleuze and Guattari and in Foucault is an analysis of "events" whose complexity of formation is traced. In the 1977 interview "Questions of method," Foucault talks about multiple causal processes at one level, each of which breaks down into further multiple causal processes at a lower level and so forth. As he says, "eventalisation works by constructing around the singular event analysed as process a...polyhedron of intelligibility, the number of whose faces is not given in advance and can never properly be taken as finite"

(Foucault, 1980/1991c, p.77) He goes on to say that the further we fractalize, the more the fractal elements must be analytically linked to salient phenomena, for example, if we are talking about incarceration, then salient phenomena are schooling and military discipline. Thus the complex explanatory network grows. The image of detailing the determination of the event is very similar to Deleuze and Guattari's idea of "rhizomatic" (tracing evolving networks of connections) as opposed to "arborescent" (determinate stable hierarchies of factors) explanatory form. The multi-layered, massive complexity of social work relations needs to be thought against "governmental" black-box models. In an analysis of social services we need to explore the interactions between molar and molecular forces, between, say, managerial regimes and local practices. At this level, both Foucault and Deleuze and Guattari are loosening up Althusserian notions such as structure in dominance and structural causality.

Deleuze and Foucault have identified themselves as functionalist, but of an anti-structuralist type. A Deleuzo-Foucauldian analysis of social work starts with the process of differentiation. Within this, we identify flows and rigidities of social work instead of using critical social work's bureaucratic model of established social work.

> It is not sufficient to define bureaucracy by rigid segmentarity with compart-
> mentalization of contiguous offices, an office manger in each segment, and the
> corresponding centralization at the end of the hall, or on top of the tower. For at
> the same time there is whole bureaucratic segmentation, a suppleness of and
> communication between offices, a bureaucratic perversion, a permanent inven-
> tiveness or creativity practiced even against administrative regulations. (Deleuze
> & Guattari, 1988, p.214)

They go on to point out that, in real time, functional organizations are actually polysemic. "Immersed in a molecular medium (a milieu) the office manager proliferates into microfigures impossible to recognize…discernible only when they centralisable" (ibid.). Here it is being argued that we should tease out the tiny eddies and movements – momentary meanings and aspects of character – of, say, the care manager. Only at what Deleuze and Guattari call the molar level, the structured group, do we notice any single "microfigure." Insofar as the manager or any social worker exceeds some "pure" manifestation of their function or role, say, by chatting about the weekend to their manger and so forth, they are making the rigid supple and are "inventing" life. They are weaving smooth into a predominantly striated space. But this plays back into the system as "good working relations."

When in everyday life social workers take their lives for a chat round the office, therewith is "smooth" space; when we pass "rigidly" from one point to another — "I am going to consult my team manager" — we are segmenting our work lives through striated space. However, and this is important to understand complex structures, activities are fractal, and thus distinctions such as smooth or striated space can be applied all the way down. We can consider report writing as participating in smooth space when we are giving a profile of the service user and their situation — we let the words flow in a circumspective way. Whereas, when we are drawing conclusions, then striated space is passed through verbally because we are concerned with linking points of evidence to points of prescription. Equally, when a supervisor or a manager reads the report, they may read it for the key points and connections to policy rather than for its narrative tale. Such reading passes through striated rather than smooth space. The fractal nature of life and analysis insists that we pay attention to the multiple strata of the social. The smooth and striated do not naturally collocate to any particular stratum of work. The distinction can be used to make sense of tiny as well as more macro levels of social work.

Organizationally, social work is decentred. The very diversity of the work — this case, that case, home visit, meetings and so forth — suggests an open network of activities whose codings are particularly visible. Deleuze characterizes these apparently open arrangements as societies of control. The practice of social work is built out of communicative acts, the passing of information from one determinate point to another. Each is a signal that is recorded upon somebody or another by memory or virtual systems. Each speech act is in this sense monitored, stored, relayed, recoded. The increasing insistence in a defensive social work culture to have a record of everything is not just "for one's own safety" but is a material condition of the instantaneity of its recall. Information technology increases the speed at which this all happens and to the proliferation of the surveillance society. Each moment of the complexity of these processes is an expression of the diagram of power.

We have then to show up the "swarming" of connections that de- and re-territorialize social work. This is done at the molar and the molecular levels. We have to trace out the connective, disjunctive and conjunctive movements that create the differentiating power structure; that speed up or slow down its rate of change. Finally, in this discussion, we need to take account of non-archival memory and resources. Here we wish to make explicit a link with the idea of social capital.

We said earlier that a Foucauldian aim was to give a history of the present as opposed to one that is archival. For this we need a notion of active memory — the present network of resonating factors that are available to us at each segment of our becoming. A forgotten memory that would have been relevant to what I am doing now is no good to me. The drawing up of "relevant" information is a form of variable capital that I can use, but only insofar as the understanding I have of it *is* relevant. Equally, the varying situations I find myself in provide a form of situational capital that I can use to execute my plans. My relations with others are a form of social capital, but constrained by subjective proximity (Will they help me? Will they recall the relevant information?) and institutional proximity (Can I talk to my team manager today?). Again, these are variable. This could point to a new line of analysis. We could look at the currently fashionable idea of social capital — a resource enabling for individual action that emerges from social interactions, for example, trust. Usually interpreted as a stable resource, this, under a Deleuzo-Foucauldian scheme, must be understood as mobile. In social work terms, social capital would turn on available memories and knowledge, relevant understanding and interpersonal and professional solidarities, where each affects the others, leading to an expansion or a diminution of available social capital that could enable effective social work by me "now." Thus the becoming of my social work is immanently connected to the becoming of variable resources. Nothing is fixed, only slowed down or speeded up.

Conclusion

What we have done here is to try to provide a critique of critical social work from a theoretical baseline of Foucault and Deleuze. Our motivation was the sense that, critical social work, while making some valuable comments about the inadequacy of analyses of power in existing social work, does not carry through the largely Foucault-inspired project of undoing power relations all the way down to the micro-level. Critical social work does not get at the movement of differing that is difference. Critical social workers' acceptance of a set of differences in society, which has been pre-defined by critical social work's own political concerns, is as much the offspring of ideology as the idea they so criticize.

Our more detailed points of criticism focused on the incompatibility of critical theory with postmodern analyses and with the way in which critical social workers had narrowly misused Foucault's work to practice a form of political criticism over more traditional social work. In particular though, we wanted to highlight the relative absence of an analysis of the micro-physics of the relation between social workers and their institutions — the sites of disciplinary power that are the invisible networks of power impressed upon the body of the worker and get translated into actual practice. Foucault's ideas about governmentality are little used by critical social workers, yet seem so crucial to understanding the full life of power on the social work "plane." When we drew on Deleuze's developments of Foucault's themes, we were enabled to see in more detail the importance of analyzing the "construction" of social work as a positive joining of different flows into a multiple movement. The arena in which the social worker operates is not simply a confined automated cipher of rules and processes. Matters of interpretation of evidence, of walk and talk within the office, of the professional face of the social worker, all give a flexibility to social work practices while being under increasingly narrow frames of policy and accountability. This is quite different from Foucault's *modern* power. This is what we identified as contemporary power or the "society of control."

To unravel the unceasing fluctuation of lines or flows of power as they de- and re-territorialize the imagined plane of the body without organs – to make this usually invisible visible — is the very work of both Deleuze and Foucault and is a form of critique critical social workers for the most part have left alone. Their idea of the governance of social work is very much in the 1960s functionalist tradition of black-box modelling, but this gives an aura of the Leviathan state, a beast of fabulous proportions that we never quite see. We have argued that, this is not because it is always a trick of ideology to mask the deceits and the very presence of the great deceiver — the bourgeois state, the capitalist, the dominant — but because such unities are a chimera. They are fictions that left and right offer up (in their hiddenness) as obvious realities to convince us that necessarily there is a world to win, and to not wish to fight is particularly supine. How we imagine these unities of power through synthetical processes is a modality of life itself for Deleuze and, in this way, contributes to our analysis of power. Critical social workers' kindly commitment to social justice has set limits to their analysis of power and to their use of Foucault. In failing to take an in-human view of matters — to *not take seriously* the claim that power is "always already" and to positively seek moral modes of practice — critical social workers produce a new in-humanism — that of limited analysis and thus of life.

References

Armstrong, T. (Ed.). (1992). Michel Foucault philosopher. Hemel Hempstead: Harvester Wheatsheaf.

Bauman, Z. (2002). *Liquid modernity*. Oxford: Polity.

Burchell, G., Gordon, C., & Miller, P. (Eds.). (1991). *The Foucault effect*. Hemel Hempstead: Harvester Wheatsheaf.

Callinicos, A. (1981). *Is there a future for Marxism?* Basingstoke: Macmillan.

Castells, M. (1995). *The rise of the network society*. Oxford: Blackwell.

Casti, J.L. (1994). *Complexification*. London: Abacus.

Cato, J.W. (2002) Theory versus analytics of power: The Habermas-Foucault debate. *Agora, 3*(1).

Chambon, A.S., Irving, A, & Epstein, L. (Eds.). (1999). *Reading Foucault for social work*. New York: Columbia University.

Colebrook, C. (2002). *Understanding Deleuze*. Australia: Allen and Unwin.

Deleuze, G. (1968/1994) *Difference and repetition*. London: Athlone.

Deleuze, G. (1983). *Anti-Oedipus: Capitalism and schizophrenia*. USA: University of Minnesota Press.

Deleuze, G. (with Parnet, C.). (1987). *Dialogues*. London: Athlone.

Deleuze, G. (1988). *Foucault*. USA: University of Minnesota Press.

Deleuze, G. (1994). *Negotiations 1972-1990*. USA: Columbia University Press.

Deleuze, G., & Guattari, F. (1988) *A thousand plateaus: Capitalism and schizophrenia* (Pt. 2). London: Athlone.

Derrida, J. (2002). Force of law. In *Acts of religion. London: Routledge.*

Dreyfus, H., & Rabinow, P. (1982). *Michel Foucault: Beyond structuralism and hermeneutics*. Brighton, Sussex: Harvester Press.

Faubion, J. (1998). *Michel Foucault: Aesthetics — essential works 1954-1984*. Middlesex: Allen Lane, Penguin Press.

Fawcett, B., Featherstone, B., Fook, J. & Rossiter, A. (Eds,). (2002). *Practice and Research in Social Work: Postmodern Feminist Perspectives*. London and New York: Routledge.

Fook, J. (2001). Linking theory, practice, and research. *Critical Social Work, 2*(1) (Spring).

Fook, J. (2002). *Social Work: Critical Theory and Practice*. London: Sage Publications.

Foucault, M. (1970) *The order of things*. London: Tavistock.(Original work published 1966)

Foucault, M. (1972) *The archaeology of knowledge*. London: Tavistock. (Original work published 1969)

Foucault, M. (1977a) *Discipline and punish*. Middlesex: Allen Lane, Penguin Press. (Original work published 1975)

Foucault, M. (1977b). Intellectuals in power. In D. Bouchard (Ed.). *Language, counter-memory, practice: Selected essays and interviews* (pp. 205-217). Ithaca, NY: Cornell University Press. Translated by Donald F. Bouchard and Sherry Simon.

Foucault, M. (1980a). Body/power. In C. Gordon (Ed.), *Power/knowledge: Selected interviews and other writings 1972-1977*. New York: Pantheon Books. (Original work published 1975)

Foucault, M. (1980b). The confession of the flesh. In C. Gordon (Ed.), *Power/knowledge: Selected interviews and other writings 1972-1977*. New York: Pantheon Books. (Original work published 1977)

Foucault, M. (1980c). The eye of power. In C. Gordon (Ed.), *Power/knowledge: Selected interviews and other writings 1972-1977*. New York: Pantheon Books. (Original work published 1977)

Foucault, M. (1985). *The use of pleasure: History of sexuality* (Vol. 2). NY: Vintage. (Original work published 1984)

Foucault, M. (1988). An aesthetics of existence. In L. Kritzman (Ed.), *Michel Foucault: Politics, philosophy, culture — interviews and other writings 1977-1984*. London: Routledge. (Original work published 1984)

Foucault, M. (1989a). Clarifications on the question of power. In S. Lotringer, *Foucault live (interviews 1966-1984)*. Columbia, NY: Semiotexte. (Original work published 1978)

Foucault, M. (1989b). How much does it cost for reason to tell the truth? In S. Lotringer, *Foucault live (interviews 1966-1984)*. Columbia, NY: Semiotexte. (Original work published 1983)

Foucault, M. (1991a). Governmentality. In Burchell et al. (Eds.), *The Foucault effect*. Hemel Hempstead: Harvester Wheatsheaf. (Original work published 1978)

Foucault, M. (1991b). Politics and the study of discourse. In Burchell et al. (Eds.), *The Foucault effect*. Hemel Hempstead: Harvester Wheatsheaf. (Original work published 1972)

Foucault, M. (1991c). Question of method. In Burchell et al. (Eds.), *The Foucault effect*. Hemel Hempstead: Harvester Wheatsheaf. (Original work published 1980)

Foucault, M. (1998a). Course summary: The birth of bio-politics. In P. Rabinow, *Michel Foucault: Ethics – essential works 1954-1984*. Middlesex: Allen Lane, Penguin Press. (Original work published 1978)

Foucault, M. (1998b). Course summary: The will to knowledge. In P. Rabinow, *Michel Foucault: Ethics – essential works 1954-1984*. Middlesex: Allen Lane, Penguin Press. (Original work published 1971)

Foucault, M. (1998c). Language to infinity. In J. Faubion, *Michel Foucault: Aesthetics — essential works 1954-1984*. Middlesex: Allen Lane, Penguin Press. (Original work published 1963)

Foucault, M. (1998d). Nietzsche, genealogy, history. In J. Faubion, *Michel Foucault: Aesthetics — essential works 1954-1984*. Middlesex: Allen Lane, Penguin Press. (Original work published 1971)

Foucault, M. (1998e). On the archaeology of the sciences. In J. Faubion, *Michel Foucault: Aesthetics — essential works 1954-1984*. Middlesex: Allen Lane, Penguin Press. (Original work published 1968)

Foucault, M. (1998f) Structuralism and post-structuralism. In J. Faubion, *Michel Foucault: Aesthetics — essential works 1954-1984*. Middlesex: Allen Lane, Penguin Press. (Original work published 1983)

Foucault, M. (1998g). Theatrum philosophicum. In J. Faubion, *Michel Foucault: Aesthetics — essential works 1954-1984*. Middlesex: Allen Lane, Penguin Press. (Original work published 1970).

Foucault, M. (1998h). The thought of the outside. In J. Faubion, *Michel Foucault: Aesthetics — essential works 1954-1984*. Middlesex: Allen Lane, Penguin Press. (Original work published 1966)

Gordon, C. (Ed.). (1980).*Power/knowledge: Selected interviews and other writings 1972-1977*. New York: Pantheon Books.

Gutting, G. (1989). *Michel Foucault's archaeology of scientific reason*. Cambridge: CUP.

Healy, K. (1999). Power and activist social work. In B. Pease & J. Fook, (Eds.), *Transforming social work practice: Postmodern critical perspectives* (pp. 115-134). St. Leonards: Allen and Unwin.

Healy, K. (2000). *Social work practices*. London: Sage.

Healy, K. (2001). Reinventing critical social work: Challenges from practice, context and post-modernism. *Critical Social Work*, 2(1).

Ife, J. (1999). Postmodernism, critical theory and social work. In B. Pease & J. Fook, (Eds.), *Transforming social work practice: Postmodern critical perspectives* (pp.211-223). St. Leonards: Allen and Unwin.

Kritzman, L. (Ed.). (1988). *Michel Foucault: Politics, philosophy, culture — interviews and other writings 1977-1984*. London: Routledge.

Leonard, P. (1997). *Post-modern welfare*. London: Sage.

Leonard, P. (2001). The future of critical social work in uncertain conditions. *Critical Social Work*, 2(1).

Lotringer. S. (1989). *Foucault live (interviews 1966-1984)*. Columbia, NY: Semiotexte.

McBeath, G., & Webb, S. (1991). Social Work, Modernity and Post Modernity. *Sociological Review 39*(4), 745-762.

Mullaly, R. (2002). *Challenging oppression: A critical social work approach*. Don Mills: Oxford University Press.

Pease, B, & Fook, J. (Eds.). (1999). *Transforming social work practice: Postmodern critical perspectives*. St. Leonards: Allen and Unwin.

Pozzuto, R. (2000). Notes on a possible critical social work. *Critical Social Work*, 1(1).

Rabinow, P. (1998). *Michel Foucault: Ethics – essential works 1954-1984*. Middlesex: Allen Lane, Penguin Press.

Rose, N. (1999). *Powers of freedom*. Cambridge: CUP.

Urry, J. (2000). *Sociology beyond societies*. London: Routledge.

PART 4
The Future of Critical Social Work

12

Where in the World Are We? Notes on the Need for a Social Work Response to Global Power

Amy Rossiter

This chapter sketches my concerns about critical social work in a time of rapid change in the nature of power at a global level. I relate this to our school's first experience teaching young, direct-entry-from-high school students, and to the kind of dystopic technical future that the present seems to predict. I then will look briefly at work that integrates redistribution and recognition as a potential place of solidarity for social work, so that we can find language that might allow us to respond from a different conception of the world. Such a response is imperative in our current global context.

My thoughts are motivated by my need to reflect on what I can offer our young, inexperienced social work students, given that the world that they will face as practitioners contains considerable threats to social work. In particular, I want to think about what shifts critical social work might take in this "brave new world." I think there are three major factors that will indirectly and directly shape their practice world: (1) globalization and free trade, (2) the neo-conservative reorganization of society, and (3) the re-articulation of the United States as a world hegemonic power.

Globization and free trade

The current thrust of globalization today is to develop binding international trade rules that will turn all possible areas of human endeavour over to business (Sinclair & Grieshaber-Otto, 2002). This is the basic goal of free trade. This process entails privatization and deregulation; that is, turning over more and more to the private, for-profit and deregulating sectors so that profit can be maximized by developing minimum standards (McBride & Shields, 1997, p.168). As I write, successive rounds of the General Agreement on Trade in Services are being negotiated at the WTO. The goal of the GATS is to bring all services under trade agreement rules in order to pave the way for foreign investment in services. This will ultimately diminish government's capacity to regulate services and weaken local decision making. These agreements are negotiated without adequate consultation with stakeholders (Swenarchuk, 2002, p.30). How many of us really know what Canada committed us to in service negotiations in 1994? The fact is that many trade experts believe that the trade agreements are so broad and so poorly defined that potentially every social service can be up for sale (Sinclair & Grieshaber-Otto, 2002, pp.72-73). Can we picture our current students working for a private child protection service owned by an American multinational? Do we know that the GATS has a Working Group on Domestic Regulation that is busy formulating global competency standards for professions so that professional qualifications are "no more burdensome than necessary"? (Gould, 2003, GATS Necessity Test Section, para. 1).

Neo-conservative reorganization of society

The neo-conservative or neo-liberal undertakings of governments have had dire consequences on the world of social work and there is no end in sight. As social spending was slashed in order to fund tax cuts designed to increase consumption and decrease the cost of doing business, we have made ourselves "attractive to business" at the cost of our social safety net. At the same time, real wages have decreased. We are developing an underclass in the midst of the increasing concentration of wealth into smaller numbers. We need to look south to really understand what is happening. In the United States, after years of neo-conservative policy, state budgets have been decimated. States are simply unable to pay welfare and education costs. Here in Canada, we have, at least to date, avoided such harsh measures as a two-year cut-off for welfare benefits, but it may be coming down the pike as harsh welfare restrictions are normalized over time. There are structural reasons for the growth of a large, poor underclass, and we know that neo-conservative policies have created a growing gap between rich and poor. Yet the ideology of individuals' ability to simply exercise individual will to better themselves is rampant. So our students will be facing a growing number of poor people, with diminished welfare provision, and continued contempt for that group as a strategy to decrease the scope of government in order to redirect money to business.

The United States as a world hegemonic power

The Project New American Century think-tank suggested new foreign policy for the United States in 1997 (Project New American Century). That policy involved increasing military spending in order to promote the values and inter-ests of the United States on a global basis, with particular reference to the Middle East. Whatever one's thoughts around the invasion of Iraq, it has signalled a repositioning of the United States as advancing its own interests at the expense of world co-operation. Refusing to ratify the Kyoto Treaty and refusing to join the World Criminal Court are signals that the anticipated fruits of free trade regarding new world co-operation and harmony are taking a back seat to U.S. interests. The major question in my mind is the global threat to democracy and national sovereignty, as well as a rise of bitter religious and cultural animosity that is bound to fuel increased global conflict, expressed as mounting repression of the Middle East and resulting terrorism. Canada is in a particularly difficult position with respect to sovereignty. Eighty-five percent of our exports go to the U.S. market. That makes the protection of more progressive social values much harder, particularly with the integration of markets through NAFTA and the FTAA. How will we protect Canadian social policy from the pressures of harmonization created by the hegemonic projects of the United States?

What about Critical Social Work with Respect to Global Changes?

In previous work (Rossiter, 1996, 2001), I have been interested in a Foucauldian notion of power — of power that works through discursive practices to construct identities and perpetuate power relations. I was interested, and still am, in the problem of how social work exercises power in the performance of help. I believed that the discovery of consent and obedience enacted within regimes of truth led to the mutability of social organization. I felt it was necessary to resist turning to a grand theory that would supply me with an innocent place in social work so that I could really teach students to help. I repudiated grand theories and models because they exclude at the very moment they are articulated. I tried to think about how to live inside the contradictions of social work that were fashioned by the history of social work in capitalism and in gender relations.

Critical social work began to take the problematic of social work *itself* as a focus for social action once prescribed by grand theory. If prescriptions produced exclusions, which in turn fostered new forms of domination, then we could safely work only on ourselves. Social work's relation to the state, its investment in social control, its enmeshment in relations of domination in terms of gender, race, class, became the object of scrutiny. Peter Leonard, for example, talks about the activist as the "resistant moral agent" (1997, p.162) engaged in process rather than plan. Attempts to substitute process for plan hope to avoid the domination inevitably produced by unitary narratives.

This space for self-critique was ironically protected by a more benevolent welfare state than currently exists in North America. We could critique it and our place in it because there was an assumption that it was possible to influence public policy and socially constructed identities towards a progressive vision. Change in the small, local sites of power was change that could influence the larger social order.

World events have cast doubt on my belief in progressive improvement in which I could participate by offering critical self-reflection. When the lifeworld is being organized by trade agreements based on the interests of multinational corporations, when the language of democracy has been distorted to legitimize aggression, and when bad education, no welfare, poor health and a large, desperate underclass are the conditions needed to attract investment... Is self-critique a form of power?

A great deal of the work of critical social work in the last decade has centred on how power operates at the level of the taken for granted. We in social work have been trying to examine our practices for the operation of power so that we could attempt to democratize social work rather than implement social control. At a larger level, critical work such as Chomsky's *Manufacturing Consent* described the manipulation of media in order to gain consent to the agenda of power. Studies of power concerned how we internalized norms consistent with the interests of power. In essence, we were looking at how the individual is a vehicle of power because if we could understand the mechanism, we could stop giving consent.

When I look at this agenda now, I see that the basis of this work was that we felt at some level that our consent was *needed*. We believed that out consent was hooked to power. Governments could still be called to account on grounds of the kinds of injustices encountered by social workers. Now, with the centres of power moving out of governments and into non-elected bodies such as the WTO and the boardrooms of transnational corporations, I feel that my consent is irrelevant. Our notion of the capillary nature of power, of ground-level power that constructs, plays David in the face of the Goliath of globalized power.

Foucault (1980, 1982) taught us that power is productive, not simply repressive This was an extraordinary advance because it allowed social work to analyze social control mechanisms of practice. It allowed us to grasp how we were implicated in power. The notion of productive power, however, is ironically democratic: it depends on assumptions about the high degree to which power is spread diffusely through society at ground levels, and is therefore mutable. Far from pessimistic, this was the excitement, the optimism of postmodernism. In recent years, however, it appears that power has become more nakedly seized, concentrated in fewer hands, and is less locally based. As a consequence, power seems to need less democratic legitimization: the agenda of power is able to proceed without fears of being called to account. From the gassing of protesters in Quebec City to the invasion of Iraq, power remains above and untouched by dissent.

In a class I taught a few years ago, I gave a lecture on Foucault and micro power. I talked about power as capillary; working through small social sites to produce consent and self-governance. There was an African refugee in the class. At the end of the lecture he raised his hand and very gently said, "Only an American could talk about power that way." And for a moment I was jolted by his recognition of me as having the luxury to talk about power as micro, as producing consent. I think of this student often as I wonder how to include in our examination of how we participate in power the problem that our participation seems less relevant at this moment because power seems able to go on without it.

I am faced with retaining my commitments to postmodernism because it has provided irreplaceable insights into the formation and vulnerability of domination and the ethical choices that present themselves. "Postmodernism welcomes this expansion of choices and even the chaos and chronic uncertainty which accompany the collages of many of the self-authorities of the past" (Leonard, 1997, p.150). But I fear that current power takes advantage of the incoherence that is celebrated by postmodernism. Chronic uncertainty and tentativeness are the necessary ethical responses to our implication in domination (B. Heron, personal communication, 2003). As I face my own racism as a white woman, choosing to remain unsettled and unfinished is a more ethical choice than instituting a new grand plan to achieve my own innocence. But if there is a liberatory chaos at one level, there is paralysis in the face of power at another. In a recent *Harper's* essay, Curtis White describes the paralysis of action that occurs in the face of "the New Censorship."

> The New Censorship does not work by keeping things secret...The genius of the New Censorship is that it works through the obscenity of absolute openness. Iraq-gate wasn't a secret. The real secret is that it wasn't a secret, and certainly wasn't a scandal. It was business as usual. The betrayal of public trust is a daily story manipulated by the media within the narrative confines of "scandal." When in fact it's all a part of the daily routine and everyone knows it. The media makes pornography of the collective guilt of our politicians and business leaders. They make a yummy fetish of betrayed trust. We then consume it, mostly passively, because it is indistinguishable from our "entertainment" and because we suspect in some dim way that, bad as it surely is, it is working in our interests in the long run. What genius to have a system that allows you to behave badly, be exposed for it, and then have the sin recouped by the system as a sellable commodity! I mean, you have to admire the sheer, recuperative balls of it! (2003, p.18)

How are we going to orient our postmodern selves in a world where betrayal, corruption and injustice do not need secrecy? Is postmodern analysis complicit with the openness of the New Censorship? I am worried about how critical social work will take account of shifts to overt force and repression as increasing modes of power. What implications does this have for a Foucauldian notion of diffuse power spread across the social body? How do we retain the chaos engendered by the step back from the certainty of modernism while being certain that we need to refuse the chaos of the "absolute openness" in which current modes of power flourish?

SOWK 1010: Who Are These New Students?

This past year, we admitted our first direct-entry class. They are eighteen or nineteen years of age, who have come straight from high school into our social work program. Next year they will be even younger because Ontario has ended Grade 13.

These students live in a different world from the one in which I practiced social work. They were twelve years old when neo-conservative premier Mike Harris was elected. The decimation in social services, education and health is the normal world for them: it's their reality. They don't remember a time when there were no homeless people on the streets of Toronto. They went to school during the period of the development of strict, rigid curriculum, standardized testing for all students and teacher-bashing that left their teachers in a state of chronic rage, burnout and frustration. This to them is just the way school is. Let's return to the ground of my pessimistic dystopic vision and try to predict what current global changes may mean to my Social Work 1010 class.

- The drive to competencies in order to facilitate movement of personnel across borders as part of investment in services may drive professional standards down, because the object of the trade rules is to make qualifications the least "burdensome" possible. With competency-based standards, there will be much more emphasis on technical and prescriptive methods at the expense of practice wisdom, judgement and reflective practice. We see the foreshadows of this now in risk assessment models, in the computerization of welfare and so forth.

- There will be pressures on social work education to be less intellectual and more technical. The emphasis will be on finding the ways to do it, and less on relationship and the context of the issue. With privatization and deregulation, education standards may be forced downward.

- There will be continuing pressure to curb social spending, resulting in fewer resources and poorer quality resources. We see the beginnings of this in the ways agency funding has changed over the past decade.

- There will be ever-increasing privatization of health, education and welfare. With a for-profit system, the needs of people and the mission of public services will become secondary to profit. The values of social work will be under attack in a privatized service system.

- There will be considerable pressure on social work's commitments to social justice and human rights.

In sum, I think less will be asked of social workers of the future. They will need technical competency and the ability to practice in a fast turnover environment, but they will have fewer options to deploy. They will need the least education possible to do the job and the least attention to democratic ideals. These trends add up to a practice of social work that deepens what postmodern critical social work has been fighting against for the past decade — a rise in instrumental, technical practice.

Ken Moffatt explores the meaning of technique in the human services. He uses a broad approach to the concept, where technique is understood as practices with goals and where efficiency and rationality in meeting those goals is the purpose of technique — which may be the hallmark of services of the future. Moffatt (2001) identifies five elements of technique:

- Technique involves the management of human behaviour for instrumental ends.

- Technique is based on an understanding of human well-being that invokes rational thought to legitimize itself.

- Technique involves the control of behaviours and attitudes, including the behaviours of the person developing or utilizing the technique. (Most often users of the technique direct the control at others.)

- Technique generally has productivity, efficiency or the management of human behaviour as its goal.

- Technique is meant to be an interaction divested of emotion, and is assumed to be replicable from one interaction to the next (Moffatt, 2001, p.109).

Technique has always been part of the discursive practices of social work. As a profession, social work requires legitimate knowledge, and so practitioners and academics alike bemoan its state of knowledge — either its lack of empiricism, or its borrowed status. Our worry about social work's status as a profession results in our insecure attachment to technique, which might dispel fears about our own legitimacy as a profession. As Carolyn Taylor and Susan White state, "Practice is inadequate, runs the argument, and more and better knowledge is the answer, combined with elements of the technical-procedural model, namely better monitoring and evaluation of the effectiveness, efficiency and economy of service provision" (Taylor & White, 2001, p.29).

Critical social work from a postmodern perspective spent a great deal of energy resisting the siren call of technique in social work, arguing that it contradicts values based in social justice and solidarity. It is deeply ironic that we may now see the imposition of technique from without, where "effectiveness, efficiency and economy of service provision," far from legitimizing professional social work, may reduce it to an activity little more than tinkering.

What conceptions of the world of social work practice did our Social Work 1010 students bring to their first class? We were quite unprepared. We had a vision that we would make relationships quickly, get down to intellectually stimulating work and introduce them to the interesting debates in the field. Instead, we were amazed at the barriers to relationships with them. We tried to organize seating in circles to facilitate discussion. Every week for at least sixteen weeks, they actively resisted moving the chairs out of rows. Each assignment, which we had devised to allow them flexibility to think independently, left them in a panic. These students from the neo-conservative years had difficulty responding to our attempts to create a less formal atmosphere in the class. They knew how not to know us and how to keep themselves unknown. We found ourselves becoming the teachers they wanted — telling them exactly what we wanted from them, becoming the authorities they knew how to handle.

Their conception of the world involved antagonistic relationships with authority, where the preservation of their integrity depended on withholding themselves in relationship to their professors. Their job was to find out what we wanted and to produce it as best as they could. They did not see themselves as participants in their learning but as receivers of our authority about what was to be learned. These were the recipients of education cuts, of the turn to discipline, of strict curriculum guides and of objective competencies. They worked hard to keep most of themselves outside the class.

Students are already socialized into a culture of technique when they start their identification with social work practice. They know in technical relations that somebody is supposed to do something to somebody else, that the purpose of the relationship is to ferret out a problem and fix it. They know that their knowledge and competency needs to produce an outcome that they control; that the authority behind technique comes from a claim to a superior knowledge; that they and clients are supposed to be quite different, just as teachers and students are. Let's look at a piece of writing compiled from a class assignment where the students were asked to describe the learning needs that emerged from their experiences in their volunteer sites (I have created a fictional piece based on what I think is a fair representation of student responses to the assignment). Two things are interesting here: one is that the students had a hard time identifying learning needs: they are not used to being asked to think in terms of their own needs. The other is the degree to which they assumed the subject positions of the kind of authority they seem to know: judgemental, problem-centered, anti-dialogical

> For part of my volunteer experience, I am working with some of the developmentally delayed people who attend programs at the Centre. I find I am learning to observe the behaviour patterns of the developmentally delayed people I am working with so that I can understand their limits in the activities I am working with them in. I am also trying to learn to communicate with them without treating them like children.
>
> One problem is that I find sometimes that the clients do not treat each other with respect — they put each other down and try to humiliate someone who is having a hard time. When this happens, I try to tell them that it's not necessary to talk like this. I think it's important for them to listen so that they don't continue that behaviour. I want to get them to realize that it's inappropriate to put each other down. I am trying to model appropriate social behaviour for them. When we go out into the community for outings, I am really happy when they behave appropriately. We've had some good times where they behaved really well and I was satisfied.
>
> At the Centre, I also help kids with their homework. Often parents are there too. I need to learn how to talk to the parents because often they are part of the problem. One parent gets angry with his son if he doesn't write neatly. I want to talk to him about easing up — it isn't necessary to be so hard on him. If fact, it usually makes the kid not listen even more. I want to get the father to be nicer to the son. Then maybe the son can improve in school. I also need to learn to deal with one of the kids who just doesn't care. She'd rather yak on the phone to her friends than do her school work. I tell her that it's her choice about whether she wants to pass English, but she doesn't really listen.
>
> My supervisor asked me to spend some time with a couple of girls who have been getting into trouble at school. Apparently, they have been doing some shoplifting and have been skipping school. I am going to have some sessions with them so that I can find the root of the problem and try to introduce some resolutions to it.

This writing represents students' beginning notion of practice. It is their image of what social workers do. That imperative brings their relationships with the clients under the influence of technique. We can see the separation of their "me" and "them." The clients are "them" as a group to which correction must be applied. They put themselves in charge of correcting attitudes such as anger at kids or disinterest in schoolwork. The search for problems and solutions are drawn, I think, from their family and school experiences. They call on their knowledge of the difference between appropriate and inappropriate behaviour. In doing so, they replicate relations of power in which they have been the less powerful actor. They take on the moralistic overtones of parental and pedagogic corrections. If a kid wants to "yak on the phone" instead of doing her work, it's "her choice." Clients are divided in terms of whether or not they "listen."

Here, their relationships with people are subsumed by a benevolent paternalism. Students are bringing their histories into the application of technique. They know they are to manage behaviour, to root out problems, to apply methods, and they have, in first year, only their histories to draw from. Their relationships embody the exercise of technique: They "model appropriate behaviour." They "try to get them to listen," so clients can be persuaded to behave within the prescribed norms inside which they are good — so the worker is satisfied — and outside of which they are inappropriate, inviting the exercise of power through the corrections provided by technique. Methods of correction come from their immediate histories in power, within the history of professions themselves, where, as they replicate now, power is obscured as benevolent. When students have to enact a social work purpose with parents, relationships becomes difficult. The exercise of power falls apart as young students are positioned in contradictory moments of being young people in relationship to parents, and social workers needing to use power to find the problem. Students are uneasy here, and wish for more skills to solve this problem of power.

In critical social work, I think we often analyze these kinds of accounts as critiques of professionalism, with the historical operations of power cum Foucault. I think it is not enough given the current nature of power. We need to offer a different conception of the world to these students. Otherwise, they will be perfectly suited to the dystopic vision I outlined above. And they will be both subjects and objects of technique that values control, efficiency, manipulation and outcome.

We need to offer a conception of the world that can act as a difference, as a clear alternative to a future that is increasingly forced on us by current modes of power. How might we use the growth of critical theory in social work of the past decade to formulate such a place? As I discussed in the previous section, postmodernism quite rightly insisted on the death of grand theory because it contained stratagems of exclusion and, therefore, could not meet the social justice requirements of a plural, multi-vocal world. But we now appear to need a conception of the world to hold onto, since the old ways of pressuring, of holding governments to account, of incremental progress are associated with a disappearing dynamic of power. I think that we have the seeds of that conception in critical social work theory. I am not suggesting a new grand theory, a new program with its inevitable exclusions. I am suggesting that we find points of agreement, convergences, common values and aspirations from our history that will allow the spectrum of points of view in social work, a fragile, temporary, limited, but united alliance around the need to hold ourselves to a different conception of the world in light of current world changes.

Recognition and Redistribution as Social Work Concerns

I want to offer my interest in recent critical theory as one of many possibilities for building a convergence of interests in social work. This work involves the debates concerning redistribution and recognition. I am interested in this debate because it has potential to pull together parallel social justice goals in social work, thus creating a better framework for solidarity. Social work has long been interested in problems of redistribution through its involvement in social welfare and its mandate with respect to poverty. The moral imperative for redistribution — the equalization of resources — comes from the rights-based arguments of Kant, Marx and Rawls. These are theories that hold that the fair distribution of resources is a moral duty. Social work has enacted that duty across a spectrum between residual social welfare and democratic socialism.

More recently, theories of recognition, spearheaded by Axel Honneth (Honneth, 1992; Honneth & Margalit, 2001), have drawn attention to the ethics of individual identity formation, stating that human integrity depends on respectful intersubjective recognition. Honneth (1992) defines recognition by saying,

> [H]uman individuation is a process in which the individual can unfold a practical identity to the extent that he is capable of reassuring himself of recognition by a growing circle of partners to communication. Subjects…are constituted as individuals solely by learning, from the perspective of others who offer approval, to relate to themselves as beings who possess certain positive qualities and abilities. (p. 189)

The theory of recognition spells out a basic paradox in identity formation: people can develop consciousness of self and individuality only through recognition from others. This is the basis of intersubjectivity and also of the vulnerability that accompanies it: our individuality depends on recognition from others.

Honneth uses the concept of recognition to ground a theory of human integrity that is quite pivotal to social work relationships. Human integrity, he says, depends on freedom from disrespect that harms recognition. He specifies three broad categories of disrespect: physical degradation or humiliation, lack of the same rights as others possess, and lack of respect for individual or group differences. We in social work witness the damage of these forms of disrespect, for example, in cases of rape or abuse as forms of physical degradation; in the withholding of welfare and other resource entitlements as forms of denial of rights; and in the enactment of power and privilege with respect to race class, gender, sexual orientation and so forth as forms of disrespect for difference.

Honneth helps us to understand the connection between intersubjective relationships of recognition and social justice: the well-being of individuals depends on identities formed within social justice. Social work struggles with the connections between justice, identity and difference. The development of anti-oppressive theory and practice with respect to gender-based discrimination, anti-racism, and homophobia and other oppressions has occupied social work education for the past decade. But it has operated on a parallel track with concerns about redistribution, albeit with acknowledgement that the two are often mutually constructing.

More recently, debates about recognition explore the necessity of holding together issues of redistribution with recognition. I am interested in this debate because it unites social work's concern for equitable distribution of resources *and* for relations of recognition that respect difference and diversity. Nancy Fraser (1995, 2001) describes this debate as follows:

> For some time now, the forces of progressive politics have been divided into two camps. On one side stand the proponents of "redistribution." Drawing on long traditions of egalitarian, labor and socialist organizing, political actors aligned with this orientation seek a more just allocation of resources and goods. On the other side stand the proponents of "recognition." Drawing on newer visions of a "difference-friendly" society, they seek a world where assimilation to majority or dominant cultural norms is no longer the price of equal respect. Members of the first camp hope to redistribute wealth from the rich to the poor, from the North to the South, and from the owners to the workers. Members of the second, in contrast, seek recognition of the distinctive perspectives of ethnic, "racial," and sexual minorities, as well as of gender difference." (Fraser, 2001, p.21)

Fraser goes on to discuss the possibilities for reconciling redistribution and recognition, using an expanded concept of justice. While in-depth discussion of her integration model is beyond the scope of this chapter, it is perhaps an example of a possibility for bringing together points of convergence in social work. Briefly, Fraser (2001) proposes to treat redistribution and recognition as distinct dimensions of justice through a concept of "parity of participation." Parity of participation requires two forms: (1) the distribution of resources needed to ensure participation, and (2) "the intersubjective condition of participatory parity" (p. 29), meaning freedom from discrimination that denies the possibility of full participation in social interaction.

I think it is possible to pull the themes of redistribution and recognition together to help us articulate an alternative to the current conception of the world. Social work is historically rooted in opposition to structures of economic injustice that ground personal problems. Recent structural approaches consolidate that history in critiques of social organization. We have also been learning to work against forms of misrecognition that organize status and identities into relations of privilege and powerlessness. Our work with diversity and difference in terms of class, race and gender brings together issues of identity and power. Thus, at the heart of social work is the imperative for redistribution and relations of recognition that insist on intersubjective respect as a condition of social justice.

Social work's recent attempts to deal with social justice have been labelled weakly as empowerment. This word has become tired and empty and offers little in the way of an alternative concept of the world. It has been all too easily harnessed to technique, as when we read so frequently in student papers, "I intend to empower her to get a job." I would suggest that the specific frame of redistribution and recognition held together under the rubric of parity of participation is a much more powerful possibility for conceptualizing social work practice because it offers a concept of a world that insists on parity of participation, and it offers concrete means of holding ourselves accountable to that vision through the conditions of redistribution and recognition.

I hear the alarm bells signalling "the grand theory trap." Even as this bell tolls with an increasingly pedantic timbre, I don't want to develop new prescriptions, but rather to suggest a time-limited agreement that can offer a badly needed strategic alternative at this particular and ephemeral moment of history. I think current social work does contain a degree of agreement about alternate and oppositional visions that, if framed and articulated, can serve as a conception of the world that we offer in contrast to current global trends. I am concerned with how we achieve solidarity through a frame such as parity of participation because I think we need an agreement that provides us with a language with which to describe a conception of the world that is actually useful in everyday, local practices.

Back to 1010

Over the course of the year, things gradually changed in our 1010 class. Students lost their stony looks in response to our feeble jokes. They started changing their seats for small groups. And, gradually, they started to imagine that they might be social workers, and that this would compel them to think about the larger social world with its inequalities and inequities. If I look over the successes of that class, they would be that we started to develop relationships with the students, and they started to learn that social work is connected intimately to the larger social world — something not so distant from redistribution and recognition. Indeed, their final papers showed the extent to which they were able to find themselves outside the prescriptive approach of technique. By the end of the term, the reflective papers showed the beginnings of students' delight in the relationships they established in their settings. Students who previously talked in paternalistic tones about modelling and correction now described an entirely different experience. One student wrote: "I have come to understand the fact that they are normal individuals that deal with many of the same issues I deal with." This student transcended the social space engineered by technique. She experienced a sense of mutuality and equality. I think she found moments of relationship outside the imperatives of purpose — moments of pleasure, moments of appreciation of her clients, that allow her to confirm their senses of selves, not as disabled people, but as people, surprisingly enough, like her in many ways.

Another student said: "They always welcomed me as a person who wanted to get to know them, as well as they wanted to get to know who I was because I was in some way different than they were. Even though I did not have a disability we still managed to find a common ground and communicate on the same level." Here, opposed to technique, the imprisoning stereotype of "delayed" disintegrates as unique individuals emerge and make a contribution to the students. As a resource, the relationship finds a kind of mutuality — expressed by the student as "the same level." To my mind it is a moment of possibility when a student social worker and a delayed adult find themselves at the same level in full view of their differences. These may be small moments of recognition that contribute however minutely to "parity of participation," and I would like to be able to frame them as such so that my students have a conception that such moments in relationships have reference in justice, and that they are working, not in an empathy-driven amelioration of individual pain, but from a frame of justice that insists on facilitating participation because it is a condition of justice. In other words, it is a conception of the world I would like my students to hold themselves to.

There is no conception of the world that will give us access to an innocent practice. Nor is there a conception of the world that can speak for everyone. To do social work is to live in a contradictory space where the unavoidable micro power of the social space of professions is in constant tension with egalitarian, progressive ideals. Should we teach students how to do social work, or should we help them "just be themselves"? What happens if "just being themselves" doesn't make them social workers? How do we have a professional identity when inherent in that identity is power and technique? How do we establish relations of recognition in view of difference? I am suggesting that, while recognizing the inevitability of these tensions, we need to cast an eye towards a future that jeopardizes social work. It is not only internal tension in the profession that we must continue to struggle with, it is external threats to our values and foundations in changed world outside the profession that will require us to articulate alternate conceptions of the world and our place in it. These conceptions need to be based on commitments already valued in the profession, which fall within redistribution and recognition. I think critical social work has a role to play in responding to the future with alternatives and active resistance that accounts for the changing nature of power in the world.

It may be that current global threats offer a new space for solidarity in the profession. Internal divisions between caseworkers and community work, therapy and self-help, the traditional splits between putative radical and conservative social work, can perhaps not be solved by formula or prescription, but maybe they can be abandoned as sharper divisions between a social work conception of the world and its current direction become increasingly apparent. We need a frame for the hard work of creating global relations of justice, solidarity, peace and sustainability that lies ahead. We need a language of justice that names the world we want to live in, so that our practice can become a way of constructing that world.

References

Foucault, M. (1980). *Power/knowledge: Selected interviews and other writings 1972-1977.* New York: Pantheon.

Foucault, M. (1982). The subject and power. *Critical Inquiry, 8*(4), 777-789.

Fraser, N. (1995). From redistribution to recognition. *New Left Review, 212,* 68-93.

Fraser, N. (2001). Recognition without ethics? *Theory, Culture & Society, 18*(2-3), 21-42.

Gould, E. (2003, March 16). *Recent Developments in the GATS Negotiations: The Good and the Bad News for Local Governments.* The Council of Canadians report. Retrieved from <www.canadians.org>.

Honneth, A. (1992). Integrity and disrespect: Principles of a conception of morality based on the theory of recognition. *Political Theory, 20*(2), 187-201.

Honneth, A., & Margalit, A. (2001). Recognition. *Theory, Culture & Society, 18*(2-3), 111-126.

Leonard, P. (1997). *Postmodern welfare: Reconstructing and emancipatory project.* London: Sage.

McBride, S. & Shields, J. (1997). *Dismantling a nation: The transition to corporate rule in Canada.* Halifax: Fernwood

Moffatt, K. (2001). *The poetics of social work: Personal agency and social transformation in Canada, 1920-1939.* Toronto: University of Toronto Press.

Project New American Century. August 15, 2004, from <http://www.newamericancentury.org/index.html>.

Rossiter, A. (1996). A perspective on critical social work. *Journal of Progressive Human Services, 7*(2), 23-41.

Rossiter. A. (2001). Innocence lost and suspicion found: Do we educate for or against social work? *Critical Social Work, 2*(1). Retrieved from <http://www.criticalsocialwork.com>.

Sinclair, S., & Grieshaber-Otto, J. (2002). *Facing the facts: A Guide to the GATS Debate.* Ottawa: Canadian Centre for Policy Alternatives.

Swenarchuk, M. (2002, May). From global to local: GATS impacts on Canadian municipalities. Electronic version retrieved from <www.policyalternatives.ca/publications/publ.html>. Canadian Centre for Policy Alternatives. ISBN 0-88627-302-1, 1-50.

Taylor, C., & White, S. (2001). Knowledge, truth and reflectivity: The problem of judgement in social work. *Journal of Social Work, 1*(1), 37-59.

White, C. (2003, August). The new censorship. *Harper's, 307,* 15-20.

13

Feminist Social Work: Past, Present and Future

Brid Featherstone

n this chapter I will provide some historical background before exploring the emergence of feminist social work in the United Kingdom in the late 1970s. I will trace its main themes as it developed into the 1980s and 1990s. While a critical approach will be taken to key aspects of its trajectory, it will be argued that, within the diverse and contested spaces occupied by feminisms today, important possibilities exist for those of us who wish to understand and engage with the lived experiences and relationships of men, women and children. The chapter will conclude by exploring how feminist thinking can contribute to a necessary critique of aspects of welfare restructuring across a range of countries.

Locating Feminist Social Work

Lewis (1992) in an analysis of nineteenth-century social work in the U.K. argues that the ideas and practice of early individual social work were more complicated than often presented in the standard histories that have constructed it as "women controlling women." Through exploring the ideas and work of two influential proponents of individual social work, Octavia Hill and Helen Bosanquet, she concludes they were by no means the "reactionary handmaidens of classical political economy" (p. 81).Their insistence on the importance of social workers reaching an understanding and appreciation of the values and ways of living of the poor was genuine, although there was a clear set of beliefs and behaviours according to which the poor family would be judged. They were sympathetic to the position of working-class women and appreciated their importance in securing the welfare of their families. For example, Lewis argued that "Bosanquet's sympathy for the working woman's efforts to do well by her children sprung both from the belief that they were well intentioned but ignorant, and from a latent feminist understanding that they were by no means the arbiters of their fate" (p. 91).

Generally, there was a belief both in the importance of the family and in a particular gendered order where men and women played their respective roles. In particular, there seemed to be some sympathy for women whose husbands did not meet their responsibilities as economic providers.

According to American historian Linda Gordon (1986), first-wave feminism in the nineteenth century in the U.S. was actively involved in the development of social work in that organized feminism was a liberal reform program, a program for the adaption of the family and civil society to new economic conditions. She argues that, whether consciously or not, feminists at that time felt that these conditions provided greater possibilities for the freedom and empowerment of women than that offered by constructions of the family, which rested upon power relations where men had property rights over women and children. In her study of developments in Boston at the turn of the twentieth century, she argues that "child protection work was an integral part of the feminist as well as the bourgeois program for modernising the family" (p. 75).

She further notes that feminists were longstanding advocates of modern forms of social control, and this was to be viewed with some suspicion by the feminism that emerged at the end of the 1960s.

Feminist Social Work in the Twentieth Century

Generally, the feminism that emerged in many Western countries such as Australia, the U.S., Canada and the U.K. at the end of the 1960s was much more wide ranging in its critiques than its historical predecessors. A complex but vigorous critique emerged of a particular model of the "family" — the post-war nuclear model that comprised a male provider and his economically dependent wife, whose key site of identity was familial and whose key role was maternal (Bryson, 2002). This critique proved too partial and specific in that it did not adequately engage with the experiences of black and working-class women. However, what feminism did fuel was a deconstructionist project that contested dominant understandings within the social sciences of the family as a unit composed of those with complementary interests. It exposed the amount of violence and exploitation that lay hidden behind a veil of family privacy and made visible the amount of work that women engaged in to nurture bodies and minds, work that was neither recognized nor valued appropriately (Segal, 1995). There was also considerable attention paid to understanding and exploring the role of "the state," and in general there was much more concern about the way state laws and institutions operated to discipline women (see, for example, Wilson, 1980). Analyses in both of these areas were of key importance for social workers in the U.K. where the state was a key employer of social workers and where "supporting the family," particularly in terms of keeping children within their families, was central.

A project that sought to articulate feminist social work became apparent from the late 1970s onwards in countries such as the U.K., the U.S. and Australia (Marchant & Wearing, 1986). In 1979, the first conference on feminist social work practice was held at the University of Warwick in the U.K., organized by women social work students, and the notes of this conference were published as a small pamphlet (Notes on the Conference, 1979). Three other national conferences were held, in Birmingham in 1980, Bradford, 1981, and London, 1982, although the practice of holding *national* conferences seemed to disappear in the mid-1980s.

An account from one of the Women and Social Work groups that began to emerge in the late 1970s and early 1980s has also been published (Birmingham Women and Social Work Group, 1985). Similar groups often formed by social work students emerged elsewhere. For example, I was involved in a Women and Social Work Group that was established in Nottingham in the early 1980s and continued to meet for a number of years. There would appear to have been similar groups around the country for a period at least, certainly in Warwick, Birmingham and Bradford.

The chapter by the Birmingham Women and Social Work Group (1985), in a volume edited by Brook and Davis, was an important attempt to outline what feminist social work was from their perspective. They argued against either views of the state as a neutral force on which demands can be made or as a directly coercive force — the latter position they attributed to the radical social work of the time. They saw their interaction with the state as contradictory. On one hand, many of the benefits the state provided were necessary, but on the other hand, people, and particularly women seeking welfare services, were often involved in oppressive relationships that defined them as "inadequate" or "scroungers." They advocated working "in and against" the state. Alternative resources set up by and for women were viewed as invaluable, not only because clients could be referred to them for specific types of help and support, but also because they served as models for the future development of state services.

They identified a key principle of feminist social work as based on the recognition that society is patriarchal. Therefore, while struggles against oppression based on "race" and class were crucial, they were not primary. They argued that women's opposition to patriarchy had neither an immediate parallel in the fight for socialism, nor were male socialists, whether black or white, reliable allies (1985, p.119).Furthermore, they refused too close a link with radical social work, arguing that women's oppression arose from a structural inequality in society that is not necessarily combatted by adapting the theories and tactics of the left. They wished to assert the importance of their roots in the Women's Liberation Movement.

Furthermore, they were critical of early radical social work approaches, which they saw as constructed in unequivocal opposition to a monolithic state. Although they did recognize this at the time of writing their chapter, radical approaches had moved on to approaches that were "in and against" the state. A further criticism cohered around the radical social work belief that casework was automatically oppressive, and they advanced a case for the feminist practice of consciousness raising as a key method of working with women.

In terms of "the family," they contested the belief that the stereotypical nuclear family was either the most common or most effective institution for the care and upbringing of children. However, they recognized that the "family is complex and ambiguous. It can be both good and bad — a place where we experience caring, loving relationships, but also a destructive, oppressive force in our lives" (1985, p.126). An approach to family difficulties and breakdowns was argued for, which would result in provision that was flexible.

This project was centrally concerned with working with women. Indeed it was argued that work with men should be done by men as feminists should not have to devote time and energy to challenging men's attitudes and behaviours. They were also the strongest advocates at one of the national conferences that the presence of men at that conference was problematic and should not be accepted.

The notes from the same conference (Notes on the Conference, 1979) reflect the differing positions held by feminists about working with men in their differing roles. According to the conference organizers, it was important to contest the version of feminism promoted by the Birmingham Women and Social Work Group as it was based upon separatism and failed to connect feminism with class politics. Allowing men to attend the conference was linked to the desire to apply feminism to social work where men were both clients and colleagues. An analysis emerged from those identifying as socialist feminists that linked sexism and class politics by explicitly underscoring the importance of the family to capitalism. It was argued that it was important

> to link women's individual position in the family, and the form of the family, which is tightly controlled by, for example, lack of nurseries, after school activities and holiday provision for children, lack of employment and an inadequate level of social security ultimately defined by relationships to men, is to see the connection of women's role to the maintenance of capitalism. If as social workers we wish to change these, we need at some point to form alliances with unions, parties and colleagues unfamiliar with feminism. (pp. 61-62)

The practice of holding national conferences seemed to die out in the mid-1980s. Furthermore, the prospects for political engagement or dialogue generally became less and less available in the U.K. The mid-1980s saw a significant setback for the trade union movement with the defeat of the miners' strike by a neo-liberal Conservative government that ruled from 1979 to 1997. Presided over for much of the time by a woman prime minister, the 1980s and much of the 1990s were difficult times for many, especially those who were poor. The numbers of lone mothers grew dramatically as did the numbers of children in poverty. The growth of female involvement in the labour market was not accompanied by any form of infrastructure for child care provision or support. There was a decline in traditional industries with corresponding consequences for full-time male employment. Feminism lost any national focus and seemed to be mired in a range of divisive internal battles both theoretically and politically (see Segal, 1987).

Attempts to develop feminist social work approaches did continue. There was an emergence of what were called "woman-centred" approaches, which advocated that the shared gender identities of service users and workers were a key resource for developing empowering practices (Hamner & Statham, 1988). This continued the focus by feminist social work on working with women, although there was a recognition that women were not a unitary category. Langan and

Day's book in 1992 directly took up the challenge of addressing differences between women — "race," age, sexuality, disability — and located feminist social work within an anti-discriminatory project. This fit with wider developments of that time where awareness of "race" issues in particular had become more high profile. Langan and Day's attempt to specify a particularly feminist approach was to become lost in the wider projects that emerged as the decade wore on. For example, it became harder to articulate how gender oppression worked across a range of categories and could be challenged. Moreover, the deconstruction of the category "women" in Langan and Day's work was not accompanied by a focus on deconstructing the category "men."

In the 1990s a number of writings emerged that raised significant issues about feminist social work theory and practice. Lawrence (1992) pointed out from a psychoanalytic perspective that the commonalities between women should not be assumed to provide an automatic route into more empowering practices. Indeed, she argued that the similarities in women's developmental trajectory could preclude women social workers being able to allow women service users to be needy or not cope.

Wise (1995) questioned the assumption that women were always the most oppressed in a given situation and that it was therefore their definitions of needs that should be prioritized. She argued that feminist social workers had paid inadequate attention to the importance of utilizing the powers they possessed in order to protect the most vulnerable in given situations, who were usually children. White (1995) pointed out the importance of acknowledging how and why differences between women mattered in practice.

Graham (1992) linked into wider feminist scholarship when she argued that gender and gender relations rather than women should be the focus of feminist theoretical and practice concerns. This involved interrogating rather than assuming categories such as women, identifying the process of construction and crucially highlighting the relational nature of such constructions. As Flax (1990) noted, a complex set of social processes are captured by the category "gender relations." Femininity cannot be understood except in relation to masculinity and vice versa. Furthermore, these relations are not static but constituted through practices with ongoing negotiations over time and space about their fluid and multiple meanings.

Issues in relation to men and masculinities did become the focus of some feminist attention in the 1990s. Cavanagh and Cree's 1996 edited book *Working with Men: Feminism and Social Work* argued in its preface that "feminist social work practice must include direct work with men as part of a broader strategy whose ultimate goal is the empowerment of women." It included chapters on working with men in prisons, men who were violent, male social work students, men coping with marital breakdown and boys.

Almost inevitably in an edited book, there were differences in the approaches taken and why, although the editors did attempt to establish a code of practice for feminist work with men (pp. 183-186). Not surprisingly, given the statement above, the principles underpinning this code emphasized the following: "[W]omen are our first priority and... work with men is done in order to improve the quality of life for women. It is about recognising that unless men change, then the lives of women and children will not change for the better" (p. 183).

There was a recognition that men could experience oppression on the basis of class, "race" and sexual orientation, although there appeared to be a overriding consensus that men continue to inhabit a privileged position in relation to women. "This is undeniable irrespective of their race or class" (p. 182). Consequently, the authors leave an unexplored paradox — men are deconstructed but still ultimately powerful.

In general, by the end of the 1990s, work such as that by Cavanagh and Cree was uncommon. There were fewer attempts to develop a specifically feminist approach to theory and method. Feminist insights had become incorporated into and to some extent subsumed within a broader anti-discriminatory project. What had became more and more apparent was a more focused and often pragmatic approach by feminists to developing an understanding of and campaigning around specific issues such as domestic violence and child sexual abuse.

Domestic violence

Awareness of the violence experienced by women within the privacy of the home coupled with an understanding that women's economic dependence upon individual men restricted women's ability to challenge or leave such violence was crucial in supporting the deconstructionist project highlighted above in relation to the family (Segal, 1987, 1995). It also led to the development of alternative spaces — refuges — for women and to campaigning for changes in relation to the law, housing and benefit provision. It became part of a much wider project that linked such violence with male violence more generally.

Initial attempts to get social workers to address such violence for the sake of women's welfare, however, was to prove unsuccessful in a system predominantly focused around ensuring children's welfare. It was the linking of such violence with the implications of children's welfare that was to be influential. The implications were argued to be twofold (Mullender & Morley, 1994). Men who harmed women were also likely to harm children, and children could be harmed by the witnessing of such violence.

In general, the analysis advanced as to why men were violent was a singular one, which linked such violence to the power men held in the wider society. There was an active repudiation of attempts to deconstruct men as a category and explore whether such violence might have multiple meanings or sources (Featherstone & Trinder, 1997).

Children and women's welfare were tied together, and it was common for feminist research to elicit children's views through their mothers (for a critique, see Featherstone & Trinder, 1997). This has changed more recently as feminists have become more involved in addressing children's own views themselves, and there have been calls for broader research projects that can encompass children holding quite complex views of their violent fathers (Peled, 2000).

Sexual abuse

This was *the* issue, which, in my opinion, feminists put on the child welfare agenda. Not only did they demonstrate the prevalence of such abuse, but they contested how it had been defined and dominant explanations in relation to causation.

Such work continues and is extremely wide ranging in scope (see, for example, Itzin, 2001). It has important strengths as well as some limitations, and the impact has been complex and contradictory. What is apparent is that the more sexual abuse has become part of a mainstream policy and practice agenda, the less a language in relation to gender informs either understandings or ways of working. The implications of the recognition pioneered by feminists of the preponderance of males as offenders (see Frosh, 2002, for a review of the strengths and limitations of the research base) has not been adequately taken on board. For example, no public awareness campaigns have emerged in this area in the U.K. that explicitly engage with gender issues. There appears to be little recognition that such campaigns are necessary and should address male patterns of emotional and sexual socialization in the context of wider cultural tendencies. It is possible that the refusal by many feminists to deconstruct the category "men" and explore why many men resist sexually abusive behaviour has not helped change the climate in relation to pushing for such preventive strategies in that it has fed into men's anxieties and defensiveness and encouraged tendencies not to engage with the issues. However, it is more likely that, in the U.K. at least, such campaigns are simply not recognized as a priority because of a policy context that simply does not make addressing such issues a priority. I will return to this below.

Feminists have also pioneered the recognition that many mothers wish to be or are protective and the importance to children's longer term welfare of such protectiveness (Hooper, 1992). However, this has fed into a policy and practice agenda that often removes men and leaves women and children to fend for themselves unsupported. Resources are clearly crucial here as statutory agencies in particular have struggled and continue to struggle to provide anything other than a reactive service premised on dealing with those who are considered "high risk."

Furthermore, little room appears available to explore mothers' more ambivalent feelings, and they are positioned narrowly as either protective or collusive. Again this can be linked to resource issues, as little opportunities are available to offer mothers and/or protective carers flexible provision and supports in order to explore their complex feelings or have time out from caring responsibilities. However, it is also apparent that broader feminist insights into the complexities of mothering and motherhood have not always been promoted by many of the feminist writings on sexual violence common in the social work literature (Featherstone, 1999).

To conclude, by the year 2000, it was hard to find any explicit adherents to feminist social work although some issues such as child sexual abuse and domestic violence that had been promoted by feminists had been placed on a wider agenda, if often in ways that did not acknowledge their gendered dimensions.

A New Century

In the U.K., a host of writings have emerged from feminists concerned with re-evaluating the role of feminism at the end of the twentieth century (see, for example, Segal, 1999; Walter, 1999), Such developments have seemed to be prompted both by end-of-century concerns to reflect but also make sense of or influence the policy landscape ushered in by the emergence of New Labour in 1997 after a long period of New Right dominance (Franks, 1999; Benn, 1998). What is clear from many, such as Segal, particularly, is that feminism is seen as a project that must be located in a complex gender landscape where old markers around masculinity and femininity are being rethought and reworked due to economic, cultural and demographic shifts. There have also been those, however, who argue that the difficulties faced by men and boys, particularly those who are poor and marginalized, necessitate the jettisoning of feminism and that it is increasingly a block to engaging with such difficulties. Coward (1999) is the most strident exponent of this view, although, in my view, her analysis caricatures the complexity of feminist thought. For example, alongside those listed above, Stacey (1999) from the U.S. has pointed out the urgency of addressing how poorly equipped many men (especially those who are economically marginalized) are to deal with a landscape where access to traditional forms of masculine legitimation is heavily circumscribed.

Under New Labour a project aimed at "engaging fathers" has emerged at a policy and practice level within social work and allied professions since 1997, and there have been some attempts to redress the neglect of family policy evident under the Conservatives (Featherstone, 2003). There is therefore some potential for bringing gender issues onto the agenda more generally as well as within social work.

In the next section I explore this within a broader discussion about why I think an ongoing engagement with contemporary feminist ideas could contribute to a vibrant critical social work project. In order to anchor my discussion, I will use the example of family support in the area of child welfare, and I will look at three interlinked areas: language, practices and policies.

Feminism for Family Support

Language and practices

In the U.K. the term "family support" is used to cover a range of practices across a spectrum of aims (see, for example, Gardner, 1996). While there is general agreement that it is an ambiguous concept, it is commonly assumed to be "good thing" of which more is needed and has been both recast and expanded under New Labour (see Featherstone, 2004). What is notable about the considerable and expanding literature devoted to family support, however, is how little explicit attention is paid to the multiple meanings that can be attached to "family" today.

Contemporary feminist developments are, by contrast, particularly concerned to engage with bottom up understandings of *who* is considered family and to explore *why* a range of diverse arrangements are apparent. In so doing, they underscore the multiple meanings that can be attached to "family" and explore why an array of diverse arrangements have emerged. They offer us important insights, for example, into why women may "choose" divorce and/or to mother alone. In a complex and changing world, they oblige recognition of the possibilities available to many women to refuse violent settlements or those that thwart their impulses towards self-actualization. They also direct attention to why men may struggle to offer women the kinds of relationships they want (see, for example, Smart & Neale, 1999).

The term "family practices" has emerged to sum up the shifts that have occurred in feminist theoretical and empirical work (Smart & Neale, 1999). The term is used to challenge the idea that the family is a "thing" or an institution and thus to challenge previous feminist critiques of it as the key site of women's subordination. This reflects the influence of a range of critiques from differing categories of women as well as the influence of theoretical currents such as postmodernism. It also reflects the evidence of a dispersal of practices across a range of households involving a range of blood, marital, kin and non-kin relationships.

Smart and Neale (1999) and Smart, Neale, and Wade (2001) explore, for example, men's, women's and children's accounts of "doing family" in post-separation and/or divorce contexts. They locate themselves within a multi-perspective approach, and while indebted to earlier feminist scholarship that sought to offer a voice to women to redress their historical invisibility, theirs is clearly a broader project (see also Stacey's 1991 ethnographic study of families in the U.S.).

They look at what "family" means to those sharing care across households with a range of participants who are not linked by blood or marital ties. They interrogate how mothers rethink and do mothering in contexts where they share care and how fathers redefine fathering in situations of non-residence. What is happening to gendered settlements in terms of caring? What kinds of new settlements emerge? What are the implications of treating men and women as equal before the law when, in practice, many may have negotiated unequal settlements around caretaking and paid work? How do children negotiate the terrain of post-divorce and/ or separation family life? In a changing context, how do "family" members understand and act out their feelings of responsibility towards each other? Is it appropriate to continue to impose top-down understandings of what mothers and fathers should do, for example?

While the term practices signposts the importance of engaging with *what* is done, by *whom* and *why,* and reinforces the importance of attending to bottom-up understandings, it also holds important additional possibilities. It directs attention to the importance of addressing what practices it is that are to be supported and/or proscribed and refuses the counterposition of supportive and controlling activities. It therefore challenges constructions of "family support" that have emerged in the U.K., which seek to promote it as a project that is counterposed to that of "child protection." In an analysis that is gender informed, Ferguson (2001), for example, articulates the need for family support in the context of child welfare today to be concerned with the building of "democratic families." Such families are those "where children are heard as well as seen and feel safe, women as well as men are treated with respect, and men as well as women are enabled to have emotional expressive lives and relationships" (p. 8). In order to facilitate the building of such families, Ferguson clearly demonstrates the necessity for both controlling and supportive activities and reinforces the importance of recognizing that to control the violent behaviour of one member of the family is to support and protect others. This echoes historical feminist concerns, as highlighted by Gordon (1986), to mobilize the power of the state on behalf of women and children in order to contest men's violent and abusive behaviour. What is apparent today, however, is a clear concern with offering possibilities to women and children to define and shape the contours of state intervention (Ferguson, 2001).

Attention to language by feminists obliges caution about the use of ungendered terms such as "parent" and "parental responsibility," terms that currently litter the legislative and policy landscape. The term "parent" can obscure both the fixity and fluidity that is apparent, and while it can herald welcome moves towards gender equity, it can also act as a rhetorical device to obscure and confuse. To give an example, gendered divisions in child care continue to be significant with women of all classes and occupations doing such work, although there is evidence of important shifts among some groups of men (O'Brien & Shemilt, 2003). There is evidence, therefore, of fixity and fluidity in relation to child care to some extent — the term "parent" can however act to construct a world where distinctions between men and women, mothers and fathers, no longer pertain.

This is highly problematic. For example, research in the U.K. into those involved with parenting programs under legislation to tackle criminal and anti-social behaviour by children, would indicate that it is women, in the main, who are involved in the reality of exercising parental responsibility (Ghate &

Ramalla, 2002). Indeed, perusal of the evidence would indicate that these programs are primarily for women who are struggling with troublesome sons (Featherstone, 2004). Mobilizing the term "parent" is both misleading and unjust in such circumstances.

As indicated above, possibilities have been opened up by some of the current policy initiatives around "engaging fathers" to bring in a gendered language and gender concerns. Emerging from a diverse array of sources and agendas, there has been an attempt in the U.K. to fund services directed at fathers and encourage some mainstreaming. This agenda does offer spaces to men, often those who are marginalized, to articulate their needs and concerns (Featherstone, 2004). The work is rife with dilemmas, however, and feminist insights can be used in helpful and unhelpful ways both to highlight and work with such dilemmas.

Feminist insights can help avoid tendencies for discussions to dwell solely on what skills and techniques may be required to "engage fathers" and to open up debates about what constructions of fathering are to be promoted and what is required by those concerned, men, women and children. Feminist insights, for example, draw attention to the importance of offering possibilities for women and children to construct lives free from fear and violence and thus question blanket approaches that assume that father involvement is uniformly positive and to be encouraged. Thus, they contest the current policy context that separates the agenda in relation to engaging fathers from that aimed at tackling domestic violence. The consequence of such a split approach is that those who are violent are constructed as offenders without any adequate recognition or supports for engaging with them as fathers (Featherstone, 2003).

There are dangers, however, in using feminist insights. As the analysis in preceding sections has argued, there has been a very limited commitment by much of the feminist and social work literature to exploring the complexities of men's positionings. Deconstructing the category "men" is vital to attend to the marginalization of many of those who come to the attention of services and to fully appreciate the differing ways in which their lives have been impacted upon by the economic, cultural and demographic changes of the last decades. A focus on violence as a reflection of men's power is too simple and pays scant attention to the complex interweaving of power and powerlessness in many men's lives. Furthermore, there can be a danger that it is only their violence or potential for violence that is focused on. Thus there can be a neglect of those who are not violent and need help with accessing services and engaging in more democratic settlements with women and children. As well, such analyses are ill attuned to exploring the multiple meanings that violence can carry for men and the multiple sources of such violence.

Policies

Finally, within feminist scholarship a linked but very diverse project from a range of disciplines around "the ethics of care" has become highly influential.

This offers a host of possibilities for rethinking practices and policies in relation to social work and allied "people work" (see Parton, 2003). Here I will concentrate briefly on policy issues. Located within concerns to open up the historical invisibility of caring work and women's need to access a range of entitlements for such work, a host of analyses have emerged that, in placing caring activities at the heart of the human enterprise, argue for a rethinking of how such activities should be recognized, valued and supported at the policy level (Williams, 2001). This rethinking encompasses calls for policy measures, for example, that actively support both men and women to combine paid work and caring responsibilities.

It also challenges a policy context very evident in countries such as the U.S., Canada and the U.K. that appears to institute involvement in paid work as *the* badge of responsible citizenship. According to Jenson and Saint Martin (2001), who write from a Canadian perspective but argue that their analysis is relevant to a number of Western welfare states, we are living through a paradigm shift. They argue that such a shift encompasses moving away from key tenets of the old welfare state towards what they refer to as the "social investment state." While the old welfare state sought to protect people from the market, a social investment state seeks to facilitate people into the market. People's security therefore comes from *their* capacity to change rather than from the state. The key guideline for states is investment in human capital rather the direct provision of human maintenance (Giddens, 1998). They explore the notion of time, which underpins the social investment approach to the role of the state. The results of an investment are located in the future whereas consumption is something that occurs in the present. For state spending to be effective and worthwhile, it must not simply be consumed in the present but must be an investment that will pay off and reap rewards in the future. Thus spending may legitimately be directed to: supporting and educating children because they hold the promise of the future, promoting health and healthy populations because they pay off in lower future costs, reducing the probability of future costs of school failure and crime with a heavy emphasis on early intervention in children, and fostering employability so as to increase future labour force participation rates. State spending for current costs, by contrast, must be cautious and targeted and is motivated not by concerns about social justice but to reduce threats to social cohesion.

Feminist analyses have been at the forefront in countries such as Canada and the U.K. in pointing out the difficulties posed by the shift towards a social investment state (Lister, 2003). A key theme is that the focus on children can divorce considerations of their welfare from those of their mothers. Moreover, the overall emphasis on all adults taking responsibility for their own welfare, crucially through engagement in paid work, can ride roughshod over mothers' and to some extent some fathers' beliefs about how best to discharge their caring responsibilities towards their children. Thus analysts such as Williams (2001) call for a new politics. In such a project the assumption that "independence" is both desirable and normatively endorsed is contested by quite a different set of values that argue that all human beings are interdependent throughout the life cycle. Thus the work done in terms of caring for and caring about should be adequately recognized and remunerated. Concrete proposals have been advanced in relation to the changing of employment practices particularly. This is being increasingly taken up by some fathers' organizations and some elements of the trade union movement (Fawcett, Featherstone, & Goddard, forthcoming). As Bryson (2002) notes, there appears to be an increasing recognition that the financial and social costs of current working patterns are unacceptably high for all concerned. Demands in relation to change are no longer seen as "feminist luxuries but central political demands" (p. 147).

Concluding Remarks

While a project called "feminist social work" is no longer evident and possibly desirable in its construction as a universalist approach to theorizing and working with women, feminist insights from a variety of disciplines are crucial. They help us to think beyond a language of "family" and "parents" and oblige engagement with what practices should be fostered to engage with a changing world where men, women, boys and girls no longer "know their place." Furthermore, they offer important pointers towards developing policy infrastructures and practices that support more democratic settlements between men and women and those they care for and about.

References

Benn, M. (1998). *Madonna and child: Towards a new politics of motherhood.* London: Jonathan Cape.

Birmingham Women and Social Work Group. (1985). Women and social work in Birmingham. In E. Brook & A. Davis (Eds.), *Women, the family and social work* (pp.70-90). London: Tavistock.

Bryson, V. (2002). *Feminist debates: Issues of theory and political practice* (2nd ed.). Basingstoke: Palgrave.

Cavanagh, K., & Cree, V. (Eds.). (1996). *Working with men: Feminism and social work.* London: Routledge.

Coward, R. (1999). *Sacred cows.* London: Harper Collins.

Fawcett, B., Featherstone, B., & Goddard, J. (Forthcoming). *Contemporary child care policy and practice.* Basingstoke: Palgrave.

Featherstone, B. (1999). Taking mothering seriously: The issues for child protection. *Child and Family Social Work, 4,* 43-53.

Featherstone, B. (2003). Taking fathers seriously. *British Journal of Social Work, 33,* 239-254.

Featherstone, B. (2004). *Family life and family support: A feminist analysis.* Basingstoke: Palgrave.

Featherstone, B., & Trinder, L. (1997). Familiar subjects: Domestic violence and child welfare. *Child and Family Social Work, 2,* 147-159.

Ferguson, H. (2001). Promoting child protection, welfare and healing: The case for developing best practice. *Child and Family Social Work, 6*(1), 1-13.

Flax, J. (1990). *Thinking fragments: Psychoanalysis, feminism and postmodernism in the contemporary West.* Oxford: University of California Press Ltd.

Franks, S. (1999). *Having none of it: Women, men and the future of work.* London: Granta.

Frosh, S. (2002). Characteristics of sexual abusers. In K. Wilson & A. James (Eds.), *The child protection handbook* (2nd ed.) (pp.71-89). Edinburgh: Bailliere Tindall.

Gardner, R. (1996. *Family support.* Birmingham: Venture.

Ghate, D., & Ramalla, M. (2002). *Positive parenting: The national evaluation of the Youth Justice Board's parenting programme.* London: Policy Research Bureau.

Giddens, A. (1998). *The Third Way: The Renewal of Social Democracy.* Cambridge: Polity.

Gordon, L. (1986). Feminism and social control: The case of child abuse and neglect. In J. Mitchell & A. Oakley (Eds.), *What is feminism?* (pp.63-85). Oxford: Basil Blackwell.

Graham, H. (1992). Feminism and social work education. *Issues in Social Work Education, 11* (2) 48-64.

Hanmer, J., & Statham, D. (1988). *Women and social work: Towards a woman-centred practice.* Basingstoke: Macmillan.

Hooper, C.-A. (1992). *Mothers surviving child sexual abuse.* London: Routledge.

Itzin, C. (Ed.). (2001). *Home truths and child sexual abuse: Influencing policy and practice: A reader.* London: Routledge.

Jenson, J., & Saint–Martin, D. (2001, 21-22 June). *Changing citizenship regimes: Social policy strategies in the social investment state.* Workshop on Fostering Social Cohesion: A Comparison of New Policy Strategies, Université de Montreal.

Langan, M., & Day, L. (Eds.). (1992). Women, oppression and social work: Issues in anti-discriminatory practice. London: Routledge.

Lawrence, M. (1992). Women's psychology and feminist social work practice. In M. Langan & L. Day (Eds.), *Women, oppression and social work: Issues in anti-discriminatory practice* (pp.32-48). London: Routledge.

Lewis, J. (1992). Women and late-nineteenth century social work. In C. Smart (Ed.), *Regulating womanhood: Historical essays on marriage, motherhood and sexuality.* London: Routledge.

Lister, R. (2003). *Citizenship: Feminist perspectives* (2nd ed.). Basingstoke: Palgrave.

Marchant, H., & Wearing, B. (1986). *Gender reclaimed: Women in social work.* Sydney: Hale and Irenmonger.

Mullender, A., & Morley, R. (1994). *Putting the abuse of women on the child care agenda.* London: Whiting and Birch.

Notes on the Conference. (1979). *Feminist social work practice.* Warwick: University of Warwick.

O'Brien, M., & Shemilt, I. (2003). *Working fathers: Earning and caring.* London: Equal Opportunities Commission.

Parton, N. (2003). Rethinking professional practice: The contributions of social constructionism and the feminist "ethics of care." *British Journal of Social Work, 33,* 1-16.

Peled, E. (2000). Parenting by men who abuse women: Issues and dilemmas. *British Journal of Social Work, 30,* 25-36.

Segal, L. (1987). *Is the future female? Troubled thoughts on contemporary feminism.* London: Virago.

Segal, L. (1995). Feminism and the family. In C. Burck & B. Speed (Eds.), *Gender, power and relationships* (pp.248-66). London: Routledge.

Segal, L. (1999). *Why feminism?* Bristol: Polity.

Smart, C., & Neale, B. (1999). *Family fragments?* Cambridge: Polity Press

Smart, C., Neale, B., & Wade, A. (2001). *The changing experiences of childhood: Families and divorce.* Cambridge: Polity Press.

Stacey, J. (1991). *Brave new families.* New York: Basic Books.

Stacey, J. (1999). Dada-ism in the 1990s: Getting past baby talk about fatherlessness. In C.R. Daniels (Ed.), *Lost fathers: The politics of fatherlessness in America* (pp.51-83). Basingstoke: Macmillan.

Walter, N. (1999). *The new feminism.* London: Virago.

White, V. (1995). Commonality and diversity in feminist social work. *British Journal of Social Work, 25,* 143-156.

Williams, F. (2001). In and beyond New Labour: Towards a new political ethics of care. *Critical Social Policy, 21*(4), 476-494.

Wilson, E. (1980). *Women and the welfare state.* London: Tavistock.

Wise, S. (1995). Feminist ethics in practice. In R. Hugman & D. Smith (Eds.), *Ethical issues in social work* (pp.85-101). London: Routledge.

14

Under Reconstruction: Renewing Critical Social Work Practices

Karen Healy

The core mission of critical social work is to promote social justice in practice and policy making. To this end, critical social workers have pursued practice theories that prioritize analysis of structural oppression and promote collaborative approaches to action. Critical social workers are adept at responding to challenges to their practice frameworks from outside their tradition, that is, challenges or contests from social conservatives, neo-classical economists and, more recently, from proponents of managerialism (see Dominelli, 1997; Harris & McDonald, 2000; Ife, 1997; Rees, 1997). However, less attention has been paid to the challenges arising among those who identify as critical social workers but who question aspects of the dominant discourse in critical social work theory.

This chapter will examine three sites of challenge to critical social work. These are contests from those engaged in: critical social practices, changing organizational environments, investigations of the relevance of postmodern interrogations and reconstructions of critical social work. While some commentators argue that the halcyon days of critical social work have now passed, I contend that these contests offer potential sites for the reconstruction of critical social work practice.

In the first part of this chapter I will define critical social work. I will then outline the contemporary contests to practice, and I will consider how critical social workers can address these challenges. I will consider how critical social workers can respond to the challenges, with particular emphasis on increased collaboration between academics and social workers engaged in policy making and direct service delivery.

Critical Social Work: What Is It?

Critical social work refers to a broad range of social work approaches that share the following orientations:

- recognition that structural social processes, particularly those associated with class, gender, race, disability and sexuality, contribute to the social oppression experienced by most social services users;
- adoption of a critical and self-reflexive stance towards the often-contradictory effects of social work practices and policy processes;

- a commitment to co-participatory rather than authoritarian practice relations in policy making, direct service delivery, and in social work education; and
- a commitment to working with, and for, oppressed populations for progressive social change.

The critical tradition has a long and rich history in social work (see Addams, 1961). However, it was not until the 1960s, under the influence of popular social movements, that a distinct and internally diverse critical social work canon emerged. During the 1980s and 1990s, critical social workers continued to develop models of practice with, for example, the articulation of structural social work, anti-oppressive and anti-discriminatory approaches (see Dalrymple & Burke, 1995; Mullaly, 1997; Thompson, 1997). Despite these advances, most critical social work commentators are united in the view that the changing conditions in human service organizations signal reduced possibilities for critical practice, if not the demise of critical social work altogether.

To be sure, critical social workers today face continuing and emerging threats to their social justice mission. For example, the neo-classical assumptions underpinning recent reforms of post-industrial welfare states have contributed to the reprivatization of public concerns, such as poverty. In the context of reform, there is no question that critical approaches to practice and policy making are needed as much now as ever before. What *is* at issue is the capacity of established critical social work perspective to guide activist practices today (Healy, 2000; McDonald & Jones, 2000). However, critical social workers' capacity to explore alternative theoretical perspectives is limited by the truth status assigned to the critical social science perspectives that have shaped the past four decades of critical social work theory building. Using the insight from a range of critical social science theories, including Marxism, feminism, anti-racist and anti-communitarian perspectives, critical social workers have claimed to reveal the "truth" of social work, including both its social control dimensions and its social change possibilities (see DeMaria, 1993; Saulnier, 1996). Notwithstanding the benefits these truths have offered critical social work, their status as unquestionable axioms has also limited the dialogue within critical social work traditions (Healy, 2000; see also Rahnema, 1990, p.205). In this chapter, I examine how emerging contests from practice, changing administrative contexts, and from postmodern analyses can extend and further develop critical social work policy and practice.

The Challenges from Practice

Many human services, including social work, education and nursing, exhibit an uncomfortable fit between theory and practice. The complex and contextual dimensions of human services work demand open and flexible interchanges between theory and practice (Fook, Ryan, & Hawkins, 2000; Parton & Marshall, 1998). Social work theorists frequently observe that many social workers are reluctant to engage with theory, particularly theory that is not readily accessible to direct practice and policy making (Fawcett, 1998; see also Featherstone & Fawcett, 1995). Rather than something that enables social workers to understand and develop their practice, theory is often experienced, at best, as an intellectual curiosity and, at worst, as authoritarian, esoteric and grossly insensitive to the complexities inherent in practice and policy making (Healy, 2000, p.1).

Despite critical theorists' commitment to "praxis," that is, the linkage of theory and practice, many social workers experience difficulties in translating critical theoretical perspectives to practice. Rather than recognizing these difficulties and using them as a site for the exploration and reconstruction of critical social work, critical practice theorists have been less than sympathetic to the obstacles to critical practice. Instead, critical commentators identify barriers to critical social work as lying in: the social control functions of social work, the limited commitment of social workers to radical transformation, the lack of political sophistication of social workers (Ife, 1997, p.169), and the limited change aspirations of service users (see Dixon, 1989; Mowbray, 1993). While critical theorists urge social workers to familiarize themselves with critical practice frameworks, rarely do these theorists turn their attention to the limits of these perspectives for guiding critical practice and policy-making contexts in contemporary human service contexts.

Over the past decade, a small body of critically orientated practice literature drawing on postmodern perspectives and practice-based research has contested the assumptions of critical social work theories (Fawcett et al., 2000; Pease & Fook, 1999; Healy, 2000; Larbalestier, 1998). Through ethical and epistemological challenges, these theorists seek to open critical social work theories to the contextual and complex character of social work and, in so doing, create new possibilities for dialogue between those who practice social work and those who build formal knowledge about it (see, for example, Wise, 1990).

Critical social workers, whether drawing on modern or postmodern perspectives, have a responsibility to highlight the structural contexts of the apparently private problems faced by service users. However, critical social workers must also address the interpersonal and institutional contexts of practice as more than effects of overarching social structures. In other words, the continuing relevance of critical social work today depends on our recognition that the local complexities of practice deserve analytic attention *in their own right*, not merely as an afterthought to structural analyses. For example, to this point, critical social work theorists have contributed little to our understanding of how to practice critically in authoritarian, bureaucratic and corporatized service contexts where most contemporary social work occurs. Nor have critical practice theorists offered much to social workers in fields of practice where the use of statutory power is an integral part of social workers' role, other than to suggest that social workers should minimize or avoid the use of such power altogether (Healy, 1998; see Ban, 1992; Spicker, 1990).

Insights from advocates of reflexive practice also point to ethical problems in modernist critical social work theory (Schön, 1983). Critical reflexive approaches call into question the critical social science axiom that, through rational thought, and action based on such thought, people can change the way they live. This rationalist assumption is evident in the critical practice theory proposal that radical analysis will necessarily lead to actions that are ethical and progressive. Yet such an assumption appears naïve to the inconsistencies of human action. Indeed, we need look no further than our own contexts of service work to identify gaps between espoused philosophies and actual practices. These contradictions can be attributed to a number of reasons, including human frailty, and, just as important, the enormous impact of legal and institutional contexts on the practices of social workers.

The Changing Organizational Environment

Over recent decades, the contexts of social policy formation and human service delivery in the welfare states of Canada, the United Kingdom, the United States, Australia and New Zealand have been subject to market reforms and the rise of a new public management discourse. In this new environment, social workers face increasingly stringent expectations from funding agencies and service managers to demonstrate cost-effectiveness and evidence of service outputs and outcomes (Healy, 2002). The changing policy and organizational context has significant implications for social work practices, as McDonald and Jones (2000, p.8) contend: "Social work is being subsumed within a new frame-work of production, one that is constructing practice in new and quite different sorts of ways."

The market reform of modern welfare states has been accompanied by demands that social work schools produce graduates with competencies needed to work in the new human services marketplace (Garcia & Floyd, 2002; Laragy, 1998; McDonald & Jones, 2000). The competency movement has gained strength as, in the context of fiscal constraint in the human services sector, professional workers are called upon to justify why their services are preferable to non-professional and volunteer labour that is much less costly to engage. The competencies social work educators are expected to produce in graduates include demonstrable practice skills and detailed knowledge of specific domains. Notably, however, less attention is paid within the competency movement to the kinds of attitudes and dispositions — such as willingness to reflect on self and practice role — required to practice as a social work profes-sional. According to Dominelli (1996), "competency based approaches herald the commodification of social work and underpin the shift away from concern about people and relationship building (an important feature in keeping the 'client' less alienated from society and his or her lot) towards the product that is being purchased from a contractor" (pp. 163-164).

Critical social work educators critique elements of the competency movement that discourage recognition of the political responsibilities and ethical priorities of critical social work towards progressive social change. Notwithstanding these concerns, critical social work educators cannot ignore the demands from funding bodies and service managers for technically competent practitioners. The challenge for critical educators is that of reconciling this demand with the critical social workers' primary ethical commitment to social justice and humanitarian practices. We should not view competent and ethical practice as mutually exclusive concerns; nor can we expect modernist critical perspectives to provide entire educational and practice frameworks in the post-industrial era (Healy, 2000). If critical social work is to remain a relevant and vital tradition into this century, it must engage critically with the new imperatives on human service workers. Such critical engagement could usefully focus on thorough analysis of organizational systems through which human services are now delivered. For example, researchers can make critical interventions into new systems of performance management and appraisal by demonstrating the scope and the limits of these systems for capturing essential components of critical social work practice and policy making.

The Challenge of Post Theories

Post theories, that is postmodern and post-structural approaches, pose a third set of challenges to critical social work. Post theories call into question the assumptions about power, identity and change on which modern social work theories, critical or otherwise, rest. Critical practice theorists and policy analysts have raised strong objections to "post" theories, viewing them as unnecessary and unwelcome interventions in critical social work (see Taylor-Gooby, 1993). The emphasis on ambiguity and fragmentation, so appealing in many areas of the social sciences and humanities, has proven problematic for critical social workers. Many critical social work academics condemn postmodernism for its failure to offer new alternatives for achieving social justice (Leonard, 1995, p.16).

However, despite substantial opposition to postmodern and post-structural perspectives, it has been increasingly difficult for critical social work commentators to ignore the challenges levelled through them. First, social work's reliance on an interdisciplinary knowledge base means that social work theorists cannot overlook the considerable influence post theories have had on the social sciences and humanities. Second, there is growing contest within critical social work traditions, as a growing band of critical social work and social policy authors have embraced some elements of postmodern analysis (see Carter, 1998; Fook, 2002; Healy, 2000; Leonard, 1997; Pease & Fook, 1999; Parton & O'Byrne, 2000). In various ways, these authors argue that post theories allow for more productive engagements with power, identity and processes of change than is possible within modernist critical traditions alone.

Postmodern analyses have much to offer for the contemporary development of critical social work theories. Postmodern and post-structural interventions challenge the drive within modern social work, whether critical or non-critical, to unify social work processes around common identifications, concerns and practices. In contrast to a unitary understanding of social work, post theories contribute to a view of social work as a product of discourse that varies from context to context (Healy & Mulholland, 1998). By drawing attention to the productive power of discourse, post-structural theories require critical social workers to locate their understandings not only in the material structures of oppression, but also within the historical and local discourses of practice.

Whereas critical social workers have attempted to situate their practice as innately different to non-critical forms of social work, post theories show both traditions to be implicated in the modernist project. The modernist project has sought to bring order and progress to humanity, but in these attempts, it has also contributed to the oppression and dispossession of those who are seen as a threat to its agenda. Critical social workers' claims to pursue enlightenment and liberation with and for oppressed populations must be viewed with suspicion because of their association with the broader modernist framework. Jan Larbalestier (1998) challenges the emancipatory aspirations of critical social work with her assertion that

> [a]ssisting people to change their lifestyles, to rethink their priorities and options may be particularly fraught in countries with histories of colonialism and migration like Australia, North America and the United Kingdom. In these countries "norms of truth," as well as exhibiting class based differences, may have culturally specific meanings in opposition to the dominant Anglophone discourse and be embedded in histories of exploitative and oppressive policies. (p. 71)

Post theories alert activist social workers to the "will to truth" that lies concealed within the desire to emancipate others. In so doing, post theories can enhance our reflexivity about the constraining effects of modern critical perspectives and practices.

Post theories also challenge critical social workers' focus on power as an oppressive force. Foucault (1980) argued that power is everywhere and, further, that is both a productive and a negative force (see also Bartky, 1988). The insights from postmodernism are crucial to enabling critical social work theorists to engage productively with the statutory and decision-making power that social workers wield in many practice contexts (Healy, 1998; Wise, 1990). It also opens critical practice theories to the forms of power that are necessary aspects of the practices advocated by them. For example, critical practice theories and policy researchers routinely invite social workers to initiate practice processes and projects (Alder & Sandor, 1990), promote participant involvement and leadership (Ward & Mullender, 1991), raise consciousness and promote activist attitudes (Corrigan & Leonard, 1978; Dominelli & McLeod, 1989; Moreau, 1990), and even initiate the sharing of power itself (Thorpe, 1992). Rather than advocate that social workers should seek to reduce or avoid power, as critical practice theorists have often done (see Spicker, 1990; Ban, 1992), post theories challenge us to articulate how such power can be exercised humanely and justly within our service contexts (Healy, 1998, 2000; van Krieken, 1992).

Post-structural analyses have exposed critical social workers' assumptions about what constitutes activist practice sites and processes (Healy, 2000; Rojek, Peackock, & Collins, 1988). These investigations have shown critical practical perspectives to be biased towards a minority of service providers and policy analysts working in atypical practice environments (Healy, 1998, 2000). For example, many elements of critical practice theory, such as an emphasis on shared decision making and collective social action, are most appropriate to small, non-bureaucratic practice sites where workers are relatively unconstrained by policy and organizational obligations. It is highly questionable as to whether these strategies can be transferred to other practice sites such as large bureaucracies, statutory authorities and private agencies dependent on short-term government contracts or philanthropic contributions. In effect, the assumptions of critical practice theory have contributed to the invisibility of activisms in a range of practice contexts, particularly conventional practice sites. Yeatman's (1998, p.2) reflections on activism amongst government bureaucrats supports this view: "My evaluation work deepened my impression that here is a type of activist work that has been relatively unrecognized: namely, the highly skilled, strategic and visionary commitment to public policy and public services."

Postmodernism draws attention to the analysis of how activist discourses themselves shape and constrain possibilities for critical social work. Opening these assumptions to critical scrutiny enables recognition of activist practices outside those typically endorsed by modern social work theories.

Postmodern interventions can sensitize activists to the discursive contexts of their work. Social workers, whether radical or orthodox, cannot evade suspicions aroused by the desire to help or liberate because of the historical deployment of these terms in the colonization and marginalization of oppressed people. Postmodern analyses can contribute to a more circumspect view of the truth claims, whether generated through scientific research or critical analyses, that have guided practice, and such interventions can lead to greater reflexivity towards critical social work objectives and processes.

Reconstructing Critical Social Work: Responding to the Diversity Within

Critical social workers' concern with just and progressive practice remains relevant today. Critical perspectives are needed for social workers to understand and respond to the structural contexts of the oppression and disadvantage faced by service users. I do not seek, then, to dismantle critical social work projects, but rather to strengthen them through recognition of, and response to, the contemporary debates among critical social workers. We must resist harking back to the halcyon days of critical social work, if indeed such days did exist, and use the current internal contests to reinvigorate critical social work practices.

The reconstruction of the process of theory development is integral to the reconstruction of the content of contemporary critical social work theory and practice. The task of reconstructing critical knowledge requires nothing less than the collaboration between those charged with formal theory building, that is, academics, and those who experience service development and delivery, that is, practicing social workers and service users. Of course, this requires a reorientation, a reconciliation perhaps, of the relations between these different domains of critical social work. Critical social workers in academia can make a constructive contribution to grounded knowledge building by making theoretical advances available to scrutiny from the field. This role is a necessary corollary of critical social workers' emphasis on collaboration and the postmodern insistence on the recognition of differences.

Critical postmodern approaches challenge activist social workers to incorporate a range of knowledge sources into formal theory building. It challenges us to allow the insights arising from the lived experiences of service providers and service users to disrupt the assumptions of the humanities and social sciences that underpin much critical theorizing.

Additionally, critical social workers located in the academy can support social workers in the field to voice concerns about policy and practice affecting marginalized populations. Although academics' opportunity for freedom of expression is becoming increasingly constrained, it remains greater than that of most of their colleagues in the field. As the human services are subject to market reform, workers experience significant constraints on their capacities to engage in public debate and critique (see Dominelli, 1997; Lane, 1997; Laragy, 1997). In this environment, the greater freedom of the academic becomes a significant resource to be used in collaboration with the field to express shared concerns.

Postmodern perspectives can make contributions to the reconstruction of knowledge building envisaged here. First, postmodern offers conceptual tools, such as deconstruction, which can be used to destabilize the oppositions that endure between theory and practice and to challenge those approaches to critical social work that silence the diversities of activisms in social work. For example, deconstructive intervention can enable us to recognize both the constructive and oppressive operations of power in practice and, in so doing, open us to new understandings of statutory and other forms of power in practice and policy making.

Second, postmodern perspectives call into question the different ways in which academics and practitioners have positioned themselves as the holders of truth about social work. Postmodernism challenges claims to absolute truth, regardless of whether these claims are based in science, theory or experience (Scott, 1992). Postmodern authors emphasize that truths are always constructed through language, context and interpretation (see Parton & O'Byrne, 2000, p.24). This recognition of the partiality of all knowledge can be used to foster critical dialogue among different stakeholders in social work knowledge building.

Third, postmodern analysis can contribute to the reconstruction of social work knowledge by drawing attention to the complex arrangements of power, identity and change in social work practice and policy making. Post theories challenge us to resist totalizing or oversimplifying social work processes by bringing to the fore the complexity, contextuality and fragmentation of social work processes. Alongside the macro-analysis of power prioritized in modernist critical approaches, postmodern theories demand recognition of the micro and mezzo operations of power. This recognition is especially important for engaging the insights and interests of social service practitioners and service users, who daily encounter operations of power across these levels.

Conclusion

Post-industrial welfare states are in a period of transition. Social work practices are being restructured as a result of changes in the social and institutional structures of human services work. Throughout the history of modern social work, critical social workers have contributed to innovations in social work practice and policy making, yet these perspectives have limited utility in this post-industrial era. In this chapter, I have proposed that the challenges from practice, context and theory require critical social workers to rethink not only the content but, also, the process of knowledge creation. I have argued for dynamic and collaborative approaches to knowledge building that draw on the understandings of stakeholders in the critical social work enterprise, whether they are situated as "academics," "practitioners" or "service users." These approaches require all stakeholders to forego their certainties about the "truth" of critical practice while recognizing that each has much to contribute to the ongoing reconstruction of critical social work. The challenges from "within" critical social work do not necessarily signal the demise of critical social work, but may herald a new chapter in it history.

References

Addams, J. (1961). *Twenty years at Hull-house.* New York: Signet, Macmillan.

Alder, C., & Sandor D. (1990). Youth researching youth. *Youth Studies, 8*(3), 38-42.

Ban, P. (1992). Client participation: beyond the rhetoric. *Children Australia, 21*(2), 23-30.

Bartky, S. (1988). Foucault, feminism, and the modernization of patriarchal power. In I. Diamond & L. Quinby (Eds.), *Feminism and Foucault: Reflections on resistance* (pp. 201-219). Boston: Northeastern University Press.

Carter, J. (Ed.). (1988). *Postmodernity and the fragmentation of welfare.* London: Routledge.

Corrigan, P., & Leonard, P. (1978). *Social work under Capitalism: A Marxist approach.* London: MacMillan.

Dalrymple, J., & Burke, B. (1995). *Anti-oppressive practice, social care, and the law.* Buckingham: Open University Press.

DeMaria, W. (1993). Exploring radical social work teaching in Australia. *Journal of Progressive Human Services, 4*(2), 45-63.

Dixon, J. (1989). The limits and potential of community development for personal and social change. *Community Health Studies, 13*(1), 82-92.

Dixon, J. (1993). Feminist community work's ambivalence with politics. *Australian Social Work*, 46(1), 37-44.

Dominelli, L. (1996). Deprofessionalizing social work: Anti-oppressive practice, competencies and postmodernism. *British Journal of Social Work*, 26, 153-175.

Dominelli, L. (1997). *Sociology for social work.* Houndmills: MacMillan.

Dominelli, L., & McLeod, E. (1989). *Feminist social work.* Houndmills: MacMillan.

Fawcett, B. (1998). Disability and social work: applications from postmodernism, poststructuralism and feminism. *British Journal of Social Work*, 28, 263-277.

Fawcett, B., Featherstone, B., Fook, J., & Rossiter, A. (2000). *Practice and research in social work: Postmodern feminist perspectives.* London: Routledge.

Featherstone, B., & Fawcett, B. (1995). Oh no! Not more isms! *Social Work Education, 14*(3), 25-43.

Fook, J. (2002). *Social work: Critical theory and practice.* London: Sage.

Fook, J., Ryan, M., & Hawkins, L. (2000). *Professional expertise: Practice, theory and education for working in uncertainty.* London: Whiting and Birch.

Foucault, M. (1980). Truth and power. In C. Gordon (Ed.), *Power/knowledge: Selected interviews and other writings 1972-1977* (pp. 109-133). New York: Pantheon Books.

Garcia, J.A., & Floyd, C.E. (2002). Addressing evaluative standards related to program assessment. *Journal of Social Work Education*, 38(3), 369-382.

Harris, J., and McDonald, C. (2000). Postfordism, the welfare state and the personal social services: A comparison of Australia and Britain. *British Journal of Social Work*, 30(1), 51-70.

Healy, J. (1998). *Welfare options: Delivering social services.* St. Leonards: Allen and Unwin.

Healy, K. (1998). Participation and child protection: The importance of context. *British Journal of Social Work*, 28, 897-914.

Healy, K. (2000). *Social work practices: Contemporary perspectives on change.* London: Sage.

Healy, K. (2002). Managing human services in a market environment: What role for social workers? *British Journal of Social Work*, 32, 527-540.

Healy, K., & Leonard, P. (2000). Responding to uncertainty: Critical social work education in the postmodern habitat. *Journal of Progressive Human Services*, 11(1), 23-48.

Healy, K., & Meagher, G. (2004). The reprofessionalisation of social work: Collaborative approaches for achieving professional recognition. *British Journal of Social Work*, 34(2), 243-261

Healy, K., & Mulholland, J. (1998). Discourse analysis and activist social work: Investigating practice processes. *Journal of Sociology and Social Welfare*, 25(3), 3-27.

Ife, J. (1997). *Rethinking social work: Towards critical practice.* Melbourne: Longman.

Larbalestier, J. (1998). Feminism, difference and social work: Positions, practices and possibilities. In E. Fernandez, K. Heycox, L. Hughes, & M. Wilkinson (Eds.), *Women participating in global change.* Proceedings of the International Association of Schools of Social Work (IASSW), Hong Kong, Women's Symposium Publications Committee.

Lane, B. (1997). A question of justice. *Australian Social Work*, 50(4), 37-39.

Langan, M., & Lee, P. (1989). Whatever happened to radical social work? In M. Langan & P. Lee (Eds.), *Radical social work today* (pp.1-18). London: Unwin Hyman.

Laragy, C. (1997). Social workers in the year 2000. *Asia-Pacific Journal of Social Work*, 7(1), 47-58.

Leonard, P. (1995). Postmodernism, socialism and social welfare. *Journal of Progressive Human Services*, 6(2), 3-19.

Leonard, P. (1997). *Postmodern welfare: Reconstructing an emancipatory project.* London: Sage.

McDonald, C., & Jones, A. (2000). Reconstructing and re-conceptualising social work in the emerging milieu. *Australian Social Work*, 53(3), 3-12.

Moreau, M. (1990). Empowerment through advocacy and consciousness raising: Implications for a structural approach to social work. *Journal of Sociology and Social Welfare, 17*(2), 53-67.

Mowbray, M. (1993). The medicinal qualities of localism: A historical persective. In R. Thorpe & J. Petruchenia (Eds.), *Community work or social change? An Australian Perspective* (pp.50-66). Sydney: Hale and Iremonger.

Mullaly, B. (1997). *Structural social work: Ideology, theory, and practice* (2nd ed.). Toronto: Oxford University Press.

Parton, N., & Marshall, W. (1998). Postmodernism and discourse approaches to social work. In R. Adams, L. Dominelli, & M. Payne (Eds.), *Social work: Themes, issues and critical debates* (pp. 240-249). Houndsmills: MacMillan.

Parton, N. & O'Byrne, P. (2000). *Constructive social work: Towards a new practice.* Houndmills: MacMillan.

Pease, B., & Fook, J. (Eds.). (1999). *Transforming social work practice: Postmodern critical perspectives.* St. Leonards: Allen and Unwin.

Rahnema, M. (1990). Participatory action research: The "last temptation of a saint" development. *Alternatives, 15*, 199-226.

Rees, S. (1997). The fraud and the fiction. In S. Rees & G. Rodley (Eds.), *The human costs of managerialismn* (pp.15-27). Leichhardt, NSW: Pluto Press.

Rojek, C., Peackock, C., & Collins, S. (1988). *Social work and received ideas.* London: Routledge.

Saulnier, C.F. (1996). *Feminist theories and social work: Approaches and applications.* New York: The Haworth Press.

Schön, D. (1983). *The reflective practitioner: How professionals think in action.* New York: Basic Books.

Scott, J. (1992). Experience. In J. Butler & J. Scott (Eds.), *Feminists theorise the political* (pp. 22-40). New York: Routledge.

Simpkin, M. (1983). *Trapped within welfare: Surviving social work.* London: MacMillan.

Spicker, P. (1990). Social work and self-determination. *British Journal of Social Work, 20*, 221-236.

Taylor-Gooby, P. (1993). *Postmodernism and social policy: A great leap backwards* (Discussion Paper no. 45). Sydney: University of New South Wales, Social Policy Research Centre.

Thompson, N. (1997). *Anti-discriminatory practice.* Basingstoke: MacMillan.

Thorpe, R. (1992). Community work and ideology: An Australian perspective. In R. Thorpe & J. Petruchenia (Eds.), *Community work or social change: An Australian perspective* (pp. 20-36). Sydney: Hale and Iremonger.

van Krieken, R. (1992). *Children and the state: Social control and the formation of Australian child welfare.* Sydney: Allen and Unwin.

Ward, D., & Mullender, A. (1991). Empowerment and oppression: An indissoluble pairing for contemporary social work. *Critical Social Policy, 11*(2), 21-30.

Wise, S. (1990). Becoming a feminist social worker. In L. Stanley (Ed.), *Feminist praxis: Research, theory and epistemology in feminist sociology* (pp. 236-249). London: Routledge.

Yeatman, A. (1998). Introduction. In A. Yeatman (Ed.), *Activism and the policy process* (pp. 1-15). St. Leonards: Allen and Unwin.

15

Challenges and Directions for Critical Social Work

Jan Fook

Where have the discussions in this book taken us in terms of our understandings of critical social work, both in its theoretical conceptualization and in our thinking about its practice? In this chapter I attempt to summarize the central ideas about these issues raised in the book, and to discuss some of the challenges and directions posed for the future work of critical social workers. The chapter is organized in the following way: After a brief summary of themes raised in the introduction, and ideas about the definition and meaning of critical social work, I note the main challenges for its further development as discussed in the book. I then summarize the suggestions for new directions that have arisen, and end with some discussion of the implications of these suggestions in terms of the initial issues raised in the introduction.

Tensions in Critical Social Work

Several main issues inherent in debates about critical social work were noted in the introduction to this book. These were:

- tensions regarding the nature of power in the relationship between worker and client — how do we recognize power inequities between clients and workers, the relative disempowerment of clients, and the contradictions and complexities this entails while avoiding their further disempowerment and working towards empowering them?

- the relevance of critical social work perspectives in direct practice — there is still a struggle in conceptualizing the broad social and structural analysis of critical theory in a way which is readily applicable in the everyday experience of social workers in diverse front-line practice settings. Yet developing practice strategies that are too concrete can run the risk of defining critical social work in exclusionary ways that do not take account of changing and diverse contexts.

- linking the everyday and the structural — the challenge inherent here is in making the link without resorting to grand theories or oversimplified dualisms that exclude multiple perspectives.

Some Common Features of Critical Social Work

How can critical social work be defined to allow room for the working out of these tensions? How can we conceptualize it in ways that allow for complexity, diversity and changing contexts? There was extensive discussion by most of the contributors about the possibility and wisdom of "defining" critical social work. Some hold the view that a single definition would function to exclude varied viewpoints and that, because of varied viewpoints, it was difficult to pin down the definitive characteristics of critical social work. Nevertheless, several common themes about its characteristics emerge, either explicitly stated or assumed as underlying analytical or value positions.

First, the idea of praxis appears as a recurrent theme. It appears crucial to critical social workers that the principles of critical social analysis are integrated with its practice. Critical social work is therefore neither exclusively a theory, a perspective or a practice but is an embodied social activity informed by particular social analysis and sets of values. Second, the praxis of critical social work embraces an analysis that links the social, structural and personal as intertwined political arenas. Third, the value stance is expressly transformative in that the explicit goal is social change based on egalitarian and democratic principles. Fourth, the processes of critical social work are dialogical and participatory. Changes are developed through inclusionary dialogue, recognizing differences and power imbalances.

Fifth, both analyses and processes are reflexive, incorporating an awareness of the interactive and social nature of knowledge creation and identity formation. Lived experience thus becomes crucial as both a window on how individuals create their own social place and as an expression of the social and structural world. Finally, this reflexivity leads to a recognition of the potential of social work to construct exclusionary arrangements. Social workers can never assume an "innocent" or non-implicated position and must therefore work with this tension and contradiction in all relations and settings. One of the challenges that this reflexive position poses for critical social workers is that they must constantly be both "inside" and "outside" — to construct themselves as social workers at the same time as deconstructing their position.

Steve Hick sums up one of the essential tensions of critical social work nicely in the introduction: "The book challenges us to 'unbecome' social workers and then struggle with clients to uncover the contours of the world implicated in a shared lived reality."

In the next section I discuss the specific contours of this challenge in more detail.

Challenges

The tensions and common themes noted above point to specific challenges for critical social workers. For many contributors, an overriding current challenge that critical social workers must address are the questions posed by postmodern thinking. There is a marked ambivalence about postmodernism and mixed debate about whether its thinking contributes to the ideals of critical social work or whether it merely deconstructs, and therefore pulls the rug from underneath, the core values and metanarratives. Does postmodern thinking actually help critical social workers to resolve some tensions and issues, or does it irrevocably raise new ones that, by their very nature, must remain as tensions, constantly unsettling our stated broad and good intentions, and meaning we are never certain of the good we hope to do?

For instance, postmodernism raises our awareness of the importance of context and, indeed, changing contexts, in the practice of social work. How are metanarratives to be interpreted and remain meaningful in different and changing contexts? Does the social justice activity intended in one context function the same way in another?

Postmodern thinking alerts us to the importance of lived experience, not only of service users, but also of social work practitioners. This may exhort us to develop critical social work thinking in ways relevant for direct practice, but what of practice that is also relevant to changing contexts, and to the many varied contexts in which direct practice takes place simultaneously — from differing and multi-faceted micro contexts, organizational sites, local communities, nations and global contexts? (Karen Healy raises this issue in Chapter 14.) How can we conceptualize the practice of critical social work in a way that allows it to be relevant across all these differing sites? Indeed, is it possible and even desirable for us to strive for this? If not, how can we talk meaningfully, with some shared dialogue, about critical social work?

Globalization, in all its economic, political and cultural forms, poses another set of challenges for critical social workers. While postmodernism in one sense represents some of the cultural and theoretical changes associated with globalization, many of the contributors remind us of the economic and also the materialist aspects of globalization, and how any notions of critical social work need to take the embodied nature of our experience into account. Any current conceptualizations of critical social work thus need to be mindful of the very real materialist conditions that in some ways determine the thinking and experience of all of us.

Thus the reflexive positioning of social workers, as simultaneous creators and inheritors of global and local conditions, gives us both a privileged and a non-privileged position from which to join with others to transform these conditions into ones that work more equitably.

Following are the types of directions the contributors have suggested for critical social workers in meeting this challenge.

Suggested Directions

Some contributors have suggested a return to existing concepts such as that of human rights. Jim Ife in Chapter 4 argues that the discourse of human rights is relevant if we see it as referring to more than the legal realm. "Human rights rest on a foundation more encompassing than the legal system; they touch every aspect of our humanity and our interaction with other humans, often in contexts well beyond the reach of the law." Giving critical social work a human rights framework can work as a framework for practice at many levels.

Other contributors seek to develop existing theoretical directions further by posing methods that might meet the practical demands of critical social work values. Trevor Spratt in Chapter 7 and Richard Pozzuto, Brent Angell and Paul Dezendorf in Chapter 2 do this in slightly different ways. Spratt revisits practice in the child welfare system in the U.K. and concludes that there is a still a need for more awareness of structural forces in the shaping of social work practice and for collective activities. He concludes that Boal's image theatre methodology might offer an appropriate set of practices to realize these goals in practice.

Richard Pozzuto and his colleagues critique social work's traditional therapeutic alliance. They argue that, since this ethos is based on an acceptance of the existing social order, new approaches to therapy are needed that link the individual and the social. They propose that narrative therapy offers one such direction.

Ben Carniol in Chapter 10 contributes to the development of critical social work theory by enlarging on seven areas of analysis that he believes will enable social workers to better develop emancipatory practices. These include: the main sources of inequalities, harmful polarizations within oppressive realities, invisible privileges created by oppressive realities, our own social situation, the social location of others, sources of emancipation and further practice implications. Ben's seven areas share some commonalities with directions suggested by other contributors. For example, the analysis of hidden oppressions and awareness of social locations and therefore the need for reflexivity or critical reflection are key themes for several, regardless of the original (structural or postmodern) theoretical position taken. This leads Ben to conclude:

> My hunch is that a different kind of common ground may be feasible if we can develop a healthy climate of acceptance for differences, for example, between postmodern and structural approaches. An acceptance of these theoretical differences may free us as social work educators and as service providers to build greater solidarity among ourselves in resisting the multiplicity of illegitimate privileges.

Other contributors have based their suggestions on an analysis of existing changed conditions and try to pose new frameworks that take this into account. For instance, in Chapter 12, Amy Rossiter starts from her own experience as a social work educator and notes how the world of her new first-year students is palpably different from her own formative one. The world of students threatens foundational social work values. "To do social work is to live in a contradictory space where the unavoidable micro power of the social space of professions is in constant tension with egalitarian, progressive ideals." She proposes that we need alternate conceptions of our world and place in it. These alternate ideas are that of redistribution (of resources) and recognition (of identities),

> I think critical social work has a role to play in responding to the future with alterna-
> tives and active resistance that accounts for the changing nature of power in the
> world...[W]e need a frame for the hard work of creating global relations of justice, sol-
> idarity, peace and sustainability...[W]e need a language of justice that names the world
> we want to live in, so that our practice can become a way of constructing the world.

This sense of the inadequacy of current theoretical frameworks for framing future critical social work is echoed by a number of contributors. For instance, Brid Featherstone, in Chapter 13, reviews the state of feminist social work, principally in the U.K., and notes that "feminism is seen as a project that must be located in a complex gender landscape where old markers around masculinity and femininity are being rethought and reworked due to economic, cultural and demographic shifts." Yet she concludes that "an ongoing engagement with contemporary feminist ideas could contribute to a vibrant critical social work project." Essentially an awareness of feminist issues and debate broadens the terrain. "They help us think beyond a language of 'family' and 'parents' and oblige engagement with what practices should be fostered to engage with a changing world where men, women, boys and girls no longer 'know their place.'" And by exploring all positionings through the pointers feminist analysis offers, it may be possible to forge a better world where both women and men can engage more democratically.

Graham McBeath and Stephen Webb in Chapter 11 analyze some of the critical social work approaches that incorporate critique and analysis of modernist conceptions of power. They are critical of the apparent lack of the use of the Foucauldian view of power at a micro level. "Critical social work, while making some valuable comments about the inadequacy of analyses of power in existing social work, does not carry through the largely Foucault-inspired project of undoing power relations all the way down to the micro-level. Critical social work does not get at the movement of differing that is difference." They suggest a more detailed usage of Foucault's ideas about governmentality, the complex workings of power and in particular "the sites of disciplinary power that are the invisible networks of power impressed upon the body of the worker and [that] get translated into actual practice."

Gerald de Montigny, in Chapter 8, is also concerned with the embodiment of critical social workers and makes his suggestions for its development starting from the question of who critical social workers are, their motivations, desires, experiences and locations, and how these influence the practice of critical social work. He terms this a "reflexive materialist analysis."

> A reflexive analysis provides a troubled and troubling ground for social workers' use
> of language, understandings and knowledge. Yet it is in the acknowledgement of the
> troubles of a social ground, which not only is, but becomes and is transformed by dint
> of action and will, that the arrogance of positivism and the rhetoric of power founded in
> objectivity is displaced by a profound epistemological humility.

Interestingly, Jan Fook and Christine Morley in Chapter 5 illustrate some of this reflexive analysis in the practice of empowerment. After reviewing the concept of empowerment and its different uses, they argue that there is a need to develop a more complex and contextually appropriate usage of the term and its practice. They illustrate this task by examining its actual operation in a particular case through a critical reflection upon an example of empowerment practice with a woman in a sexual assault centre. They show how the worker's assumptions about what was empowering were not the same as those of the woman client, and therefore they are critical of conceptions of critical social work that are simply diluted to empowerment practice. They conclude that in order to ensure that empowerment practice actually does function as empowering for the client, it needs to be aligned more closely with postmodern and critical analysis. "A practice of empowerment...needs to be accompanied by broader postmodern and critical analysis if the intended empowering goals are to be achieved in ways that are appropriate to the specific needs of the individual in question."

This theme of the usefulness of reflexivity in forging new directions for critical social work practice is carried through by several other contributors. June Yee, in Chapter 6, illustrates this well with her analysis and critique of anti-racism practice. She argues, for example, that accepted practices used in addressing culturally diverse populations are often underpinned by a hidden complicity to a basic system of domination. She terms this hidden system "whiteness" and argues that we must be aware of its operation if we are to realize the transformative goals of critical social work. Therefore, instead of focusing on phenomena such as culture and identity, we may need to focus on how racism operates in one's own social location. She argues for "practical reflective activity."

> This involves questioning and critiquing how people come to know what they know, why people no longer question what is taken for granted as valid knowledge and when will the outcomes of social work practice cause everyone to want to transform the structures of oppression.

Similarly Sarah Todd conducts a reflexive deconstruction of feminist community organization practice. Her analysis reveals some of the ways feminist workers may unwittingly seek to maintain the existing social order. She concludes that

> we may be able to develop a more critically reflective practice that challenges us to seek out innovative ways of unbecoming white feminist organizers. The goal of such reworkings cannot be to secure innocence in oppressive relations, but rather to engage with the present in all of its ambivalences; to see ourselves as ambivalent subjects, invested in achieving social justice, but also in maintaining a familiar social order in which we secure a significant amount of privilege. The result of this will always be an unfinished web of stories that hold onto traces of past narratives, often weaving together in contradictory ways that allow us to both avoid and explore new terrains towards future possibilities.

Concluding Remarks

This volume has presented us with a number of rich and varied perspectives on critical social work, both in its former and current state. Where has the foregoing discussion taken us in terms of the initial issues raised, and what broad themes might guide our future thinking about critical social work and its practice?

The tensions raised for critical social work in the introduction to this book revolve around the implicated positioning of the worker, as both powerful and powerless, as people both subjected to the social order while implicated in its creation. With this awareness, and with the necessity to avoid prescribing grand narratives for action that exclude differing viewpoints, the challenge is to find clear guidelines for action that can achieve transformative goals in changing and diverse situations.

In broad terms I believe it is fair to say that the contributors have approached these issues directly. First, for me there is a clear sense of the importance of context, and our need to be more responsive to this, whether it be our own personal, social or embodied location, our organization, our local community, or our global and material circumstances. Context for me has taken on much more form, substance and diversity after reading this volume, and I believe this is a major contribution to the theorization of critical social work as we struggle to understand that most traditional of social work concepts, "person in environment."

Second, I am struck by the ways in which the contributors used and related to conceptions of theoretical positions. For instance, some argued that we need to use more "pure" or better applications of some concepts or theoretical traditions. Others suggest a further development of these and even went some way to creating their own. Overall I found that there was a clear exhortation to be more flexible in the use of theory or concepts, to perhaps be less concerned about differences and more concerned about the ways in which different theoretical positions or traditions might be used to illuminate the problem at hand.

Third, the contributors brought to light the need to be more aware of the complexity of experience, the ways in which power and oppression operates differently in grounded and embodied ways at the everyday level, and the corresponding need to find ways and processes of practising that allow openness and responsiveness to these complexities.

The idea of critical reflection and reflexivity as a stance and a process was thus important, not only as a way of staying open, but also of guarding against the dangers of assumed innocence. What I found interesting throughout was the strong argument for the importance of an awareness through a process of reflexivity and dialogue, rather than emphasis on the achievement of transformative goals. While these goals were of course assumed, the focus of the chapters is more on the complexities and difficulties of how to get there. And of course, many contributors framed the critical social work struggle in much more open-ended terms than we might have done a decade ago.

To again quote Steve Hick from the introduction: "The book challenges us to 'unbecome' social workers and then struggle with clients to uncover the contours of the world implicated in a shared lived reality."

This may well be the future task of critical social workers

AGMV Marquis

MEMBER OF SCABRINI MEDIA

Quebec, Canada
2004